The Mama's Boy Myth

Kate Stone Lombardi

AVERY

a member of

Penguin Group (USA) Inc.

New York

THE

MAMA'S
BOY MYTH

Why Keeping Our Sons

Close Makes Them

Stronger

ꝏ

Published by the Penguin Group
Penguin Group (USA) Inc., 375 Hudson Street, New York, New York 10014, USA ·
Penguin Group (Canada), 90 Eglinton Avenue East, Suite 700, Toronto, Ontario M4P 2Y3,
Canada (a division of Pearson Penguin Canada Inc.) · Penguin Books Ltd,
80 Strand, London WC2R 0RL, England · Penguin Ireland, 25 St Stephen's Green,
Dublin 2, Ireland (a division of Penguin Books Ltd) · Penguin Group (Australia),
250 Camberwell Road, Camberwell, Victoria 3124, Australia
(a division of Pearson Australia Group Pty Ltd) · Penguin Books India Pvt Ltd,
11 Community Centre, Panchsheel Park, New Delhi–110 017,
India · Penguin Group (NZ), 67 Apollo Drive, Rosedale,
North Shore 0632, New Zealand (a division of Pearson New Zealand Ltd) ·
Penguin Books (South Africa) (Pty) Ltd, 24 Sturdee Avenue,
Rosebank, Johannesburg 2196, South Africa

Penguin Books Ltd, Registered Offices: 80 Strand, London WC2R 0RL, England

Most Avery books are available at special quantity discounts for bulk purchase for sales
promotions, premiums, fund-raising, and educational needs. Special books or book excerpts
also can be created to fit specific needs. For details, write Penguin Group (USA) Inc. Special
Markets, 375 Hudson Street, New York, NY 10014.

Library of Congress Cataloging-in-Publication Data

Lombardi, Kate Stone.
The mama's boy myth : why keeping our sons close makes them stronger /
Kate Stone Lombardi.
p.   cm.
ISBN 978-1-58333-457-7
1. Mothers and sons.   2. Mothers—Psychology.   3. Sons—Psychology.   I. Title.
HQ755.85L66   2012   2011047483
306.874'3—dc23

Printed in the United States of America
1 3 5 7 9 10 8 6 4 2

BOOK DESIGN BY KATY RIEGEL

Some names of parents and children featured in this book have been changed to protect
their privacy.

While the author has made every effort to provide accurate telephone numbers and Internet
addresses at the time of publication, neither the publisher nor the author assumes any responsibility for errors, or for changes that occur after publication. Further, the publisher does not
have any control over and does not assume any responsibility for author or third-party websites
or their content.

To Michael, Jeanie, and Paul, with love

Contents

_ঽ_

The Mama's Boy Myth

Introduction

ॐ

ON A WINTER'S DAY some time ago, I fell into conversation with Susan, a woman I barely knew. At the time I had been writing a regional column for *The New York Times* but had recently been reassigned to cover local news. Casually, I mentioned that my son had used a sports analogy to describe the situation.

"He told me, 'Mom, the problem is that they're playing you out of position.' And he got it exactly. It's not that I can't do straight reporting—I did that for years—it's just that my strengths lie elsewhere. My son understood my frustration immediately. And he always knows just what to say to make me feel better."

When Susan didn't answer, I got a little nervous, and

added, "I hope you don't think it's odd that I get career feedback from my nineteen-year-old son."

Her response both reassured and surprised me. She told me that she also talked to her son about work regularly. Her son was older than mine, and he often called her on the way home from his own office to rehash both of their days.

"But you have to understand," Susan told me. "My son and I are particularly close."

Let me flash forward here and tell you that this very phrase—"My son and I are particularly close"—was one I would go on to hear repeated again and again when I would later interview dozens of mothers and survey hundreds more for this book. Each of these women believed her closeness to her son was unusual, if not unique.

But back on that cold, gray afternoon, I was still dealing with only a sample of two. As we began to discuss our relationship with our sons, the two of us—who had only met that day—slowly began to reveal a shared level of intensity about our boys that stunned us both. Susan talked about how simpatico she was with her son, and how they had the exact same sense of humor. I countered that no one really "got me" like my son, and how we could intuit each other's moods without even speaking. She said that time spent with her son evoked a profound level of tenderness that she didn't experience with anybody else. This precisely described my own experience.

The conversation was far deeper than talking about what good boys we believed we had raised. Sure, we thought our sons were smart, sensitive, and sweet, and like all proud mothers, we adored them. But there was something else going on. We were also talking about a level of emotional connection and a kind of closeness that was usually only associated with mother-daughter relationships.

For a few moments we didn't know what to make of discovering each other. She said she had never before opened up to anybody about the intensity of her feelings or the true nature of the relationship, assuming that what she experienced was only relevant to her and her son, a kind of family secret. Perhaps, Susan speculated, she could talk about it now because her son had left the nest a decade earlier, had gone on to marry, and was himself about to have a child. This, as she saw it, was proof that she hadn't damaged her son by their closeness.

But what struck me the most that day was what happened next. All of a sudden Susan remembered she was talking to a journalist who writes about families and stopped short. Covering her mouth, she blurted, "You must never write about what I told you, and you certainly must never use my full name."

I assured her of the latter but found I couldn't promise the former. Because as the conversation continued, I began to feel a psychological wall was crumbling, even as I was catching the scent of a great story. Why had she and I each believed that we needed to keep this precious bond with our sons to ourselves? Why did both of us feel that if we talked about it openly, our feelings would likely have been misinterpreted and we would have been criticized, perhaps harshly?

In fact, we were soon proved correct about our assumptions. Another woman had quietly joined us during the conversation, and after she listened for a while, she said, with more than a tinge of distaste, "You two each sound like you are discussing an illicit love affair." Immediately, Susan and I stammered our denials—there was nothing sexual about our feelings. If anything, it was a kind of maternal tenderness. But clearly, the mother-son relationship was considered suspect.

As I thought more about it, I realized that the reason I had never discussed my true feelings about my son with anyone—not even my own sister—was because there seem to be no words, no examples, no context whatsoever to describe a close bond between a mother and son that doesn't in some way raise eyebrows and invite strict censure. Mothers who stay emotionally close to their sons for "too long" are seen as those smothering moms who won't let their boys grow up. Instead of pushing them out of the nest to make their way in the rough-and-tumble world, these moms hold their sons too tightly. They create effeminate "mama's boys" who will invite contempt from their peers and will be forever maladjusted.

Take this to the next extreme, and what are we really talking about? Homophobia is one of the big bogeymen behind fear of mother-son closeness. The unspoken fear is that if the mother is too great an influence on the son, she will somehow make him gay. Few people rationally believe this to be true, and certainly there is no science behind it. And the whole discussion doesn't even address the assumption that having a gay son would by definition be a bad thing. But the truth is that much of the uneasiness around a close mother-son relationship is fed by the fear that too much influence from the mother will feminize the son.

That doesn't even address the other reaction of alarm that Susan and I got—that perhaps something untoward and sexually inappropriate was going on with sons who were loved so deeply.

A healthy relationship between a mother and son in which they remain emotionally close? It seems a contradiction in terms. We don't even know what it's supposed to look like. Closeness between mothers and sons is perceived to be fraught with danger.

The problem was that I didn't buy this, and neither did Susan, with whom I had fallen into this unexpectedly intimate conversation. We had both quietly rejected the conventional wisdom of how to raise healthy sons. Not only didn't we believe that we had harmed our sons by maintaining a close bond, but we were also confident that this closeness would help them grow into stronger, more appealing adult males.

Now, of course, I wanted to find out if other mothers felt the same way. Was it simply some strange confluence of events that has blessed this woman and me with exceptionally caring, sensitive sons who kept us close? Or was something broader going on?

I began with interviews—with women I knew personally and women I barely knew professionally, with women whose sons were in their early teens and women whose sons were long married, with women who were grandmothers and women who were under forty. I set up a website and drew responses from women from across the country from a variety of backgrounds. I heard from truck drivers from Ohio, nurses in Kentucky, teachers in Rhode Island, and psychotherapists from Manhattan. And here's what I discovered: although there were a handful who truly didn't know what I was talking about and didn't feel particularly close to their sons, a surprising number understood exactly and immediately. Most opened up only after they were assured that their privacy would be protected. Once they agreed to speak, virtually none cut the discussion short. Most figuratively and some literally grabbed on to my sleeve to prevent me from ending the interview. Not only did they talk about how close they felt to their sons, but a surprisingly large majority also talked at length about special traditions, shared sensibilities, overwhelming tenderness, and a deep satisfaction with a relationship that had been incredibly meaningful to them and their sons.

Like the very first woman I spoke to about this, most of these mothers also expressed the desire to keep the closeness secret. An odd disconnect soon became apparent. These women had all absorbed the message that society believed there was something "off" about a close mother-son relationship. They, too, remained quiet about its real nature for fear of being criticized.

But in their hearts they did not believe that they were

doing anything wrong by nurturing the relationship. They didn't buy the idea that they were damaging their sons by keeping close, and they felt strongly that they were creating more sensitive, caring men for the next generation of women.

That story—the secret closeness between mothers and sons—was the original book I set out to write.

But as I dove deeper into what mothers were specifically saying about raising their sons, a more complicated and interesting narrative began to emerge. This is also the story of an underground movement being conducted by a generation of mothers. It's not only that women are keeping close to their sons; it's that in rejecting decades of accepted "wisdom" about how to raise boys, mothers are questioning the very nature of masculinity and redefining assumptions about gender. By nurturing close bonds with their sons, mothers are developing in boys traits like sensitivity, emotional awareness, tenderness, and the ability to articulate feelings—all of which have traditionally been considered female characteristics. This is precisely the kind of "emotional intelligence" that many believe today's adult men lack. In a very real sense, mothers of sons are bringing the feminist movement full circle.

Think about it. For more than thirty years, girls have been encouraged to embrace traits that were once considered traditionally masculine. It's hardly breaking news that girls have been urged to compete athletically and academically, to develop their own strong voices, to demonstrate leadership and break the glass ceiling. We might not be all the way there yet, but the world for girls is a very different place than it used to be.

Mothers are thrilled that their daughters have these opportunities. (In fact, some mothers I interviewed who have only sons expressed "daughter envy," in part because they said they would have vicariously enjoyed the wide range of options available to girls growing up today that they themselves missed out on.) But interestingly, fathers are just as enthusiastic about embracing and supporting their daughters' ambitions. They coach their daughter's teams, take their daughters camping, and encourage their career plans. One scientist posted a comment on the MIT website not long ago about how he wept when he realized his daughter would follow in his footsteps at the prestigious school. For heaven's sake, it's been nearly a quarter of a century since Astronaut Barbie came out in 1985.

You'd be hard-pressed to find a father today who would advise his daughter to forgo an education, play dumb, and make her life's ambition to try to catch a man. Moreover, fathers are applauded when they support their daughter's non-traditional pursuits. But the same doesn't hold true for mothers and sons. If a mother tries to support her son's more sensitive side or encourages him to learn a traditionally feminine skill, she is seen as a dangerous influence who is compromising his masculinity.

Not only is this attitude unfair, it is misguided. What today's mothers are doing for their sons—primarily teaching them emotional intelligence—is a critically important gift.

Mothers, by affording their sons the emotional closeness that they once offered only to daughters, are giving them access to a fuller experience of humanity.

Mother after mother described the connection she formed with her boy, how she carved out special time for them to be alone so he could open up about his feelings, how she helped him learn to put into words his pent-up emotions. By fostering this closeness, mothers also opened up their own lives to their sons, shrinking the divide between a "man's world" and a "woman's world."

Unlike fathers with their daughters, however, mothers have not been applauded for breaking through old gender stereotypes. On the contrary, it makes society—and particularly many fathers, uncles, grandfathers—uneasy. Mothers' instincts might tell them one thing, but they are constantly bombarded with messages that tell them to back off from their sons.

There is no end to this critique, some of it subtle, some overt. It's in modern literature, parenting books, sociological movements that want to "reclaim manhood," and even contemporary television reality shows, like NBC's *Momma's Boys*, which depicts domineering mothers picking out their sons' girlfriends. The only kind of mother-son "closeness" we see consistently portrayed is one in which the mother is needy, controlling, and emasculating. The only good mother seems to be a mother who leaves her son alone and lets him be.

This is particularly ironic, given all the attention paid recently to the suffering of boys. About a decade ago, a spate of books and articles was published that claimed boys were "in crisis" precisely because of the pressure placed on them to conform to stereotypical male behavior. Boys had more trouble in school and were more likely to be both perpetrators and victims of violence. These authors argued that what was causing all this trouble was a combination of popular culture, the way we parent and educate boys, and, most of all, the fact that society was not permitting boys to fully develop their capacity for emotional depth and complexity.

This was important work and began some real soul-searching on the part of educators and parents on what boys were really experiencing. But what was the prescription for a cure in nearly all these books? They called for fathers and other men to serve as role models in teaching emotional literacy. This would be a great idea except for two key problems. First, the majority of men who are fathers of older boys and teens were not brought up this way themselves. They didn't experience being encouraged to recognize and articulate their feelings as they were growing up. On the contrary, they were urged to "be a man" and "have a stiff upper lip." Emotional guys were considered sissies, and most quickly learned how to conform to traditional male expectations of stoicism. The fallout from raising boys this way is exactly what much of this "boys in crisis" literature documents and bemoans. So how on earth were fathers brought up with these old expectations supposed to teach their sons emotional intelligence? They didn't have it to give.

Certainly, no one would argue against having fathers more involved in their children's lives. Mothers are the first to support this. But the second problem with saying that it should fall to fathers to model emotional intelligence is the reality that it's usually mothers who are on the front lines when a son pushes the gender boundaries or is at his most emotionally vulnerable. She's the one who tends to be there when it's all unfolding, not to mention the one who is attuned to perceiving what's going on.

Yet more than ten years after this crisis was proclaimed, it remains rare that a mother's tolerance, let alone encouragement, of a wide range of emotion and self-expression in her son is admired. It might be acceptable for the unusual father or another male to model these behaviors or attitudes. The "nontraditional dad" is often held in warm regard. But a mother is still expected to reel in any behavior in her son that falls outside expected gender norms, and certainly it is the mother who is held accountable if that doesn't happen.

It turns out, though, that a generation of mothers has been quietly trusting their instincts and raising sons to be part of this new world. Despite the barrage of criticism and the constant admonitions to push their sons away, mothers have been engaging in their own underground social rebellion. They have been working hard to nurture the emotional skills they know their sons need.

These women recognize that the world no longer values either über-feminine or über-masculine traits. Brute strength and dominance no longer serve men in either the workplace or larger society.

Does this mean that mothers want to feminize their sons? Not any more than fathers who by encouraging their daughters' potential are trying to create masculine girls. What it does mean is that mothers are trying to raise a new kind of boy with the opportunity to become a more fully emotionally developed human being. Maybe these sons will grow up to ask for directions when they are lost. Maybe they'll even ask for help when they're in trouble. But they'll still be men, just ones who have found their bearings and aren't quite so alone with their problems. And they'll most likely make better partners and spouses, too.

I didn't come to these beliefs overnight. They are the product of my own experience in raising both a son and a daughter, of interviews with dozens of mothers and surveys of hundreds more, and of several years of research. Given how quickly the world is changing, there is a real urgency to this issue. We have to trust our instincts when it comes to raising our sons. We have to keep them close and give them what they need. And we need to start right now.

1

Defending the Bond

Few misfortunes can befall a boy which bring worse consequences
than to have a really affectionate mother.
—W. SOMERSET MAUGHAM

～

NO MOTHER EVER HESITATED to go on and on about the
deep connection she has with her daughter. She'll proudly
tell you about the special trips they take together, about the
nature of their whispered confidences. She might even confess
they're "best friends" and that they can't go even two days
without speaking to each other. You might roll your eyes, but
you probably wouldn't be particularly alarmed. You might
even be a bit jealous.

Now switch genders. Suppose I told you that I am very
close to my son. That I love spending time with him, and that
we have dozens of inside jokes and shared traditions. Even
though we speak frequently, I still get a little thrill when I see
his number on the caller ID. Then I confess that my son is

so sensitive and intuitive that he "gets me" as no one else in the world does. Are you starting to raise an eyebrow? Are you beginning to speculate that something is off here? Are you a little worried about what kind of guy my son is growing up to be? And are you wondering about what kind of mother would raise her son this way, keeping him so close?

Well, I'm that kind of mother, the kind who—like so many others—has been surprised and delighted to find that my relationship with my son bears little resemblance to anything I'd read or been told about raising boys. Certainly from the moment I saw his newborn face, I was awash in love and tenderness. He brought out the deepest of maternal feelings, just as the birth of my daughter had a few years earlier. But as my son grew up, the level of connection and companionship that developed between us was completely unexpected. Mothers and daughters are supposed to be close; that's only natural. But mothers and sons—surely not.

Let me make it clear: though we are very close, I am not my son's best friend. We certainly don't gush all our secrets to each other. (For that matter, I'm not my daughter's best friend, either. I'm their mother.) Also, my son, a young man now, is more than six feet tall, plays ice hockey, has many male friends and a steady girlfriend. Why do I feel the need to tell you all this? Because in this culture, I must reassure you—and myself—that my deep emotional bond with my son hasn't compromised his masculinity. Look—he and his mom have this tight connection and my son is still "a guy's guy."

So then, what's going on here? What's causing this dissonance? Why should I have to qualify and apologize for my closeness to my son? The problem is the large disconnect between the myth we've been told about the mother-son relationship—that it should be one of "healthy" distance—and the reality of the close bond that many members of this generation of mothers and sons is living every day. It's as if we're watching a movie with the wrong sound track, leaving us disoriented and confused.

For at least a century, the common wisdom about mothers and sons has been something like this: a mother who stays emotionally close to her son after he reaches, say, the tender age of five, is acting inappropriately. She's that smothering mother destined to prevent her boy from growing up to be a strong, independent man. This mother is needy and controlling and refuses to cut the apron strings. She is on track to create the archetypal "mama's boy," an unappealing wimp who will never be able to form mature adult relationships with women.

This is actually the more benign view of mother-son closeness. Even worse is the notion that a tight bond between mother and son can be interpreted to mean that something even more deeply inappropriate—seductive and possibly sexual—is going on. It is pathological in nature. It is repellent. This is why initially I didn't want to tell you that my son and I have "our song," because it just sounds so creepy. (You might start imagining Norman Bates, the crazy son in *Psycho*, who dresses up as his dead mother and murders attractive young women.)

The truth is that "our song" is not romantic—it's Arlo Guthrie's recording of "City of New Orleans." If it happens to come on the radio or one of our iPods when we're together, my son and I have a goofy tradition where he pretends to hold out a microphone during the verse "penny a point, ain't no one keepin' score" and I belt out the lyrics. I can't remember how this started, but now the song reminds us of each other.

All this defensiveness about the song, the hockey, and the girlfriend reflects the confusion that many of today's mothers live with. The cultural message we have absorbed is that a well-adjusted, loving mother is one who gradually but surely pushes her son away, both emotionally and physically, in order to allow him to grow up to be a healthy man. Not only does she let him go, but she also gives him a hearty shove on the back to send him on his way, firmly and with love. This was standard operating procedure for our mothers, our grandmothers, and even our great-grandmothers.

My own mother has told me that one of the most difficult times in her marriage was when she had a disagreement with my father over how she was raising my brother. My father is a particularly warm and tenderhearted man, yet he was worried about my mother's closeness to my brother, Todd. When Todd turned fourteen, my father thought he should be sent away to school because he worried that his son was becoming a "mama's boy." My mother's instincts told her otherwise, but she deferred to my father, assuming that fathers knew best about sons. My brother was very unhappy away from home and my mother wanted to bring him back. But my dad insisted that it was important "a boy learns that you don't quit when things become difficult." More than forty-five years later, my mother still regrets not fighting for what she intuitively knew was best for her son.

My mother was not atypical for her generation. Cate Dooley and Dr. Nicolina Fedele, who codirected the Mothers-Sons Project at the Jean Baker Miller Training Institute at Wellesley Centers for Women during the 1990s, witnessed this phenomenon frequently with mothers of grown sons. The two women conducted hundreds of group sessions and workshops, teaching mothers a new model of parenting that began to question some of the old assumptions about raising boys.

"In the workshops with mothers of adult sons, the grief was so palpable," Dooley said in an interview. "Some of these mothers couldn't talk without crying. They felt they had lost their sons and now were at a loss on how to connect with them as adults. Their sons came of age immersed in that model of separation."

It wasn't just older generations of mothers who were filled with regret. Dooley and Fedele found that younger mothers of sons were struggling with how to raise their boys, too. Many wrestled with everyday parenting issues and old cultural stereotypes. Should a mother defer to her husband when he insists that she stop kissing their first-grade son when she drops him off at school? If a mother cuddles her ten-year-old son when he is hurt, will she turn him into a wimp? If she keeps him too close, will she make him gay? If a teenage boy is crying in his room, should a mother go in and comfort him, or would this embarrass and shame him? If a mother is too affectionate with her son, might it be construed as seductive?

Amazingly, many of these ideas about mothers and their sons still hold considerable power and resonance today. After all, we've been through a social upheaval that has dramatically changed the way men and women lead their lives. It has been more than forty years since the advent of the modern feminist movement, and our beliefs about the roles of men and women, masculinity and femininity, and even how gender itself is identified have been significantly transformed. So why haven't the rules about how mothers bring up their sons been revolutionized as well?

Somehow, throughout this momentous social upheaval, our view of the mother-son relationship has remained curiously and stubbornly stagnant. We have certainly changed the way we raise our daughters, encouraging them to be assertive, play competitive sports, and shoot for the stars when it comes to their educational and professional ambitions. We don't worry that we are raising our little girls to be boys; we believe we are offering our daughters an opportunity to reach their full potential. But what about our sons? It is as if the feminist revolution sputtered out when it came to expanding the possibilities for boys, and especially for how their mothers might relate to them. The mother-son relationship is still largely seen through a prism that ignores the tidal wave of change that has otherwise transformed our society. We're hanging on to an old narrative that no longer describes our contemporary reality.

This frozen perspective is problematic on many levels. For one thing, it continues to reinforce a dated, sexist, homophobic, and generally negative view of what goes on between women and their sons. It diminishes or ignores anything positive that women can and do contribute to their boys. It leaves both mothers and sons feeling confused and anxious about their relationship. And because of this distorted lens, the mother-son relationship has become the only parent-child combination in which closeness is viewed so critically and with such suspicion.

Think about it. We know the mother-daughter relationship is considered sacrosanct. There is, in fact, a small industry built around it, complete with kitschy "A Daughter Is a Friend for Life" pillows, mother-daughter spa discounts, and enough books on the relationship to stock a small independent bookstore.

No one, of course, has any problem with fathers and sons being close. They are encouraged to spend time together, to go off and do manly things and bond. There is a national fatherhood movement, supported by President Barack Obama, which particularly focuses on fathers being role models for their sons.

The father-daughter relationship? A "mama's boy" might be a reviled creature, but everyone looks tolerantly on "daddy's little girl." She has been singled out for an elevated status. Indeed, a loving and supportive father is now considered essential to a girl's self-esteem. Fathers are encouraged to be part of their daughters' lives, whether it's coaching their soccer teams or escorting their teenage girls to father-daughter dances.

Moreover, a father who flaunts gender stereotypes and teaches his daughter a traditionally masculine task, say rebuilding a car engine, is considered to be a pretty cool dad. But a mother who does something comparable—forget something equivalent, like teaching her son to knit; try simply encouraging him to talk more openly about his feelings—is looked at with contempt. What is she trying to *do* to that boy?

But here is where the discord comes in. Most mothers today do not actually buy the idea that nurturing close bonds with their sons will harm them. We are pretty tired of all the hand wringing about the future sexual proclivities of little boys who play with dolls and Easy-Bake Ovens. We have no interest in changing boys into girls. That is simply ridiculous. We love our sons with an intensity and tenderness for who they are as themselves. Like girls, boys, as every mother of a son knows, are delightful.

What we are interested in is a new narrative—something beyond the old "mama's boy's" myths and warnings. We want a fresh story that reflects the reality of our own lives. And that reality is that more and more mothers continue to keep their sons close and treasure that affectionate, nurturing bond well into their young adult lives. In my online survey of more than 1,100 mothers, nearly nine in ten describe themselves as either "extremely close" or "very close" to their sons. Not only do today's mothers dismiss the notion that we are damaging our sons by nurturing this relationship, we also believe we have an important and positive role to play in developing their emotional lives and influencing them in other ways. Far from creating wimpy guys who will forever cling to their mothers, we believe we are raising boys who will one day make strong, empathic spouses and partners. What's more, our sons will have the sensitivity, communication skills, and emotional intelligence they need to better navigate a fast-changing world.

This isn't just mothers' self-justification for "helicopter parenting," when parents hover close and become overinvolved in their child's every problem or decision. Nor is it wishful thinking. A new and growing body of scientific literature shows that sons who are close to their mothers are emotionally and physically healthier than those who are not. *Time* magazine recently ran the following headline: "Being a Mama's Boy: Good for Your Health." It was a catchy summary for a research project presented in 2010 at the American Psychological Association by Carlos Santos, a professor at Arizona State University. Santos set out to study the extent to which middle school boys buy into more traditional, stereotypic images of masculinity—the idea that being a man means acting emotionally stoic, physically tough, and self-reliant. Santos followed for three years 426 boys from sixth grade through eighth grade, asking them how much they agree with statements such as "If I have a problem, I take care of it on my own" or "Fighting others is something

I have to do to prove myself." When the boys are younger, they are less accepting of these views, but Santos found that as boys get further along into adolescence, they tend to adopt more hyper-masculine beliefs and behaviors. Younger boys are more emotionally expressive and enjoy more intimate friendships. But as they grow older they tend to toughen up, hiding their own vulnerability and pulling away from those close connections.

Santos didn't set out to study mothers and sons, but as he analyzed his findings, he discovered that there is one major factor that mitigates boys' move toward toughness and autonomy—their closeness to their moms. It turned out that boys who have warm, supportive relationships with their mothers don't accept strict, traditional definitions of masculinity. They are also more emotionally open and communicative. "The emotional language boys used when speaking of their mothers was directly at odds with the way we see boyhood constructed in our culture," Santos told me. "These boys would talk very openly about their deep love and care for their mother." In fact, a boy's closeness to his mother is the number one predictor of how emotionally available he remains. Closeness to fathers does not have the same effect. Santos speculates that the nurturing and communication skills a boy gains from a strong attachment with his mother gives him the tools he needs to help him with the other relationships in his life.

Is it necessarily a good thing for boys to remain more emotionally available and communicative—stereotypically feminine qualities—or should these young guys be learning to "man up"? The boys Santos studied were from six public schools in New York City that predominantly serve low-income students. The boys were also from a range of different racial and ethnic backgrounds—African-American, Puerto Rican, Dominican American, Chinese American, European American, and a few others. You might assume that it would benefit these boys to toughen up so they could better navigate the playgrounds and neighborhoods where they live.

But that's not true. It turns out that the boys who are less traditionally macho are actually happier and healthier than their tougher peers. Santos's research found that they have lower rates of depression and overall better mental health than boys who buy into the more traditional view of manhood. The boys who equate masculinity with stoicism and autonomy tend to become more detached in their relationships, less able to talk about what they are feeling, and more likely to use aggression and violence. The more macho boys also reveal greater feelings of sadness and of their own worthlessness. The connection between being close to mom and rejecting hyper-masculinity, which creates better mental health through middle school and beyond, cuts across all socioeconomic, racial, and ethnic identities.

This research isn't important just because it makes mothers feel good about keeping their boys close. It has societal implications. For the last decade we have been hearing that boys are "in crisis," a subject I'll explore in greater depth later.

Many boys continue to struggle in school. Not only are they falling behind academically but boys are also more likely to be diagnosed with hyperactivity and attention disorders than girls. In the classroom, boys exhibit far more behavior problems. There are competing theories about the causes of boys' academic and social troubles, including the ideas that school curriculums are excessively verbal and favor girls, that boys have more trouble sitting still and do more poorly in a classroom setting, and that boys and girls actually have different brain wiring and simply must be taught differently. Many of these arguments are controversial; some academics even contend that the "boy crisis" itself is a manufactured one.

While there may be no consensus about what is now causing girls to outperform boys academically and to get into less trouble in school, we do know a solution to the problems boys face—mothers nurturing close relationships with their sons. Surely boys who are less aggressive and violent, more articulate and better able to connect with others, will perform better in a classroom setting. And these are precisely the qualities that Santos found in boys who remained close to their mothers. In fact, his most recent research is making the connection between the extent to which boys embrace traditional macho masculinity, and their success in school. "What I saw was a domino effect," Santos explained. "The quality of the mother-son relationship was predictive of these boys' resistance to male stereotypes, and that resistance was predictive of academic engagement."

Other scholars have suggested that boys who are hyperactive and inattentive in classrooms might actually be suffering the effects of separating prematurely from their mothers. Dooley and Fedele even suggest that the real label for many boys' academic troubles should be CDD—Connection Deficit Disorder.

Santos isn't the only one documenting the benefits of the mother-son connection. It turns out that the advantages of a strong bond between mother and son extend well into young adult life. For instance, teenagers who have warm, supportive relationships with their mothers engage in fewer risky behaviors than those who report less closeness. In general, teenagers who have good communication with both their parents are more likely to resist negative peer pressure. But recent studies show that it is a boy's mother who is the most influential when it comes to preventing teenagers from using alcohol and drugs, as well as engaging in unprotected sex. Teenage boys who report a strong connection with their moms also tended to postpone early sex. Again, these findings about boys and their mothers held true for boys of all races and social classes.

Despite the mounting evidence that keeping our boys close will help make them happier and healthier, mothers continue to face relentless pressure to back off from their sons, beginning at astoundingly early ages. Mothers of one-year-olds told me that they were accused of "coddling" their sons. Mothers of toddlers reported being admonished for comforting their weeping four-year-olds. As one husband told his wife about their pre-kindergartener, "He needs to learn to man up." Mothers of school-aged boys are told to stay out of it when their sons are being bullied, because "boys will be boys." And as for mothers of teenage boys—they get the strongest message of all to pull away. Moms are told that the last thing a teenage boy needs to grow up is his mother.

Well, the time has come to ask, "How's that been working out for you?" Because the truth is that this old model no longer serves boys or their mothers. The academic "boy crisis" isn't the only one that should concern us about our sons. Over the last decade, an alarm has also been sounded about boys' emotional crisis. Boys are at risk of becoming "emotionally illiterate," according to psychologists Dan Kindlon and Michael Thompson. In *Raising Cain*, these authors argue that our culture systematically steers boys away from their emotional lives "towards silence, solitude and distrust." Boys aren't learning to read and understand their own emotions or those of others. Over time, they adopt the only socially acceptable "manly" emotions—primarily anger, aggression, and withdrawal. Dr. William Pollack, an assistant clinical professor of psychology at Harvard Medical School and Director of the Centers for Men and Young Men at McLean Hospital, wrote compellingly in *Real Boys* about the "boy code": that familiar outdated, gender-stereotyped checklist—be tough, keep your feelings to yourself, don't depend on anyone else, no sissy stuff. Boys are encouraged to disengage from family connections—including and especially their mothers—at tender ages. What happens when boys conform to this code? The same thing as when our sons become "emotionally illiterate." They become lonely, withdrawn, and depressed, and as they grow older, sometimes aggressive and violent.

This is exactly what mothers are pushing back against. We don't want this for our sons and we don't accept it for our sons. It is why we are working hard to teach our sons the language of emotions. Our boys' more tender and sensitive sides do not frighten us and we don't feel the need to suppress or stamp out these so-called feminine parts of them. We want them to be happy and whole. What's more, we believe—and the research is starting to prove—that we play an important role in influencing how well our sons develop.

Look, mothers through the ages have wanted the same things for their sons—we want to protect them and we want them to be ready to face the world. But the world our sons are entering is a very different place from the one their fathers and grandfathers navigated. A 2010 headline in *The Atlantic* magazine heralded "The End of Men." The author, Hanna Rosin, argues that we are at an unprecedented moment in history when the power dynamics of men and women are shifting very swiftly. Women, she says, are taking over everything—graduating at higher rates from college and beginning to dominate professions like medicine, law, banking, and accounting. Women are rapidly moving into managerial ranks. For the first time in 2010, women became the majority of the American workforce, mostly because men were casualties of the recession, when construction jobs and other jobs related to the housing industry disappeared.

Moreover, Rosin makes the case that in all of the fifteen professions projected to grow the most during the next decade—fields like nursing, home health assistance, child care—women dominate all but two of them—janitor and computer engineer. The social sector of the economy will gain 6.9 million jobs by 2018, according to a study by Northeastern University. And while women have for decades been steadily moving into fields that were once considered men-only, men have not proved as adaptable, still shunning traditionally female jobs like teaching and nursing.

The key point—especially for mothers who are raising sons who will enter this marketplace—is that the job market is transitioning to one that values brains over brawn, and more specifically thinking and communication skills over physical power and stamina. This isn't just a shift for working-class jobs. Management is also starting to value a different kind of leadership style. Top business schools are now teaching management theories that are less top-down hierarchical and more focused on team building, communication, and fostering creativity. Harvard just added a first-year curriculum-course that not only encourages students' teamwork but also is designed to help them "cultivate their emotional intelligence and learn how others perceive them." said Nitin Nohria, dean of Harvard Business School. In other words, a course more oriented to traditionally female strengths. As Rosin puts it, "The postindustrial economy is indifferent to men's size and strength. The attributes that are most valuable today—social intelligence, open communication, the ability to sit still and focus—are, at a minimum, not predominantly male. In fact, the opposite may be true."

Actually, recent research on gender reveals that attributes like social intelligence, open communication, and focus are not inborn sex traits but aptitudes that have been developed. Girls and women are socialized early on to learn these skills, but they are not innate to either gender. Since most mothers have been brought up to develop these very qualities, we are also in the best position to impart them to our sons. That is precisely what so many mothers that I interviewed for this book told me they were doing with their boys—patiently encouraging them to "use your words," working with them to understand what they are feeling and express it, urging them to refrain from fighting and to work out their issues with their friends. Many of these same mothers are accused of babying, coddling, and feminizing their sons. But they are forging ahead anyway, trusting the instincts that tell them their sons will benefit, not suffer, from some female influence.

In a way, mothers have to play catch up, trying to update a crazily outdated parenting model so our sons don't get left behind. Why would we raise our sons the same way as mothers did in the 1950s and 1960s, when that world is long gone? What does the world our sons will be entering look like today? Single, childless young women now make more money than single, childless men in this country. This holds true at every level of education—unmarried men now fare worse than unmarried women. Marriage itself is on the decline; the decline has occurred primarily along class lines, with lower-income people less likely to wed. In one national survey, nearly 40 percent of respondents believe marriage is obsolete.

Four in ten mothers are the primary breadwinners in the family; many of them are single mothers. In 1970, women contributed between 2 percent and 6 percent of the family income; in 2008, women in dual-earner families contributed an average of 44 percent of annual income. Not only has that figure been climbing rapidly, but the percentage of women earning more than their husbands also continues to increase.

All this has created a huge cultural shift and significant gender role reversal. A Pew Research study published in 2010 concluded that the economic benefits of marriage have now flipped. In the past, when relatively few wives worked, marriage boosted the economic status of women more than men. But lately, the economic gains associated with marriage have been greater for men than women. In a survey on gender issues, *Time* concluded that "at the most basic level, the argument over where women belong is over; the battle of the sexes becomes a costume drama, like *Middlemarch* or *Mad Men*." Across a wide range of income levels and ideologies, people agree that women's growing role in the workforce is good for the economy and society. It might sound matter-of-fact now, but the idea that women no longer view getting married as their ticket to economic stability or that marriage and motherhood don't need to go together was radical a few decades ago.

Newsweek recently featured an article urging men to adapt to the new economic and social realities, in part by pursuing traditionally female jobs, pushing for parental leave, becoming more involved as fathers, and contributing their fair share at home and at work. Authors Andrew Romano and Tony Dokoupil dubbed this approach the "New Macho," asking, "After all, what's more masculine: being a strong, silent, unemployed absentee father, or actually fulfilling your half of the bargain as a breadwinner and dad?"

How does this affect our sons? Well, they certainly can't assume they will grow up to be the breadwinners and heads of the households. And they can expect to take on their fair share of the "second shift" of child care and housework. Of course, this transition has been in the works for quite a while now, though heaven knows it's been slow going. Multiple studies have documented that younger fathers are increasingly participating in the nitty-gritty of parenting and housework. As they assume greater responsibility on the domestic front, men also now report feeling more work/life conflict—just as women have for decades.

That said, fathers are often still treated as heroes for doing what is simply expected of mothers. The author Michael Chabon writes in *Manhood for Amateurs*, "The handy thing about being a father is that the historic standard is so pitifully low." Michael Lewis admits in *Home Game: An Accidental Guide to Fatherhood*, "I expected to be chastised for doing so little but instead found myself appreciated for doing anything at all."

Chabon and Lewis are contributors to the growing body of "Dad Lit," fathers who write about their lives on the home front. Some of this is annoying for mothers to read—why are the travails of diaper bags or cleaning up a kid's vomit somehow interesting if a father writes about it? It's even worse when these descriptions of fatherhood are done in a kind of faux self-deprecating but actually self-congratulatory smug tone. But I suspect that by the time many of our sons are fathers, there will not be much of a market for such books, because the novelty of a father changing a poopy diaper will be long gone.

To succeed in the workplace and on the home front, our sons are going to need a much broader skill set than men in the past. Abilities like nurturing, working cooperatively, and articulating feelings are the very qualities that mothers can help to develop in their sons. That's not because these traits are inherently feminine or the sole province of women, but because at this juncture in history, women have been socialized to develop these skills, and up until now, men have not. By encouraging this side of our sons, mothers are not feminizing our boys. Rather, we are trying to help redefine masculinity and move away from a model that is not only limiting to our sons, but also threatens to undermine their success in a fast-changing world.

Emily, an associate professor of journalism and the mother of a twelve-year-old son, told me a story about a university department meeting she recently attended. "There was this old-school man who was being so sexist. He was nervous and making inappropriate jokes. The others in the meeting were some really highly educated, strategic women and a few younger guys. As soon as the meeting was over, the women and the younger men got on a conference call to figure out how to handle the situation because it was so clear that we really couldn't bring this guy to any presentations or larger meetings. If you are raising a boy to be like that, he is going to be left behind," she said.

And what about the influence of fathers? Of course boys benefit from good strong relationships with their dads. It is a lucky boy—and an increasingly rare one—who is afforded a close, warm relationship with two parents. But parenting is not a zero-sum game. A son's being close to his mother doesn't weaken his relationship with his father; that is another dated myth. No one wants to push fathers out of their sons' lives; that would be absurd.

The point is that for far too long, mothers have been pushed away from their sons—discouraged from keeping them close, from influencing them, even from loving them too deeply. There is still a taboo about mothers and sons, a bit of a prurient smirk and a lingering suspicion that too much mom will damage her growing boy and keep him from becoming a man. These ideas are deeply embedded in our culture. They predate Freud and his Oedipus theory. They dominate contemporary psychological "wisdom," and a good chunk of today's parenting advice, particularly from some who claim expertise in raising boys. You see this attitude reflected in contemporary movies, literature, and advertisements. And mothers deal with it every day, starting from the very first moment they reveal their pregnancy and are asked, "Do you know yet what you're having?" The correct response is not "Why, yes, a baby." We want to know if it's a boy or a girl, because then we can start to imagine just how different the experience is going to be, depending on the sex. And if a mother doesn't know her baby's sex, there will be plenty of speculation. If the baby is very active in utero, it must be a boy. (Because you know how boys are.) If you have heartburn, it must be a girl. (Because you know how girls are.) The myths start well before birth and take off from there. Studies have shown that parents observing newborns only a few hours old perceive the boys to be stronger and more active than the girls, even though this has no correlation with their babies' actual hardiness. This "boy vision" just goes on and on, to the point where a silent teenage boy is seen as strong and stoic, when in fact he might be deeply depressed.

I don't really believe that boys are "in crisis." But I do think that boys, and especially young men, are growing up in a transitional time when they are getting very mixed messages about what it means to be a guy. They are expected to be sensitive and respectful of women—basically evolved men—but at the same time they get plenty of pressure to be strong, tough, and macho. It's confusing for boys, and sometimes for their mothers, who after all are part of this culture, too.

What is clear to me, and to so many other mothers, is that the conventional wisdom about mothers and sons has become sorely outdated. It isn't healthy for our boys to push them away from us when they are young. It is cruel to insist that they "be a little man." (I can't imagine any mother, or father for that matter, turning to a weeping five-year-old girl and admonishing her to "be a little woman.") The idea that we need to shove our sons toward independence so that they can be strong men is simply flawed logic. Our sons need us when they are young, and benefit from our influence as they grow older.

But challenging entrenched beliefs is not a simple process. Cultural shifts take time. Yet every day, in kitchens, in cars, on playgrounds, and even in nurseries, mothers are pushing back the old admonitions to separate from their sons. And many find themselves surprised and delighted by the results of this new approach.

2

The Pink-and-Blue Divide

A daughter is a daughter for all of her life,

a son is a son till he takes him a wife.

—IRISH PROVERB

᠀

᠀ Not-So-Great Expectations

Certainly I wasn't the only mother who, soon after hearing "It's a boy," gazed down at this small bundle, immediately wrapped in blue by the hospital staff, with all sorts of preconceptions about what having a son would be like. Most pregnant women will tell you they don't care about the baby's gender, they are simply grateful for a healthy child. For the most part they are telling the truth. But there's another truth as well, and that is that we do have preferences, based on our strong feelings about how the experience of raising a son will differ from that of raising a daughter. Our expectations are based on the assumption of a great pink-and-blue divide.

Why do you think books like *How to Choose the Sex of Your Baby* have stayed in print for more than forty years?

There are dozens of books and multiple websites that adver-
tise ways to improve your chances of having a son or a daughter. They range from low-tech interventions—like sex timing
and positions—to high-tech—including sperm sorting and in
vitro fertilization procedures that involve pre-implantation
genetic testing.

These techniques are simply more scientifically advanced
methods of an age-old obsession. Aristotle believed a baby's
sex relied on the direction of the wind during conception. Men
in ancient Greece tried tying off their left testicle to produce
a male heir. In medieval times, people believed that the sex
of a baby could be influenced by which side of the bed a man
hung his pants on—right for a boy, left for a girl. Over time,
couples have experimented with sex positions, maternal diets
(if you want a girl, gorge on chocolate; for a boy, stick to salty
snacks), and even timing intercourse during certain phases of
the moon, all in an effort to influence their baby's gender.

Listen to this advertising copy from a contemporary website: "Good News! Now You Can Choose! Our proven baby
gender selection program will successfully add some pink or
blue to your unbalanced family so that you can finally hold
this longed-for little prince or princess in your arms and stop
feeling guilty about your secret desire for this gender!"

There are a variety of reasons parents prefer one sex over
the other, some based in medical history—like avoiding sex-
linked genetic diseases—and others in cultural expectations—
such as the idea of passing on the family name through a son,

or the notion that a daughter will more likely take care of you in old age. Some families have had a string of boys or girls and want to experience "the other."

Certainly in patriarchal societies, boys historically have been more valued than girls. The tradition of male primogeniture— the rule that a firstborn son inherits the entire estate—has existed since biblical times. We remember King Henry VIII primarily for his determination to produce a male heir, working his way through six wives, two of whom he beheaded. China, India, and Korea have long been known for a preference for male children; abandonment of infant girls in China was a significant problem not long ago. And in the United States, as recently as my own mother's generation, it was a point of pride for women to "give" their husbands a firstborn son. Lynn, a post–World War II Texas mother, remembers having her first child—a healthy girl—in 1955 and receiving condolences. "People would say, 'Oh, well, that's too bad. Maybe you'll get a boy next time,'" she recalled.

But in today's world, which has since undergone such a dramatic social upheaval when it comes to men and women, just how do we expect the little "princes" and "princesses" described on that gender selection website to differ? Many of these beliefs go straight to the heart of how we view the mother-son relationship. The nursery rhyme proclaiming little girls as "sugar and spice and all things nice" and little boys as being made of "snips and snails and puppy dog tails" sounds sweetly quaint and old-fashioned. Yet when it comes to mothers anticipating how they should relate to their sons and the messages we get about how to raise those boys, our ideas remain startlingly retro, eerily close to the nursery rhyme ethos.

We are familiar with the long-held stereotypes about what boys and girls are like, and how those characteristics will play out in the mother-child relationship. Girls are emotional and empathetic. They have deep feelings of warmth and sadness, and a strong capacity for connection. Daughters might fight bitterly with their mothers during the teenage years, but the bond will not be broken. Mothers and daughters will be close for life.

That's why when Tanya, already the mother of one adopted son, had a sonogram that revealed she was having triplet boys, she was as shocked by their sex as she was by their number. "When I found out about the triplets, all I could think is, 'Where's my daughter?' I was supposed to be the mother of a daughter. I have a very close relationship with my mother, and I assumed I would have the same with a girl, not boys," she said. Tanya, a broad-shouldered blonde, had gone through years of infertility treatments before her pregnancy and feels guilty for still having daughter lust. "I have nieces, and I joke with their mom, when it comes to prom dresses, I'm there."

Claudia, an advocate for immigration reform, was even more blunt about the arrival of her son: "I kept cleaning his balls and thinking, 'How the hell did this happen to me?'" Claudia, who grew up in Colombia, believed that she would relate to a girl better, because in a sense she would be re-creating herself.

Certainly there are mothers who dream about engaging in very traditional "girl activities," like Sue, a Mississippi mother who was crushed when an ultrasound revealed she was carrying her second son. "I wanted to experience the pretty things," she explained wistfully. "The pink things. The dance classes. I wanted to be Mother of the Bride."

But for many mothers, the relationships they imagine with their daughters don't focus on tea parties and playing with Barbie dolls. "I'm a feminist and I was going to raise the next generation of strong women," says Jen, a successful Silicon Valley career woman, the mother of two sons, now twenty-three and twenty. "When it came time to have children, what I had in mind were daughters. All of my feminist friends laughed, 'Look at the hand you were dealt.' I had to process that loss. I had daughter envy."

For Marti, who is in her fifties and still runs marathons, it was about Title IX, which passed in 1972 and prohibited sex discrimination in federally funded education programs. Marti's high school offered girls only one sport: cheerleading. She dreamed of the vicarious thrill of watching a daughter excel in competitive team sports. (As life would have it, Marti had both a son and a daughter, and neither was remotely interested in athletics.)

But even as those daughter dreams reflect a changed world of new opportunities for girls and women, they still embrace the traditional assumption that daughters will be far more emotionally available, open to influence, guidance, and simply being closer to their mothers than sons could ever be. Our expectations for boys remain unchanged.

"What do I know about being a mom to a boy?" Leslie, a New Jersey mother, remembers thinking. Her father was a biochemist and her brother operated a ham radio, and neither one of them was the least bit emotive. "They were brilliant but they were no fun at all, and that's what I thought all boys were like," she says.

About half of all women say they would definitely prefer a girl over a boy, according to a study that looked at parents across a broad spectrum of race, class, and sexual orientation. For those who go so far as trying scientific sex-selection techniques, the preference for girls is far greater. Currently, Micro-Sort, a gender-selection method that separates sperm, is in an FDA clinical trial. Only 7 percent of couples enrolled in the trial are trying to prevent genetic disease; the other 93 percent are seeking "family balance." Of those, more than 70 percent want girls; just fewer than 30 percent want boys. (In order to qualify for the family balance trial, couples must have at least one child of the other sex.)

Why this overwhelming preference for a daughter? The scientists at MicroSort declined to speculate on clients' motivation, but the women in the study gave reasons similar to those of the women I interviewed: they believe daughters will grow up to think like their mothers, enjoy the things their mothers enjoy, and perhaps most of all maintain a tight bond with their mothers even after they leave the family nest to start their own family. As one woman in the study that looked at parents' preferences for sons or daughters put it, "I envisioned that a daughter would be a great companion in old age. We would do things together . . . a lot of girl time . . . a girl would never forget your birthday, would be much more emotionally connected." None of the mothers surveyed imagined they would have shared interests or close emotional bonds with their sons.

What are the assumptions we make about our sons? They will be more aggressive and active, maybe even a little wild. If you ban toy weapons from the house, boys will create them out of anything, transforming sticks into swords or, as one mom told me, biting a piece of toast into the shape of a gun. Boys won't be very emotional, but when they are, they'll show more anger than sadness and more aggression than compassion. "I figured boys were going to be macho, unfeeling, and insensitive," says Sarah, a lawyer. "That's what you grow up thinking."

As for boys' relationships with their moms—they might be their mothers' little darlings when they are very young. But as they get older, they'll toughen up and keep their feelings to themselves. They certainly will not be hanging out with their moms. For boys, maturing means cutting those apron strings and leaving their mothers behind. Boys need to outgrow their moms to become men.

These beliefs about the mother-son relationship are so widely held that Joyce A. Venis, a psychiatric nurse, has developed a specialty in "gender disappointment counseling." Venis, who practices in Princeton, New Jersey, says that most of her

clients are expectant mothers who were deeply disappointed—
some even became clinically depressed—when prenatal testing revealed they were having boys. Why? They had dreamed
of having girls because they were convinced that daughters
would be soul mates. A daughter, these women believed,
would always be close and never leave you.

The emotional reactions of mothers who seek counseling
over their disappointment in a baby boy might be extreme,
but their assumptions about just how differently the relationship will develop between mother and child, depending on
what shadowy parts are revealed on an ultrasound, are widely
shared. Venis works at ground zero for gender preconceptions
and her experiences echo much of what mothers confessed
to me. "Some of these moms believe there's something magical about a relationship with daughters," says Venis. "They say
that you can have a great relationship with a daughter, and
share things, do 'girl things,' and relate to them better. I also
hear things like, 'I don't know how to play with Matchbox
cars; I'm better at dresses.'" Mothers also told Venis that they
were sad about having sons, because they believed that even
if they were able to develop a deep emotional bond to their
boys, it would only be temporary. "These moms are concerned
about the future," she said. "They would love to remain close
to their sons, but they're also afraid, some of them, that if they
don't have a daughter, there is going to be nothing left for
them later. There's this fear that a son leaves you."

Or as Robin, a California mother of an eight-year-old son,

put it sadly, "I just always remember that proverb—'A daughter is a daughter for all of her life, a son is a son till he takes him a wife.'"

⌁ Snips and Snails/Sugar and Spice

Are these assumptions based on any real science? The truth is, there is simply no biological basis for the idea that daughters are able to form close, lifelong bonds with their mothers, but sons are incapable of doing so. Researchers who have studied the ways in which the mother-child bond is formed and how it enables children to thrive emotionally have found no significant differences among boys' and girls' abilities to form attachments to their mothers. In fact, new research has revealed that boys who do have insecure attachments suffer far more than girls, at least outwardly. Dr. Pasco Fearon, a clinical psychologist and professor at the University of Reading's School of Psychology and Clinical Language Sciences, reviewed sixty-nine attachment studies involving almost six thousand children age twelve and younger. His study, published in 2010, found that boys who were insecurely attached acted more aggressive and hostile later in childhood—kicking and hitting others, yelling, disobeying adults, and being generally destructive. (That's not to say that poor parenting does not harm girls. Researchers speculate that girls might react differently and turn their feelings inward, resulting in depression and anxiety.)

Furthermore, research on the extent to which "girl behavior" and "boy behavior" are hardwired—reflecting real biological differences in the sexes—suggests that socialization is far more important than any innate gender-based factors in the emotional lives of both boys and girls. New research on the brain disputes the popular notions that female brains are hardwired for empathy or male brains for more rational thought. (Some female scientists have coined the term "neurosexism" to describe this kind of thinking.) Cordelia Fine, an academic psychologist, argues in *Delusions of Gender* that much of the past research claiming gender brain differences was based on sloppy science, using small sample sizes and emphasizing insignificant differences while failing to note the similarities. Such research inevitably validates the status quo. Fine argues that there are not "male" and "female" brains, but minds that are malleable and constantly influenced by our cultural assumptions about gender. In her book *Pink Brain, Blue Brain*, associate professor of neuroscience Lise Eliot completed an exhaustive review of brain research and found only two physiological inborn neurological differences between the sexes. First, boys' brains are bigger than those of girls to the degree that their bodies are bigger. Second, girls' brains stop growing approximately two years before those of boys, basically because they mature more quickly.

Eliot does not argue that there are no other innate sex differences, only that these are the two neurological distinctions that have been identified and proven. Overall, Eliot,

Fine, and other neuroscientists believe that the brains of boys and girls are more similar than their behavioral differences might imply. Much of what we assume to be differences in the brain—distinctions that would cause boys and girls to relate differently or learn differently—are simply reflections of how parents unconsciously socialize their children about gender at an early age.

In fact, there is evidence that boys might well begin life as more emotionally sensitive than girls. In the first few months of infancy, boys are more easily aroused and emotionally expressive than girls. They cry and fuss more, startle more easily, and are quicker to excite. Research has shown that boys remain more emotional than girls until they are six months old. In one study mothers were instructed to stop smiling, talking, and playing with their six-month-old babies. Sons reacted with significantly more stress and anxiety than daughters. Boys cried more and took longer to soothe once their mothers began responding to them again. Another study found that six-month-old boys exhibited "significantly more joy and anger, more positive vocalizations, fussiness, and crying, [and] more gestural signals directed towards the mother . . . than girls."

Boys exhibit their sensitivity in other ways as well. Interestingly, boys who miss out on the benefits of breast-feeding are harmed more than girls. The advantages of being breast-fed for at least six months have been widely documented, particularly its association with enhanced immunity. But a new Australian study that followed three thousand children from birth onward suggests that breast-feeding might yield academic benefits later in a child's life, particularly for boys. In a study published in the journal *Pediatrics* in 2010, researchers found that boys got a significantly bigger academic boost than girls from breast-feeding. Boys who were nursed for six months or more were not only better bonded to their mothers, but also by the time they were ten years old had better scores in math, reading, writing, and spelling than boys who were bottle-fed or breast-fed for shorter periods. These cognitive advantages of breast-feeding were far less pronounced for little girls. (This was an unexpected place to find a new way to address the academic boy crisis!)

Why are boys more receptive to the positive effects of breast milk? Dr. Wendy Oddy, part of the research team at the Telethon Institute for Child Health Research in Australia that conducted the study, says that infant boys are more vulnerable to adversity during critical periods of brain development than infant girls. Breast milk contains "neuro-protective estradiols"— basically female hormones found in long-chain fatty acids— that protect growing brains. And infant male brains need more protection than female ones in order to thrive.

Because men are generally bigger and physically stronger than women, we might assume that newborn boys are heartier, too. In fact, infant males are surprisingly more fragile than infant girls. In utero, males are particularly vulnerable; women are 30 percent more likely to miscarry a boy than a girl. Not only are boys more likely to be born prematurely than girls but their survival rate is lower. Those who do survive tend to have more complications resulting in neurological damage. Scientists aren't sure why boys at the start of life are so much more susceptible to illness and death than girls. Eliot, the neuroscientist, says that one hypothesis is that male fetuses can be more easily rejected by their mothers' immune systems. Male fetuses express a protein that could trigger an immune reaction from their mothers, though this has never been proven. Another theory is that male fetuses mature more slowly than female fetuses, especially their respiratory and immune systems, leaving them more vulnerable to infection as newborns. Males also have a faster metabolism, so they need more calories to survive.

Despite all the evidence that boys are more fragile than girls at the beginning of their lives, parents tend to respond with far less comfort to their son's distress than they do to their daughter's. For instance, when baby boys express unhappiness or fear, mothers tend to counter these emotions with positive feelings. If a baby boy cries because he is upset or in pain, his mother is more likely to bounce him up and down, while saying, "You're okay, you're fine!" and smiling at him. With a daughter, though, mothers are more likely to empathize by saying, "Oh, poor thing, what's the matter?" with an accompanying face that mimics her daughter's sadness.

That might seem like a subtle difference, but in these everyday interchanges, baby girls' emotions are being acknowledged and played back to them—"I see you're sad, and I'm responding to that sadness"—while boys are getting the message that what they feel is not acceptable—"You're not really sad. You're just fine. Buck up." We're unconsciously socializing our boys to be tough at remarkably young ages.

In one study, mothers brought their eleven-month-olds to a lab where babies could crawl down a carpeted slope. The mothers could push a button to change the slope's angle, depending on what they believed their children could safely navigate. Mothers of girls underestimated their daughter's abilities by a significant margin, despite the fact that—when they were on their own—boys and girls were equal risk takers and equally able to handle the same slopes.

Mothers of sons did not underestimate their son's physical abilities. But they did discount their boys' behavior in other ways, like not being overly concerned if their sons lagged in reading, because, as one mother summed it up, "He's a boy."

The brains of infants are extremely plastic, and as Eliot notes, it is precisely because of the brain's plasticity, particularly in the early years, that a child's environment is so influential. Learning and practice rewire the human brain to such an extent, she says, that scientists today no longer pit nature against nurture, but instead view them as elaborately entwined.

This has great relevance to mothers of sons, whether they start out with severe "daughter envy" or fall immediately and deeply in love with their sons. Gender stereotyping can become a self-fulfilling prophecy. That's why it's hard to say exactly how boys' potential emotional development is affected, according to Leslie Brody, a professor of psychology at Boston University, who has written extensively about gender differences in emotional development. But the bottom line is that to date there is no conclusive evidence to support the idea that boys are born with less capacity for emotional depth, range, or expression than girls.

Mothers who are sensitive to their sons' emotional states soon discover this for themselves. Even those who were initially sad or anxious about having boys gradually find that their baby boys and toddlers are capable of great tenderness and sweetness. These mothers are most awestruck by their sons' early, unwavering devotion to them.

"From the beginning, there was an instant connection," said Jane, who had worried when she was pregnant that she wouldn't have the same feelings for a boy that she did for her daughter. "He clung to me like he was still inside, wrapped around like an outer garment. I could let go and he'd still be on. He would nuzzle his chin into my neck like a pillow that belonged there. It was the best feeling in the world. From the minute he was born, it was like a love affair. I adored my daughter, but this was like a gorgeous, red-headed surprise package."

Lori, a social worker with two sons and a daughter, said, "There was a period where my boys were just in love with me, they were like little wet noodles. I could do no wrong." Sarah, who thought boys would be macho and insensitive, remembers watching the movie *Cinderella* with her toddler son, Alex. "We're going up the stairs and he says, 'Mom, you are so beautiful. Don't you think there's any way that Dad can marry Cinderella and I could marry you?'" (We will get to Freud later on.)

Mothers described little boys covering them with wet, sloppy kisses, toddlers softly patting and kissing their mothers' "boo-boos," and preschool sons exhibiting a level of sweetness, sensitivity, and deep need for connection that was sometimes surprising in its intensity. When Carrie's son Adam started nursery school, she had to stay with him in the classroom for several weeks, each day moving her chair a little farther away from Adam, one foot at a time. When Sally's little boy returned from an overnight visit to his grandparents, he hung on to his mother long after the first welcome home hug was over. "He just threw his arms around me and wouldn't let go," she says with a wistful smile. "He was really attached and really glad to see me." Deborah, a lesbian mother, was initially surprised by her son's emotional vulnerability. "Before I had a son, I just didn't know," she says. "I never had a brother and I didn't know many men. But with little boys there's this weird way you want to take care of them; they just seem a little helpless. When something happens they just fall apart in a way that girls don't. I asked my straight women friends, and they said, 'Oh, this is a guy thing.'"

Most mothers were not particularly alarmed by their little boys' neediness, attachment, or sensuality at this stage of development. They were often bemused by the contrast between the innocent and intense devotion their sons expressed alongside the exhibitions of their rampant "maleness." Claudia remembers James running through the house naked with nothing but the sword he had fashioned from a curtain rod, and then out of breath, plopping into her lap for a bare-bottomed cuddle.

↣ Back Off, Mom

No sooner do mothers delight in discovering that their sons long for emotional closeness and physical tenderness than they are encouraged to push their little boys away. It is as if there was an existing playbook, based on all those gender preconceptions, about how mothers and sons should interact, and mothers are constantly being held to task for straying from the rules.

Many women report critiques from husbands, brothers, and even female friends and family that they are "too close" to their sons. It begins when the boys are just babies and never stops. The early criticism tends to center around two areas: cuddling and "babying" sons. Physical cuddling and comforting seemed particularly provocative to those observing the mothers and sons.

Lee, an assistant district attorney, described exuberantly scooping up her one-year-old and spontaneously kissing him on the lips, only to have her husband chastise her—he told her it was too intimate. Bedtime routines often set off alarm bells. "When I lay down with Evan, it's this incredibly tender thing. He'll often put his little arm around my neck and his nose is pressed into my cheek and for me it's the most tender, intimate time—it's very precious," said Nan, a psychiatrist, about tucking in her five-year-old. "But there's intense family pressure not to stay with him until he falls asleep. They think I'm coddling him. Sometimes I am nervous enough about that pressure that, just to make sure I'm not doing something bad, I tiptoe out while he's still awake. I have to reassure myself that I haven't created this dependent boy."

But Nan notes that it is during this time together as they cuddle in the dark that Evan talks about his feelings, revealing if someone was mean to him at school or what he's worried about.

Pam, a single mom from New Hampshire with two boys, ages four and six, was told bluntly by both her father and her sister that she was creating "mama's boys" by having a lengthy bedtime routine that included reading and talking together.

"My sister and I were out drinking one time, we're spilling our souls, and she said I was too close to my sons," Pam recalled bitterly. "And I said, 'What do you see that makes you feel like that?' I was so angry. Like I needed the pressure. I read all the divorce books, and I don't unload my personal problems on them. But I do talk to them and I do try to meet their emotional needs."

For the most part, mothers privately dismiss the message to back off from their young sons, but some of it rankles. "I like to lie in bed and read to my boys," said Maureen, a nurse who has two sons, ages seven and five. "My husband keeps telling me to stop. When my younger son had his first day of kindergarten, I was working at the hospital and his dad was working at home. I called and asked, 'How was his first day of school?' and my husband said, 'Fine.' When I got home and my son and I laid down together, I asked Liam how school was. He immediately opened up about things that upset him. He often tells me things when I lie in bed with him, and I'll do it as long as he'll let me."

Amy, a yoga instructor in Maine, holds her six-year-old son's hand when she walks him to and from school, and even this benign contact has drawn rebuke. "I got a comment just the other day. This person asked if I thought it was appropriate that I was still holding his hand," she says. Amy was unconcerned—"I'll hold his hand until he's twenty-four"—but she also doubted that anyone would have questioned the appropriateness of a mother holding her first-grade daughter's hand.

Mothers also described being frequently criticized for running too quickly to comfort their young sons when they were hurt. "He has to learn to man up," one father told the mother of a four-year-old. A Seattle pediatrician cautioned Wendy, the mother of a three-year-old, not to cuddle her son when he fell down. "He told me I was modeling anxiety and that my child would become fearful," Wendy explained. "I'm supposed to pick him up and say, 'You're okay,' rather than kiss him." Tanya, the mother with an older son and triplets, was concerned when two of the triplets—who are identical twins—started picking on the third, the most emotionally sensitive of the brothers. She wanted to intervene, but her husband instead instructed the boy to stand up for himself and hit back. The triplets are three and a half years old. "This has resulted in everyone hitting each other and it has become gang warfare," Tanya said. "I told my husband to rescind that and say something about keeping your hands to yourself."

I remember one afternoon when my own son was four years old and had just transitioned from Velcro to tie sneakers. I was kneeling over to help him tie his shoelaces after he had tripped. My father looked over in exasperation and instructed me to "Leave that boy alone." It was a small thing, but he never would have suggested that I allow my daughter to run around with her laces flapping around.

The concern over mothers' tending to their sons in this way is yet another part of the great pink-and-blue divide. Few mothers reported getting any rebukes for being too warm, intimate, or coddling with their daughters; just the opposite. It is only the mother-son relationship that provoked the reaction. And it isn't just the physical and emotional tenderness between the two that came under criticism. Mothers also take considerable flack for allowing their sons to do or wear things that are not considered "gender appropriate."

Lori's son was still a baby and had curly blond hair. "I told my husband I'd cut it when Jeff turned two. But a month before, when he was in the bath, my husband cut his curls off.

He had to do it. He thought I was turning his boy into a girl," she said.

Joanne, a Connecticut mother of two teenagers, is still smarting over the pink jelly shoes incident. One summer day, she was out shopping with her seven-year-old daughter, her daughter's friend, and her four-year-old son, Noah. They were at the Gap, and the girls spotted some pink jelly shoes. They were on sale, and Joanne agreed to buy them. When Noah wanted a pair, too, she threw them in the bag. Later that day, her mother-in-law was running a benefit at the local country club. Joanne brought all three children to the event, clad in their new pink footwear. A magician was leading the festivities and Noah was picked as a volunteer from the audience.

"The magician says, 'Before we do anything, I want to know who your mother is who is letting you wear pink shoes in public as a little man?'" Joanne recalled.

If you really want to get a sense of the great pink-and-blue divide, and just how early children are socialized into gender, visit The Pink & Blue Project online (www.jeongmeeyoon .com/aw_pinkblue.htm), where artist JeongMee Yoon displays side-by-side images of actual girls' and boys' rooms. The toddler girls are clad in bubblegum-pink clothes, on bubblegum-pink bedspreads, surrounded by bubblegum-pink toys and accessories. The toddler boys are in a sea of blue, with blue tools and blue trucks in abundance. Interestingly, the artist notes on her website that pink was not always a "girl color" but was once associated with masculinity because it was considered a faded version of red. She quotes a 1914 edition of the *Sentinel Sun*, an American newspaper, advising mothers "to use pink for the boy and blue for the girl, if you are a follower of convention." In 1918, toward the end of World War I, Earnshaw's Infants' Department, a trade publication, wrote, "There has been a great diversity of debate on the subject, but the generally accepted rule is pink for the boys, blue for the girls. The reason is that pink, being a more decided and stronger colour, is more suitable for the boy, while blue, which is more delicate and dainty, is prettier for the girl." Only after World War II did the gender identification with color begin to reverse.

Emotions continue to run high on the pink-and-blue divide. In 2011, a mother and part-time family counselor in Santa Cruz, California, opened an all-girls preschool for three- to six-year-olds. She called it Pink Academy, and the all-pink website described the program this way: "It's pink, it's girly, and it's all about them!" While the site (now password protected) promised parents that their girls would not just make fairy wings or butterfly wands but would also be taught math, science, and sports, it was still too much for many modern moms. "An all girls, pink, girly, nurturing, fairy-winged preschool? I'd sooner send my daughters to learn to field-dress a deer," blogged KJ Dell'Antonia, on www.doublex.com.

Later that year, J. Crew ran an ad that showed a brand designer smiling into the eyes of her five-year-old son, whose toenails were painted hot pink. The caption read "Lucky for me, I ended up with a boy whose favorite color is pink." The image drew the ire of conservative pundits. A Fox News commentator opined that it was "unwise to encourage little boys to playact like little girls. This is a dramatic example of the way that our culture is being encouraged to abandon all trapping of gender identity." Erin R. Brown of the conservative Culture and Media Institute went a step further, accusing the company of pushing "liberal, transgendered identity politics" and "celebrating transgendered children." In addition, Fox, ABC, NBC, and CNN weighed in on the issue, and Jon Stewart jokingly referred to the intense reaction as "toemageddon." The fracas was also a hot topic on Mommy blogs, where the wisdom of the image was debated and for the most part defended.

Joanne, the mother who bought her son the pink jelly shoes, told her story to a group of other women, and it provoked a watershed of similar anecdotes. One mother talked about her young son's preference for floral patterns and her husband's deep uneasiness when she let her boy pick out what he wanted. Another described the Christmas when her four-year-old son wanted nothing more than an Easy Bake Oven. "Even his seven-year-old brother said, 'That's a girl thing.' And when anyone came over, they'd say, 'Whose Easy Bake Oven is this?' My husband was really mad I bought it," the woman recalled.

Becky, who hosts a radio talk show, remembers bringing her five-year-old son to "one of those damn Scholastic book fairs" where he became enamored of a purple and pink journal with a cat on it. "Boys were making fun of him and girls were, too, and for a while I was like, 'Are you sure you want that?' But he did. I struggled with it, but my husband has a really big problem with it."

Claire, who had been listening quietly, said, "I think my son Joey, who is just five, might be heading towards being one of the boys in pink jelly shoes. I've talked to my husband. He's a cop, he's really big, and he's like, 'If that's who he's going to be, then I'm going to teach him to fight.' I don't know if that's right."

What's really going on here? As these little boys—and at this point we are talking about boys who are clearly nowhere near puberty—began to break out of stereotypical "masculine" tastes and behavior even the tiniest bit, it immediately raised hackles, especially of their fathers or other men in the family. This anxiety is usually followed by a critique of the mother for letting her son stray too far from traditional gender expectations.

Little girls, by contrast, are allowed to be "tomboys" and given far more leeway in their behavior. They can climb trees or be "girly girls." They are allowed to hold hands and express their affection for one another. If little boys behave that way, adults begin to panic. When my sister's son was in kindergarten, she got a call from his teacher. Her five-year-old, Todd, was putting his arm affectionately around his friends' shoulders. It made the teacher so uncomfortable, she asked my sister to intervene and put a stop to it. To her credit, she ignored the teacher's advice.

In one study of preschool children that looked at parents' reactions to gender nonconformity, mothers and fathers celebrated their daughters for stepping out of traditional "feminine" expectations. These parents reported that they enjoyed dressing their girls in sports jerseys and buying them toys like trucks, trains, and building blocks. They also described their efforts to get their young daughters involved in activities once considered traditionally male, like T-ball, football, fishing, and learning to use tools.

However, they didn't give little boys nearly the same freedom way to explore activities considered traditionally female. Boy toddlers were allowed to stray only into certain "girl" areas—like the play kitchen. Parents accepted the idea of their sons acquiring domestic skills. But mothers were considerably more positive about this kind of play, while fathers were more neutral and often ambivalent.

"Occasionally, if he's not doing something, I'll encourage him to maybe play with his tea cups, you know, occasionally. But I like him playing with his blocks better anyway," one father said. Dads were also uncomfortable when their toddler sons cried too much over what they viewed as minor injuries. "Sometimes I get so annoyed, you know, he comes [crying] and I say, 'You're not hurt, you don't even know what hurt is yet,' and I'm like 'Geez, sometimes you are such a little ween.'"

Parents generally accepted toddler boys playing with baby dolls, but there was something about a Barbie doll—the author of the study on preschoolers and gender conformity describes her as "an icon of femininity"—that set mothers and fathers off. Several sons had specifically asked for Barbies. A few parents bought their boys the doll, but others avoided letting their sons play with one. One little boy repeatedly asked for a Barbie for his birthday, so his mother, in what she saw as a compromise, bought him a NASCAR Barbie.

Why are parents—and especially fathers—more comfortable, even proud, when their daughters embrace traditionally male activities than when their sons enter the more stereotypically feminine realm? In large part, the explanation might simply be that in patriarchal societies men are more valued than women. This assumed superior value of men explains why a girl would be seen as strengthened by her association with all things male, while a boy would be weakened by any female influence. That would also account for why it's more acceptable for a father to influence his daughter—after all, he is empowering her. But a mother who influences her son might be disenfranchising him.

There is also far more anxiety around the issue of the future sexual orientation of little boys. One father of a three-year-old son put it this way: "There are things that are meant for girls, but why would it be bad for him to have one of them? I don't know, maybe I have some deep, deep, deep buried fear that he would turn out, well, that his sexual orientation may get screwed up."

This fear that playing with "girl things" will feminize a boy underlies and reinforces the belief that a mother shouldn't be too close or too great an influence on her son. Let's face it, what are we really talking about when we talk about a "mama's boy"? We mean a boy who has been feminized. The mother has imparted too much of her own tastes, inclinations, and influence on the son. And in our sexist and homophobic culture, that's considered a disaster. Or as one mother said to me, "It's like if I spend too much time with my son, he'll somehow get the taint of woman, and the next thing you know he'll be running around begging for directions."

Listen to this, from a 1957 copy of Dr. Benjamin Spock's *The Common Sense Book of Baby and Child Care*, a child-raising bible for millions of mothers—probably many of our own. He is talking about mothers who become too close to their sons:

> The temptation of the mother . . . is to make him her closest spiritual companion, getting him interested in clothes and interior decoration, in her opinions and feelings about people, in the books and other recreations she enjoys. If she succeeds in making her world more appealing to him than the world of boys . . . he may grow up precocious, with feminine interests.

Did you catch that reference to "interior decorating"? The unspoken message behind much of this anxiety over mother-son closeness is that that by being too close or too great an influence, a mother might somehow make her son gay. I'm setting aside several questions for now: one, how it could be remotely possible for a mother to change her child's sexual orientation; two, the stereotype that all gay men are effeminate; and three, the assumption that having a gay child is a bad outcome. At present, I'm simply saying that what drives a lot of the prohibition of mother-son closeness is homophobia as well as sexism. We still live in a society where the highest insult you can throw at a guy is to call him a girl, and school hallways ring with comments such as "Dude, you're a fag" and "That's so gay." And what does that mean? According to sociologist C. J. Pascoe, who spent a year studying homophobia in high school boys, it can mean a lot of things, including "too emotional, feminine, weak, incompetent and stupid." Interestingly, Pascoe found that the epitaph "fag" was used less against boys who were known to be gay and more toward boys who were assumed to be straight, as a way of reinforcing conventional definitions of masculinity.

Let's take a minute here to talk about terminology. We sometimes use the terms *sex* and *gender* interchangeably, but they are not quite the same thing. When we refer to the sex of a person, we really mean the biology—which is defined by differences in chromosomes and anatomy. "Gender," on the other hand, is a cultural concept, made up of all those behaviors that we associate with males and females. Biology, for the most part, is fixed.

But our understanding of what it means to be masculine or feminine evolves over time and differs within cultures. Less than a century ago, having the vote wasn't considered "womanly."

(In fact, during the suffragette movement, many physicians at the time argued that women were physically incapable of political judgment.) Less than thirty-five years ago, a woman couldn't get a credit card in her own name—evidently securing financial credit was a masculine trait. In her book about the American women's movement, *When Everything Changed*, Gail Collins notes that by the mid-'70s, Billie Jean King had twice won three Wimbledon titles in a single year (singles, doubles, and mixed doubles) and was supporting her household. Still, she could not get a credit card unless it was in the name of her husband, a law student with no income.

Things have changed for men far more slowly. Men continue to be held to standards that limit their choices and range of expression. Male nurses, flight attendants, and elementary school teachers are still sometimes viewed with contempt or suspicion. Men make up only 9 percent of the country's public elementary school teachers, a forty-year low, according to the National Education Association, and only 6 percent of nurses are male, according to the Center for Nursing Advocacy.

At the same time, younger generations are pushing the boundaries of what defines gender, particularly when it comes to personal expression. As everyone who enters a public high school knows, many teenagers are into "gender bending" their dress and behavior in ways that confound their parents. One mother in Maine told me she wasn't quite sure how to react when her son's high school principal called to say that her six-foot-five son would have to come home and change his zebra-print dress. The problem? The spaghetti straps violated the school dress code.

Given that our culture is changing at such a dizzying pace, you might think that bucking the entrenched "wisdom" about mothers and sons would not be very difficult. In fact, it's not easy at all. Why? Because the war against closeness between mothers and sons, as we will see, has been going on for at least three thousand years.

3

Oedipus Wrecks

Well, a boy's best friend is his mother.
—Norman Bates, in *Psycho*

꙼

Achilles was a legendary warrior who had only one vulnerable spot—his heel. According to Greek mythology, Thetis, Achilles' mother, dipped the infant into the river Styx to assure her beloved son immortality. Everywhere the water touched him, Achilles was protected from death. But Thetis couldn't completely let go of her son for fear he would drown. Ultimately, it was his mother's grip that killed him: Achilles died from an arrow that struck him in the very spot where her thumb and forefinger had held him tight. The moral of that story is if a mother holds her son too close, she will kill him.

This mythic tale comes to us from Homer's eighth-century B.C. epic poem *The Iliad*. And for the past three millennia, when it comes to mothers and sons, it's been the same story over and over again.

It's a wonder that Freud didn't come up with an overarching, explain-it-all psychoanalytic theory called the "Achilles Complex." The myth the founder of psychoanalysis did inscribe on the modern psyche, of course, is that of Oedipus, which Freud adopted and around which he created his theory of a "complex." That's the one haunting the shared consciousness of twenty-first-century mothers, causing us to second-guess our natural emotions and gestures of affection toward our sons. Michelle, fifty-seven, a California actress, still remembers the feelings of confusion she experienced when her son was born. "Back in the day when you didn't know what sex child you were having, out comes this beautiful little boy." Michelle says she vividly recalls not wanting to tell anyone about the intensity of her emotions when her son was born. She worried that people would think her feelings were "incestuous."

"I remember feeling awkward, not safe to say that I was in love with this little boy. Not even with my husband, not with anybody, had I experienced these feelings. I have a daughter. I love her. I adore her. But this was a very different emotion, one that no mother had ever talked to me about. My own mother had never expressed it to me."

After she described Kevin's infancy, Michelle jumped to another emotional milestone that stirred similar ambivalence. One morning, when her son was fourteen, he walked out of his bedroom as usual, got his Cheerios, plopped down on the couch, and flipped on the TV to watch ESPN. As she glanced down at her son, Michelle was startled by what appeared to be Kevin's overnight plunge into adolescence.

"When he went to bed he had little boy hands, and when he woke up he had man hands," she says. "I remember how sad I was, wondering, 'What do I do with this?' If I love him as a boy, that was okay, but if I love him as a man, that's not appropriate."

All of Michelle's anxious second-guessing about her feelings for Kevin was grounded in the cultural assumption that there must be something pathological about a mother loving her son so deeply.

"You can't really talk about how you truly feel about your son, or people will think it's sexual," said Michelle, whose son is now twenty-seven. "When I can get that hug, that feeling of having that boy close to me, it doesn't get any better than that. There's no sexual tension. I don't know how we got this distorted view. I think Freud screwed it up for all of us."

Ah, Freud. You just can't escape the man or his Oedipus complex. (I certainly couldn't escape it when I was writing this book. When I mentioned that my subject was mothers and sons, the usual reaction was something along the lines of, "Boy, Freud would have a field day with that one.") Someone even sent me a cartoon that shows Oedipus at a greeting card rack on Mother's Day. His head whips back and forth between one section marked "From Your Sweetheart" and another labeled "From Your Son." In the caption below, Oedipus says, "It was shortly after this I blinded myself."

We might jokingly toss the term "Oedipal" around, but unless we are trained analysts, most of us probably don't know what Freud's "seminal" psychoanalytic theory actually postulates. But we do know just enough to make us question our natural instincts to love our sons. For a psychodynamic concept that's been around since the late 1800s, the Oedipus theory still casts an astonishingly long shadow onto twenty-first-century Western society. The problem is—that shadow is a distorted one.

What did Freud actually postulate in his Oedipus theory?

In its simplest form, the psychoanalytic theory holds that in the normal development of a child from the age of about three years old to five years old, he or she has a desire for sexual involvement with the parent of the opposite sex, along with a sense of rivalry with the parent of the same sex. Freud believed that during this stage, a normally developing little boy unconsciously sexually desires his mother and wishes to kill his father. Mothers are completely passive in this domestic drama; they are simply the objects that the father possesses and the son wishes to possess.

Freud had a penchant for using mythical texts as illustrations of his psychological insights—myths, he said, are a mixture of conscious ignorance and unconscious wisdom. Thus he named this developmental stage after the mythological

Oedipus, who, as described in the Greek tragedy by Sophocles, unknowingly killed his father and married his mother. It is worth noting that Greek literature was created by men who were writing for other men; the Oedipus story offers more insight into men's own fears and anxieties than it does into how women actually think. On top of that, Freud gave Sophocles' ancient work a dramatically altered interpretation. Sociologist and masculinity scholar Michael Kimmel says, "Freud's use of Oedipus has for years driven me batty. It's a revision of the actual play that completely transforms things." Kimmel, a professor at the State University of New York, says that in the original play, it is the father's envy and anxiety that sets all the catastrophic events into motion. Freud turned that on its head, making the action spring from the son's unconscious desire.

In the myth, Oedipus gouges his eyes out once he realizes what he has done; his mother Jocasta promptly hangs herself. The female version of the theory is known as "Electra complex," but it doesn't get nearly the play in the public consciousness that Oedipus does.

In addition, Freud maintained that at the developmental stage when a young boy wrestles with his desire to sleep with his mother and murder his father, he imagines that his rival, his father, will respond by threatening him with castration. You might wonder how this theory works with little girls, since, in imagining their mothers as sexual rivals, how could they fear castration? This is where Freud's theory of "penis envy" comes in. The analyst believed that girls are born with "castration anxiety" because they perceive that they have already lost their penises.

Stay with me now. The only way to resolve all this castration anxiety is for both boys and girls to repress their sexual desire for the parent of the opposite sex and begin to identify with the parent of the same sex. Freud theorized that children at this developmental stage start to develop superegos, which act as their consciences and allow them self-restraint. Thus children eventually move through the Oedipal and Electra crises and enter a period of sexual latency. Puberty reactivates some of the conflict, but when Oedipal issues are properly resolved, boys will redirect their desire from their mothers to other women; girls will desire men other than their fathers. Freud considered this theory, which he published in *The Interpretation of Dreams* in 1899, to be the cornerstone of the development of human relationships. He also described the Oedipal drama as "the nuclear complex of neuroses" and believed that when things went awry at this stage—when children did not successfully resolve the "Oedipus complex"—the seeds for sexual "perversions" were sown. Freud included homosexuality as one such outcome, though he did not consider homosexuality a mental illness.

For mothers of sons, the Oedipus theory raises two basic questions: one, do we understand it, and two, do we buy it? Why would we passively accept this century-old interpretation rather than scrutinize it, as we have so much more we thought we knew about men and women?

When we use the term "Oedipal" today, it is generally divorced from its roots as a then radical developmental theory based on the unconscious. Today it exists in a sort of vestigial form, mostly as a vague and general prohibition of mother-son closeness. Certainly we don't often think about the theory in its original context.

The original theory says nothing about emotional relationships between mothers and sons. Over time, we have confused the tender, loving feelings natural between mothers and sons with a distorted version of Freud's one-hundred-year-old speculations about the development of the unconscious. In the process, a sexualized taint has been cast over the mother-son relationship. What somehow got lost in all of this is that Freud was speculating on the benign, unconscious yearnings of toddlers and young children, not on the everyday relationships between parent and child.

Freud himself basked in and benefited from a close and loving relationship with his mother, Amalia. He was her first-born of eight children and said to be her favorite. She called him her "Golden Sigi," and Amalia was the one who taught her son to read. Later in life, Freud would say, "A man who has been the indisputable favorite of his mother keeps for life the feeling of a conqueror." Oddly, it is precisely when our own sons are in the Oedipal phase, roughly when they are between three and five years old, that we seem to feel most comfortable as mothers lavishing physical and emotional affection on them. That period is also when we get the least criticism for doing it. Yet at almost every stage of raising boys, our ongoing confusion about Freud's theories causes many mothers to be self-conscious and nervous.

Carin, a technical writer, said that Freud was often in the back of her mind when she was dealing with her son.

"Freud has certainly influenced many of my own interactions with my son," she said. "Privately, I wonder should I really be rubbing his back to calm him down? He's thirteen now. Publicly, I fear any real revelation of the passion I feel for my boy would be misconstrued as something sexual".

Wendy recently noticed that her fourteen-year-old son, Max, had been keeping his distance for a few days. "I mentioned it to my husband, and he said, 'Oh, you mean he's keeping his Oedipal distance because he wants to screw you.' It confused me. I didn't know what to think."

Marian, a lawyer, put it like this: "There is all this Freudian psychobabble that goes on and we've internalized it because it's definitely part of our culture. The mother-son relationship is very suspect, a very uncomfortable thing to talk about because people are going to think you have something very strange happening with your son."

So, no, we don't understand the Oedipus complex, and we tend to misinterpret the theory in ways that can drive mothers and their sons apart. We confuse the very normal love between parent and child with what Freud said about unconscious longings. We've been culturally conditioned to perceive this natural love between mother and son as some kind of psychopathology.

Let's go back to what Freud actually did mean to say.

The father of psychoanalysis was very much a product of his own time and culture. Over the past century, the Oedipus theory has been reevaluated and critiqued from every perspective imaginable: feminists, sociologists, anthropologists, psychoanalysts, and scientists have all taken their shots. Even during Freud's time, some of his female colleagues objected to his "phallic monism"—that is, his belief that the penis was central to everything. Feminists, in particular, have had a field day with his "penis envy" theory. Anne Hallward, a psychiatrist with a private practice in Maine and the mother of one son, told me: "I went through years of rejecting everything Freudian until I came up with my own feminist interpretation of penis envy: whoever gets born with the penis gets to have the power and the money, so of course women want it."

The feminist activist Betty Friedan devoted an entire chapter in her groundbreaking book, *The Feminine Mystique*, to what she called "The Sexual Solipsism of Sigmund Freud." She noted that a great deal of what Freud believed to be biologically intrinsic to human beings was in fact simply characteristic of his patient population—middle-class European men and women at the end of the nineteenth century. Much of what he wrote about women, she argues, is obsolete, "an obstacle to truth for women in America today." And Friedan herself was writing nearly fifty years ago. In her 1970 book, *Sexual Politics*, feminist Kate Millett argued that by attempting to link psychology and biology, Freud essentially tried to codify women as a second-class gender.

Since then, a generation of female psychologists has reevaluated some of the basic modern theories of human development as being inherently biased toward men. In 1976, Jean Baker Miller's influential *Toward a New Psychology of Women* held that women seek out a more relational worldview than men do. She argued that women's capacity to bond with others and seek connections should be viewed as a strength rather than a liability, and that their lesser interest in aggression and domination, compared with men, should not be considered weakness. Harvard psychologist Carol Gilligan argued in *In a Different Voice* that traditional theories failed to take into account the more relationship-centered empathetic experiences of women. More recently, psychological theorists argue that men and women are more alike than they are different. They question "difference theory"—the idea that the sexes are wired so differently that it really is as if women are from Venus and men are from Mars.

What are mothers raising sons today to make of all this? To start with, we have Freud's obvious sexism, understandable given his time but problematic for contemporary mothers who might look to his theories for guidance. Further, the Oedipus theory has come under fire for reasons that go well beyond sexism. Some criticize Freud's view of personality development as seen solely through the lens of sexuality. They argue that the love of and attraction to one parent and the hostility toward another might well be rooted in the resentment of authority and power rather than in sexual rivalry. Sociologists have also emphasized that family and social structures differ in each culture, and that, as mentioned earlier, the Oedipus theory reflected the patriarchal Victorian society of Freud's time. Scientists have also questioned the lack of empirical evidence supporting the Oedipus complex.

The issue of homosexuality seems to underlie much of the current angst around the Oedipus complex. Yes, Freud did suggest that an unsuccessful resolution of the Oedipal drama could result in a boy becoming homosexual. He believed that sexual orientation was a matter of arrested development.

Here again, though, Freud's theory has been distorted by cultural anxiety. For his time, the analyst was surprisingly humane and progressive on the question of sexual orientation. In 1935, he wrote a letter responding to a mother who had asked him to treat her son's homosexuality. "Homosexuality is assuredly no advantage, but it is nothing to be ashamed of, no vice, no degradation; it cannot be classified as an illness," he wrote. He went onto to cite Plato, Michelangelo, and Leonardo da Vinci as homosexuals and "among the greatest men," and added, "It is a great injustice to persecute homosexuality as a crime—and a cruelty too." He believed he could promise no more success in "treating" homosexuals to make them heterosexuals than he could in converting a heterosexual into a homosexual.

Since Freud's day, there has been a great deal of scientific inquiry into what makes people gay. Even the question itself has become political—why does it matter what "causes" homosexuality? Those engaged in the research maintain that if a biological cause for homosexuality can be determined, if people are "born gay," then that understanding might give them wider acceptance and better protect them from discrimination. Given how much influence the Oedipus complex has had over the years, as well as the extent to which it has been misinterpreted and wielded as a weapon, it is a relevant question of mothers of sons.

It's particularly pertinent to some mothers of gay sons, who are often held accountable for their sons' homosexuality by themselves or by others.

Mary Beth, whose thirty-two-year-old son is gay, grappled for a long time with guilt about whether her closeness to David contributed to his sexual orientation. "I remember when David was about eleven, he had a piano teacher who pulled me aside and told me, 'You better stop, you shouldn't be so close to him,' and it really stung me. God forbid you should have a good relationship with your son. Of course I didn't know he was gay at that point. He didn't come out until his twenties. I was dumbfounded. Then I immediately thought back to that conversation and that I had somehow caused it, although my son kept telling me I was being ridiculous."

Allie, a soft-spoken woman whose son Mark came out when he was fifteen years old, remembers being as confused as she was shocked. "There was so much mythology around gay men having overbearing mothers and wimpy fathers. Well, my husband is really forceful and I was this very traditional housewife. It didn't make any sense."

Mary Beth's and Allie's reactions are not uncommon. The most popular publication issued by the national nonprofit group PFLAG (Parents, Families and Friends of Lesbians and Gays) is a question-and-answer guide for parents of gay sons or daughters. Under a section titled "Why is my child gay?" it reads, "[Some] parents believe that their parenting is the cause of their child's sexual identity. For years, psychology and psychiatry have bandied about theories that homosexuality is caused by parental personality types—the dominant female, the weak male—or by the absence of same-gender role models. Those theories are no longer accepted within psychiatry and psychology."

In fact, contemporary researchers have looked at genetics, brain imagery, prenatal hormones, and birth order—even finger length!—to find the key to sexual orientation. Homosexuality does run in families, but studies have yet to determine a "gay gene." What most of the new research does point to, however, is that the roots of homosexuality appear to be in place by the time a baby is born. The notion that a boy's sexual orientation is determined by his relationship with his mother has been widely discredited.

Researchers now believe that those who observed that effeminate boys and gay men were often close to their mothers and had distant fathers were looking at effect, not cause. Straight fathers who perceived their boys to be homosexual withdrew from their sons; mothers compensated by drawing close. (Tellingly, there seems to be much less general angst over the idea that if a father is too influential on his daughter, she might grow up to be a lesbian.)

The point is, in the more than 110 years since Freud developed the Oedipus theory, volumes have been written analyzing, questioning, reevaluating, and sometimes debunking it. "The literature has by now come so far from the Oedipal complex," said Stacey, a clinical psychologist who works with families. "What remains from it is fear in mothers."

So why, after all the cross-examination, does the Oedipus complex still loom so large in mothers' minds—minds that instinctively don't believe that closeness between mothers and sons is harmful? Part of the problem is that historically, we seem to have held mothers responsible for much of what's wrong with the human condition. So it is not surprising that with vague Freudian prohibitions lurking in our minds, mothers fret about the lasting impact of even the most benign interchanges with their sons.

ꕤ A Mother's Place Is in the Wrong

"You're always so judged," said Linda, an assistant district attorney in Portland, Maine. "If your kid cries in the grocery store, you get this sense of oppressive criticism. My mother-in-law blames herself if something isn't going well with my husband or my brothers-in-law. She'll say, 'When he was four, I didn't do this. . . . '"

As mothers we tend to bear the brunt of responsibility for any dysfunction in our children. In this blame-the-mother ethos, mothers often feel that we simply cannot get it right. We are either too enmeshed or too cold. We are too controlling or too distant. With our sons, mothers are seen to be overprotective, overly involved, seductive, smothering, and devouring. That is, when we're not being castrating, hostile, unresponsive, and rejecting. Take your choice. Whatever we do, we're inflicting damage. As one frustrated mom put it, "A mother's place is in the wrong."

Authority figures, ranging from religious leaders to mental health professionals, have blamed mothers for all manner of problems in their children and in society. For centuries, ministers have been haranguing moms from their pulpits. "How can a mother expect to govern her child when she cannot govern herself?" demands the Reverend John S. C. Abbott, in *Mother at Home: Or the Principles of Maternal Duty*, published in 1833. "She must learn to control herself, to subdue her own passions; she must set her children an example of meekness and equanimity, or she must reasonably expect that all her efforts to control their passions will be ineffectual." Ironically, mother bashing is often preceded by mother idealizing. Raised to impossible heights, she inevitably falls off the pedestal and proves herself to be a huge disappointment. Here is the Reverend Samuel Phillips, in his book *The Christian Home*, published in 1859. "The mother is the angel-spirit of home. . . . Her love glows in her sympathies and reigns in all her thoughts and deeds. It never cools, never tires, never dreads, never sleeps, but ever grows and burns with increasing ardor, and with sweet and holy incense upon the altar of home-devotion."

It's an exhausting depiction of motherhood, not to mention unrealistic, but it is at least benign. Sadly, it seems that in the reverend's eyes, many of these angelic mothers end up failing in their duties. "Oh is it not too often the case that even the Christian mother, while she teaches her babe the accents of her own name, never thinks of teaching it to lisp the name of Jesus,—never seeks to unfold its infant spirit, never supplies it with spiritual food, or directs its soul to the eternal world!" he laments.

You know where this is going, right? "Strip the Christian family of its mission as a nursery for the soul; wrest from the parents their high prerogative as stewards of God; and you heathenize home, yea, you brutalize it!" Children raised thus, Reverend Phillips glumly warns, are destined for ruin and God will curse the very home in which they were raised. So the good news was that mothers were vested with moral authority over their children, but the bad news was that they were subsequently blamed for any lapse in piety or weakness in character.

In this country, particularly after Freud's work gained wider acceptance, the mental health community began to supplant religious authorities as the voice of expertise on child rearing. And from its early days, psychology and psychiatry pointed to mothers as the root cause of a wide variety of mental disorders. Schizophrenia was believed to be caused by the "schizophrenogenic mother," who induced the disease by being both dominant and rejecting. Autism was blamed on "refrigerator mothers," who allegedly lacked the warmth to raise normal children. In 1960, psychiatrist Leo Kanner gave an interview to *Time* magazine describing the mothers of autistic children as "just happening to defrost enough to produce a child." Influential child psychologist Bruno Bettelheim also championed this theory. "The precipitating factor in infantile autism is the parent's wish that his child should not exist," Bettelheim writes in *The Empty Fortress*, his seminal work on autism. Despite his use of the male pronoun, that comment appears in a section titled "The Mother in Infantile Autism." These doctors did not seem particularly troubled by the fact that if their theories were true, these cold and rejecting mothers would have inflicted mental illness on every one of their children, not only the ones who heard voices in their heads or couldn't speak.

Today, scientists consider both schizophrenia and autism to be brain disorders that are most likely set off by a combination of genetic vulnerabilities and environmental factors. (By "environmental factors," scientists refer to exposure to viruses, disease, toxic metals, and the like during critical times of brain development, rather than family environment.) Despite all the research that points to biological causes for a great array of conditions, mothers often continued to be blamed—and to blame themselves—for disabilities in their children.

Rebecca, whose twenty-four-year-old son has been diagnosed as schizophrenic, has wrestled with guilt over her son's illness for years. "I took a course at the Alliance for Mentally Ill [in Manhattan], and intellectually I know that I didn't cause this and that Tim is the primary victim of this disease. But as a mother you always look at things that you could have done differently and ask yourself how you could have prevented it," she says sadly. Rebecca remembers Tim as almost luminescent as a young child: "He had this glitter," she said, and was unusually smart and verbal. When he hit adolescence Tim became increasingly angry, troubled, and out of control. Immediately Rebecca blamed herself. She struggled to accept the reality of his illness and looked to her own parenting as the root of the problem. Over the last few years Rebecca has devoted herself to getting Tim into the right programs, securing his Social Security and Medicaid coverage, and reconnecting with him emotionally. Now that she has more fully accepted his diagnosis, she says, "I have greater access to my feelings of love for him."

Despite Rebecca's self-blame, schizophrenia runs on her husband's side of the family. Her husband's brother had the disease and killed himself when he was in his twenties. Rebecca's mother-in-law, of course, still holds herself responsible. "I talk to her all the time about how it's not her fault," Rebecca said. "She hears it but she doesn't hear it."

Mother blaming persists, almost as a popular sport. Mothers continue to be bombarded with the message that they just can't get it right. Much of this is plainly rooted in recalcitrant cultural sexism.

"Nothing gets better for women over time, because in a sexist society anything that can be used against mothers will be," said Dr. Paula J. Caplan, a clinical and research psychologist who has taught courses in motherhood at Harvard University. "A mother who takes pride in her son's accomplishments is still seen as living vicariously through him. A mother who takes pride in her daughter's achievements is often seen as competing with her. Society misinterprets what mothers do in the most pathological way. Mothers are a deeply, intensely scape-goated group."

Caplan conducted a study that reviewed 125 articles published in nine different mental health journals from 1970, 1976, and 1982. In them, she found seventy-two distinct problems—ranging from bedwetting to schizophrenia—that were blamed on mothers. Mothers were held responsible for their offspring's inability to manage color blindness, learning problems, and, in one case, something labeled "homicidal transexualism."

Caplan said she realized that as a mother, she was a member of a group that her psychology colleagues believed caused all the world's psychological problems. She even maintains that what is said about mothers often amounts to hate speech. Substitute the word "mother" for "woman" and you can get away with a really sexist joke, she says. Not many people would feel comfortable slapping a bumper sticker on their car that read "Woman in Trunk," let alone "African-American in Trunk." But "Mother-in-Law in Trunk"? Now that's funny.

This recurrent pattern of mother blaming, particularly the persistent image of the dangerous mother who damages her son, is reflected throughout twentieth-century literature and entertainment. One of the top ten movie quotes of all time, as voted by the American Film Institute: "Well, a boy's best friend is his mother." The movie? *Psycho*.

If you search movie websites for films on the mother/son relationship, *Psycho* usually comes up first. Others that come up with frequency are *The Truman Show* (odd, because the boy in the movie is raised by a TV producer and his "mother" is an actress playing the role) and *Mama's Boy*, a 2007 movie about a twenty-nine-year-old slacker man-child who still lives with his mother.

᠅ By the Books

Culturally speaking, you can aim higher than popular film, but even then the portrayal of the mother-son relationship doesn't fare much better. Review many classics of modern literature by revered authors, such as D. H. Lawrence and Philip Roth, and you'll find various archetypes of the destructive mother. Among them: the blindly adoring mother, the emasculating mother, and the martyred mother, all of whom try to control their sons to meet their own needs. Mother-son closeness in this literature also invariably undermines a boy's relationship with his father. Of course, these intrusive, overly close mothers can't bear the thought of their sons being close to another woman. So the only chance the son has to achieve manhood—if not sanity—in these fictional depictions is to break away from his mother.

The influence of literature should not be underestimated. More than popular entertainment, esteemed books carry the same kind of authority and inspire the same respect as religion and psychology do. These works are taught in universities as keys to understanding human nature. And literature that is rife with anti-mother/son themes remains standard fare in college curriculums.

Probably the most well-known book on the subject of mother-son love gone wrong is the classic *Sons and Lovers* by D. H. Lawrence, a contemporary of Freud. ("I hope you've read *Sons and Lovers*" was another comment that came my way more than a few times in the course of writing this book. I have.) In the novel, Gertrude Morel has married "down" to a rough-hewn miner. Eventually, the unhappy and alienated wife turns to her sons for emotional sustenance, making them in essence substitute husbands without the sex. Here is how Lawrence himself describes the plot of the novel, in a letter he wrote in 1912.

"As her sons grow she selects them as lovers—first the eldest, then the second. These sons are urged into life by their reciprocal love of their mother—urged on and on. But when they come to manhood, they can't love, because their mother is the strongest power in their lives, and holds them." The sons, who grow contemptuous of their father, are torn between their actual sexual lovers and their mother's emotional needs, and cannot resolve the tension. Lawrence writes about Paul, the younger son, abandoning his girlfriend because he loves his mother best. "She was the chief thing to him, the only supreme being."

Feminists such as Simone de Beauvoir and Kate Millet have roundly critiqued Lawrence for his misogyny, and more than a dozen books have been written about Lawrence and his treatment of women. De Beauvoir's *The Second Sex* has a chapter titled "D. H. Lawrence and Phallic Pride." Nonetheless, *Sons and Lovers* is a complex and beautifully wrought novel, still considered a classic, making its message about the insidiousness of mother-son closeness extremely powerful. But it is telling that the novel has become symbolic of a mother destroying her son's ability to form adult romantic relationships. After all, in the novel Paul also witnesses his drunken father frequently beating his mother. Wasn't the way Walter Morel treated his wife equally destructive to their son's view of romantic love?

Then there is Somerset Maugham, the English playwright and novelist and another of the many nineteenth- and twentieth-century male authors to bemoan the perils of a close mother-son relationship. In Maugham's observation, "Few misfortunes can befall a boy which bring worse consequences than to have a really affectionate mother."

Among his works is a short story called "The Mother," which describes the main character's relationship with her son this way: "He was all she had in the world and she adored him with a fiery, jealous passion that demanded in return impossible devotion. She wished to be all in all to him. On account of his work they could not live together and it tortured her to imagine what he did when he was away from her. She could not bear him to look at a woman and she writhed at the bare idea that he might pay court to some girl."

In the end, the mother murders the son's lover.

At least those depictions were fictional. Far more vicious was the sociological attack on the mother-son relationship in *Generation of Vipers*, a treatise on American society by Philip Wylie, published in 1943. While the book launched a broad vitriolic assault on the entire American lifestyle, Wylie bore special venom for mothers. The author coined the term "momism" for what he saw as the worship accorded to these harridans who wrought damage on their children. Here is one of Wylie's many passages describing mothers:

> Men live for her, and die for her, dote upon her, and whisper
> her name as they pass away. In a thousand of her, there is
> not enough sex appeal to budge a hermit ten paces off a rock
> ledge. She plays bridge with the stupid veracity of a ham-
> merhead shark. She couldn't pass the final examinations of a
> 5th grader.

The intensity of that language seems to illustrate the passionate hatred he harbored for women. Mothers had done such damage to their sons, Wylie argued, that they had created a generation of men wholly unfit for military duty during World War II. "It is difficult to put young men in the mood for war when they come to arms fresh from reviling arms, and in the panty-waist, besides, which their moms had put upon them," he wrote. In Wylie's view, mothers, to meet their own inexhaustible needs, had generally emasculated their sons to the point of contemptibility. Dr. Edward Strecker, a psychiatrist and contemporary of Wylie, went so far as to argue that mothers represented a threat to the national health and security. In his 1946 book, *Their Mothers' Sons*, Strecker contended that the 2.5 million men rejected or discharged from the army during World War II were too neurotic to serve their country because of "smother-love." An editorial on "momism" in *The Washington Post* called Strecker's book "a timely warning concerning a system which condemns enormous numbers of men to a miserable, maladjusted life because 'Mom' has never weaned her son emotionally."

Generation of Vipers was a particularly influential book, going through multiple editions, and it is still in print. Interestingly, both Maugham and Wylie were very young when their mothers died. Maugham was said to have been devastated by the loss of his mother and kept her picture at his bedside until his own death at the age of ninety-one. Philip Wylie, on the other hand, denied having been influenced by the early death of his mother. But in a television interview, his brother, Max Wylie, said, "I think that Phil is somewhat bitter about mothers because his own mother died when he was five and his stepmother died when he was sixteen. Now Phil's trying to compensate for the almost total motherlessness of his own life with a shell of cynicism about mothers."

John Cheever seems to have hated his mother. Because she supported her family by running a small gift shop, he accused her of "emasculating" his alcoholic father. In a 1952 journal he wrote that "all of her children, looking to her for the graceful discharge of her affection, have been rudely discouraged." In the same entry he writes of "a breakfast with the umbilical cord seeming to have been cut but to lie, ragged and bleeding on the table between us."

Another famous rant about emasculating mothers comes in *Portnoy's Complaint* by Philip Roth. The book depicts the stereotypic "Jewish mother" who shapes her son in her own neurotic image. The protagonist Alexander Portnoy says in his frantic, stream-of-consciousness narration that she is "the patron saint of self-sacrifice" and "one of the most outstanding producers and packagers of guilt in our time." His mother is so intrusive that when Portnoy is a young teenager masturbating in the bathroom, she is convinced he must have diarrhea (because he spends so much time in there) and demands to see the content of the toilet bowl. The novel might have reflected Roth's own experience with his mother, but his depiction became iconic shorthand for overbearing mothers. Reviewer Eric Weiner put it this way: "*Portnoy's Complaint* did for the Jewish mother what *Jaws* did for the shark: took an already frightening creature and made it even scarier." Portnoy, who wavers between self-love and self-loathing, is desperate, of course, to escape his mother. (This brings us to the old Jewish mother joke: A frustrated psychiatrist has been trying over and over again to explain the Oedipus complex and its consequences to the mother of a neurotic mama's boy he is treating. "Oedipus, Schmedipus," she replies. "As long as he loves his mother.")

The anxiety around destructive or seductive mothers and their sons is reflected and reinforced in a great deal of what we read and see. But perhaps you are thinking that we've come a long way, baby, from these nasty depictions of mothers and their sons. After all, the majority of those books I mentioned are written by men of an earlier generation. Our understanding of psychology has evolved greatly, particularly given the influence of feminism. In a world where the roles of men and women have so dramatically changed and with all the progress we've made in understanding gender, surely these portrayals are dated.

Well, yes and no. *The New York Times* hailed Jonathan Franzen's 2010 novel *Freedom* as "a masterpiece of American fiction." The center of the novel is the Berglund family—Walter, his wife, Patty, and their son, Joey. (The Berglunds have a daughter, too, but she is a minor player.) Franzen has a superb eye for cultural detail, and his Patty is very much a contemporary character. She is a former all-American basketball player and the daughter of a feminist mother. As a young mother, Patty lives in a gentrified neighborhood and uses cloth diapers. So much for the new; here comes the old. Patty showers her son with the love she doesn't feel for her husband. Her dreams are centered on her bright, handsome, and personable boy. "Patty was undeniably very into her son. . . . Joey was the child Patty could not shut up about," Franzen writes. "In her chuckling, confiding, self-deprecating way, she spilled out barrel after barrel of unfiltered detail about her and Walter's difficulties with him. Most of her stories took the form of complaints, and yet nobody doubted that she adored the boy. She was like a woman bemoaning her gorgeous jerky boyfriend. As if she were proud of having her heart trampled by him: as if her openness to this trampling were the main thing, maybe the only thing, she cared to have the world know about."

It gets creepier. She adores him. She spends long hours in Joey's room during his early adolescence, confiding in him about her relationship with her husband. When Joey starts dating someone his mother doesn't like, "the move was a stunning act of sedition and a dagger to Patty's heart," Franzen writes. (Cue Somerset Maugham.) Soon afterward mother and son have a drastic falling-out, and Joey moves out of the house and in with a family Patty despises. Soon he's heading down a corrupted path, in part to escape his smothering mother. Patty's great sins as the mother of a son, as Franzen sees it: first, when he is young, she tries to baby him, and then as Joey grows older, she attempts to turn her son into "her boy pal."

Franzen, a National Book Award winner, represents the top tier of cultural literacy. You can certainly set the bar far lower if you are looking for contemporary insights into mother-son dynamics. Sadly, you will get the same message, just one that's considerably cruder. Take NBC's reality television program *Momma's Boys*. It was produced by Ryan Seacrest, and debuted in 2008. The casting call for eligible men said, "If you and your mom have a unique and strong relationship, we'd love to hear from you." That sounds relatively harmless, but the show that actually ended up on the air makes Philip Roth's depiction of mothers seem benign. Set on an estate in Santa Barbara, California, *Momma's Boys* featured three single men and their mothers. Thirty-two young women are in residence at the mansion to vie for the position of "bride to be" for each of the three men. These women know they have to go through the gauntlet of demon mothers to get to the complacent sons.

The casting call for mothers asked, "Are you a mom who is frustrated that her son is not dating the right woman? Do you look forward to the day your son finds the love of his life, and you get the wedding of your dreams?" Not surprisingly, the mothers chosen for the show who fit these criteria were domineering women who infantilize their grown sons. One woman is a blatant bigot and brays on national television that she will not allow her son to date anyone who is black, Asian, Jewish, or Muslim. For good measure she throws in, "I don't want someone from a divorced family. I don't like a lot of makeup. I don't want someone who is outspoken. I don't want someone after my son's money." What does she want for her beloved son? "I need a girl just like me."

Another more recent entry into the pile of mother-son bashing entertainment is the movie *Cyrus*, starring Jonah Hill as a twenty-one-year-old man-child with a creepy deadpan stare and, of course, an unhealthy attachment to his single mother, played by a sexy Marisa Tomei. When she begins to date someone steadily, Cyrus does his best to undermine the new relationship and reclaim ownership of his mom. Tomei's character, as the review in *The New York Times* points out, is "the sexy smother-mother with the possibly psycho adult son." Reviewer Manohla Dargis also adds, "This is perilous ground—incest as comedy." Well, yes, incest isn't funny, but neither is the perpetuation of mother-son closeness through this pathologic lens.

The prime-time message of this contemporary material is no different from earlier diatribes about mothers and sons—a guy who is close to his mother is no man, and the only prism through which we can see a close mother-son relationship is the one in which the son remains a child and the mother is either inappropriately seductive or a controlling shrew.

If these depressing portrayals were confined to entertainment, either high- or low-brow, that would be bad enough. Far more dangerously, the negative assumptions around mothers and sons also underlie a good deal of the contemporary psychology focused on boys. Over the last decade, the state of boys, men, and masculinity has become a subject of intense anxiety. Boys, we are told, are "in crisis." Men, also, are suffering. Our rapidly changing notions of gender are accompanied by a deep uneasiness.

All this has only caused the mother-son connection to come under even greater scrutiny. True to tradition, mothers again find themselves in the crosshairs. Not surprisingly, rather than seeing mothers as part of the prescription for a cure to what ails boys and men, a number of contemporary and very influential "experts" on masculinity continue to put the blame on Mom.

4

Moms and the "Boy Crisis"

There is a national blindness to the fate of boys.
—MICHAEL GURIAN, AUTHOR OF THE WONDER OF BOYS

FOR ALL THE HAND-WRINGING over the last decade about boys being "in crisis," it is amazing how little attention has been paid to one obvious solution: the positive influence of mothers. If boys are struggling in the classroom to a greater extent than girls, doesn't it make sense that certain traditionally female skill sets—like working cooperatively or verbalizing frustration instead of acting out—could help? Mothers are in a perfect position to help their sons develop these traits. And if boys are in emotional pain because they've been taught that silence means strength, whom better to teach them how to articulate their feelings than their mothers? After all, women have long been socialized to put their emotions into words, and there are few safer spaces for a boy to reveal his vulnerabilities than with his mom. Moreover, studies have shown that boys who are closer to their mothers enjoy better mental health, and that when that mother-son attachment is insecure, boys act out in destructive ways. Yet even when boys are purported to be suffering on a national scale, mothers are marginalized. Not only are moms rarely considered as having a role in addressing the "boy crisis," more often than not mothers get the message that they are part of the problem.

Several prominent theories about why males seem to be in such a state of distress appear to be at odds with one another. One argument is that men and boys are struggling because they have lost touch with their innate masculinity. When fathers are absent from their lives, boys have no strong male role models. As a result, they spend too much time in the company and care of their mothers, putting them at risk of "feminization." This explanation of their crisis, by definition, leaves no role for moms to help, since they are named as one of the main causes of their sons' difficulties.

Some of these same "boy experts" also suggest that boys are doing poorly academically because the expectations for school behavior—like sitting still during lessons, reading quietly, and raising hands before speaking impulsively—go against the essential male nature. Specifically, theorists on this side of the question argue that the reason boys are more often placed in special education, prescribed drugs for attention deficit and hyperactivity disorders, and do more poorly than girls in the classroom is that they are being held to standards that don't properly recognize the immutable biological differences between boys and girls. For instance, intolerant teachers might recommend that normally boisterous, rambunctious boys need to be medicated before they can be taught. In short, boys are being disciplined simply for being boys, and they are falling behind.

This explanation, too, leaves mothers with no role to play in addressing the problem. It implies that issues like focus and self-control are based on gender. It also begs the question of why boys were able to perform well in classrooms that were once considerably more structured than they are today. Why have boys begun to slide academically only relatively recently? Classrooms in the 1950s through the 1980s were far more rigidly organized and tolerance for poor behavior was lower, yet boys were not thought to be in crisis then. It's worth noting that until fairly recently, it was not assumed that most boys (or girls, for that matter) were college-bound. For boys, there was a vocational track, one that recognized tactile skills used in fields like mechanics and electronics. Most of these programs have been removed from schools, and some students who might have flourished with vocational training are now pushed into academic programs that often don't serve them well.

Nonetheless, some advocates, like Dr. Leonard Sax and therapist and author Michael Guerin, believe that single-sex schooling is the answer to boys' academic and behavior problems, based on the theory that boys and girls learn differently.

Another theory of the "boy crisis" holds that males are in

psychic pain because they are forced to live up to punishing traditional ideals of masculinity. Our culture tells them they must elicit respect from others, that they should be physically tough, and that they shouldn't talk about their problems. These demands cause boys and men to become alienated from their emotional lives. The societal pressure on guys to toughen up, display bravado, not cry, not be a sissy, has forced them to lose connection with their true selves. Males are so out of touch with their feelings, these advocates argue, that they have been rendered "emotionally illiterate." There is actually a scientific term for this condition at its extreme: "alexithymia"—the inability to identify and describe one's feelings in words. (The clinical term "alexithymia" has Greek roots: "a" meaning lack, "lexis" meaning word, and "thymos" for emotion.)

Here is an area where mothers can really help. So many of the mothers I spoke to described their ongoing efforts to teach their sons to identify and talk about their feelings. Mothers can also challenge the strict definition of masculinity in a safe, nonthreatening environment. But often, when a mother does attempt to nurture her son's more sensitive side and works to help him articulate his emotions, she gets critiqued for coddling or feminizing her son.

Whether boys are in trouble because they are being denied their innate masculinity or they're in trouble because they are too traditionally masculine for their own good—and it's hard to see how both could be true at once—mothers continue to be nearly absent from the discussion about solutions. This is completely misguided, because mothers, who love their sons with a deep tenderness and want them to thrive, can play an instrumental role in supporting their struggling sons. To understand how mothers got cut out of so much of the crisis discussion, it's instructive to take a look at its origins.

↝ The Making of a Crisis

Popularized cultural "crises" tend to be media-generated hype, capturing a partial truth from academia and blowing it up to emergency proportions. They also seem to come in waves. The attention to the pain of boys—highlighted in headlines like "The Boy Crisis" on the cover of *Newsweek*—came after the plight of girls enjoyed a brief moment in the media spotlight. In 1992, the American Association of University Women (AAUW) published an influential report titled "How Schools Shortchange Girls," which said among other things that girls receive less attention from teachers than boys do, that they are subtly turned away from pursuing math and science, that classroom activities tend to appeal more to boys than girls, and that in general gender bias in the classroom is negatively affecting girls' educations.

In 1993, the Ms. Foundation sponsored the first Take Our Daughters to Work Day to encourage girls to think about careers. The following year, Mary Pipher published *Reviving Ophelia: Saving the Selves of Adolescent Girls*, which highlighted a culture said to "poison" girls. She wrote that American teen-age girls fall prey to depression, eating disorders, and suicide attempts, and that they had lost their voices and their own unique sense of self. Her best-selling book garnered a great deal of attention and launched a national conversation on the plight of girls.

It didn't take long before a backlash began. Critics questioned the science of the AAUW study and said "misguided feminists" had largely manufactured the crisis. In 2000, *The Atlantic* published an article by Christina Hoff Sommers headlined "The War Against Boys" (later turned into a book), documenting boys' struggles in the classroom. The author argues that contrary to what the AAUW study claimed, girls were thriving in school and boys were doing poorly. Far from being a girl crisis, there was actually a boy crisis. She argued that boys were falling behind in academic achievement, lagging in verbal skills, and dropping out of high school at higher rates than girls. Also, more girls were attending college than boys. Advocates began calling for single-sex education and more "boy-friendly" classrooms. By 2003, Take Our Daughters to Work Day had morphed into Take Our Daughters and Sons to Work Day, as if men had been so historically discriminated against in the workplace that boys needed exposure to career possibilities.

The pendulum kept swinging, and the AAUW came out with another report in 2008, arguing that the disparity between boys and girls in the classroom has been exaggerated and that the "boy crisis" is a myth. Dr. Rosalind Barnett, a senior scientist at the Women's Studies Research Center at Brandeis University, is one of many scholars who believe the academic boy crisis is a largely manufactured one. Race and class are the biggest determinants of academic achievement, not gender, she argues.

Not only does the idea that all boys are lagging behind divert attention from addressing pressing class and racial issues, but it can also serve as an overall explanation—and excuse— for individual boys who are struggling academically.

While the academic debate rages on, many mothers remain frustrated and confused about their sons' school performance. Libby, a New Jersey mother of three sons, ages sixteen, four-teen, and five, is one of many moms who get frustrated when told not to worry if their sons lag behind in reading or act up in the classroom because "he's a boy." She is tired of hearing that her sons' chromosomes can explain away academic and behavior problems. "If I hear one more time they're immature and they'll grow out of it, I'm going to be really pissed off," fumed Libby. "It's like 'That's okay, they're boys.' Don't tell me it's okay because he's a boy, because he's going to get an F. When does it stop? When is your boy immature and having fun, and when is he in real academic trouble? As a mom, I have to know when it's an actual issue."

Libby noted that she, like two of her sons, struggled with reading when she was younger. But as a girl, she was expected to overcome her difficulties. Libby developed excellent pen-manship and became an accountant. She believes her sons would perform better if they were held to the same expectations that she was. Educational research indicates that Libby's standards for her sons might be self-fulfilling. A mother's education and aspirations are a powerful influence on a young person's schooling outcome, several studies have found.

No doubt the debate over whether boys are disadvantaged will continue: the idea of a crisis is compelling and breaking down issues by gender makes for headline-grabbing news. But pitting the problems of boys against girls is a not zero-sum game. There are enough real problems for both boys and girls today to worry any parent, even if they haven't reached crisis proportions. It's true that boys are more likely to be diagnosed with attention deficit disorder, but girls are more likely to be given a diagnosis of depression. Boys are more likely to kill themselves, but girls are more likely to try. Boys do have lower rates of literacy, but girls continue to have lower scores on mathematics and science tests. As the mother of a cherished daughter, I am extremely concerned about how damaging our culture can be to teenage girls and women. As the mother of a son, I'm equally alarmed about threats to boys' well-being. And as someone who loves both my children deeply, I am of course interested in how I can help each navigate his or her way to a healthy self-image.

But with my daughter it has been far easier. We mothers of daughters feel confident in trying to counteract those damaging societal messages that hold girls back. We happily exhort our daughters to believe in themselves and to buck the gender stereotypes that discourage them from pursuing their dreams. When it comes to supporting our sons, though, mothers begin to get very mixed messages about the role they are meant to play.

✌ Real Men

Let's start with the theory that the "crisis" was caused by today's men having become alienated from their own masculinity. Robert Bly is a pioneer of this men's movement. His treatise on new manhood, *Iron John: A Book About Men*, remained on the *New York Times* best seller list for sixty-two weeks, beginning in 1990. Bly attempted to forge a new concept of masculinity, arguing that before men can get in touch with their feminine side, they need rituals to establish a positive idea of manhood. "Women can change the embryo to a boy, but only a man can change the boy to a man," he wrote.

The author, a poet, was ridiculed for his ideas that men should go off in the woods, bang drums, and find their inner warriors. But another part of his message took hold with a wide audience and is still very much in fashion today—the idea that children suffer from "father hunger." He argues that American men are depriving their offspring of their presence, instead investing too much of their time and energy outside the home. This, he believes, is a particular problem for boys, because they have no one to model masculinity.

This idea was really nothing new. In the mid-nineteenth century, similar worries about boys being deprived of masculine authority were already being voiced widely. As public education spread throughout the United States, magazine articles appeared warning that boys were spending too much time in the classroom with female teachers, and that this over-influence of women was robbing them of their manliness. Books like *Adventures of Huckleberry Finn* (1884) glorified the image of a "real boy" living away from the damaging influence of school and women. The use of the word "sissy" to describe an effeminate man was first recorded in 1887. Etymologists believe the word was derived from "sister," in keeping with the theme that there is no worse insult to hurl at a man than one suggesting he is like a woman. Senator Albert Beveridge, who represented Indiana from 1899 through 1911, gave a stirring speech in Congress warning against overeducating boys. He exhorted young men to "avoid books and in fact avoid all artificial learning, for the forefathers put America on the right path by learning completely from natural experience." Part of the impetus for founding the Boy Scouts of America in 1910 was to counteract this supposedly über-feminine educational environment by providing opportunities for boys to spend time outdoors with male leaders and other boys.

Ironically, in today's Boy Scouts, more than one-third of leadership volunteers are women. The organization might have been founded by men and for boys, but currently thousands of mothers end up leading the troops, camping overnight, and building those Pinewood Derby cars. Mothers do this because they want their boys to have the Boy Scout experience, and are often stepping in for fathers who, for one reason or another, are unavailable. (Mothers might also be motivated by the sex abuse scandals that have rocked the Boy Scouts over recent decades. In 2010 the Boy Scouts of America was ordered to pay $18.5 million to a former scout who was repeatedly assaulted by a former scoutmaster during the 1980s. The judge in the case overruled the Scouts' efforts to keep the jury from seeing roughly 1,200 files kept by the organization on suspected pedophiles.)

The concern over insufficient male influence for boys continued to mount as the country moved into the postindustrial era, when men's work largely moved outside the home, and mothers became the hub of domestic life. With the emergence of the two separate spheres of work and home, boys were spending their days under the greater influence of women. Fears began to emerge that mothers would create a generation of feminized boys, unfit for work or soldiering. Philip Wylie's comments in his 1943 book *Generation of Vipers* about boys not being in the "mood for war" after wearing the "pantywaist" their mothers had put on them, exemplifies these fears. Bly revived this latent anxiety about absent fathers, giving it a late-twentieth-century twist with psychological and new-age-y undertones. He spoke compellingly about the broken connection between fathers and sons, and men's subsequent sense of isolation and loss. He described the emptiness of men's emotional lives. But despite the new emphasis on men's emotional damage, in Bly's view the root of the problem remained unchanged: the absent father and overly influential mother.

The "father hunger" theory still has great currency today. Barack Obama has touched on the theme every Father's Day since he has been in office, and has called for a "national conversation on responsible fatherhood and healthy families." Obama often references his own absent father, who left the family when Barack was two years old, and who only visited once after that. Obama has said that growing up without a father "leaves a hole in a child's heart," and he surely speaks from experience.

But the man who made this statement also had the experience of being raised by his fiercely independent mother, who woke him up hours before school for extra tutoring and pushed him relentlessly toward achievement. The lack of a male role model doesn't seem to have impeded Obama's drive or success, or for that matter his masculinity. Perhaps a more revealing comment about Obama's path might be found in the preface to his autobiography, *Dreams from My Father*, written while his mother was alive but published after her death. He wrote: "I think sometimes that had I known she would not survive her illness, I might have written a different book, less a meditation on the absent parent and more a celebration of the one who was the single constant in my life."

Bill Clinton was also raised by a single mother with a strong personality; the two are among many leaders who managed to thrive under the sole tutelage of their mothers. Other prominent American figures—Franklin Delano Roosevelt, General Douglas MacArthur, Andrew Carnegie, and Lou Gehrig—were raised by strong-willed, sometimes dominating mothers, and they managed respectively to lead a country, command an army, amass a fortune, and become a sports hero, each with his masculinity firmly intact.

Now let's take a minute here to clarify something. Absolutely no movement exists that opposes fathers being more emotionally and physically present for their kids. Who on earth is against fatherhood? The truth is that most moms welcome the involvement of their children's fathers in both their sons' and daughters' lives (assuming there is no major dysfunction with the father or in the family). My own husband is a wonderful father to both my son and my daughter, and I couldn't even begin to describe all the ways they each benefit from his guidance, support, and of course, love. Moreover, studies have shown that a mother's support of the father is a critical factor in his level of involvement with his children. This is true in traditional two-parent families and true in families of divorce. Of course, a father does better with his son or daughter if he is not undermined or second-guessed by the mother, and vice versa. Mothers have no desire to replace fathers; they have enough to do as mothers.

The infuriating part about the fatherhood movement is

that the other shoe always drops: the championing of fathers is often followed by the denigration of mothers. Instead of the absent father being held responsible for a son's identity problems, the present mother is blamed. See if you can follow this logic: a father leaves the family, or spends little time at home. A boy has no male role model. What's the problem? His mother.

It simply doesn't make sense.

Yet many of these fatherhood experts advocate that boys must be saved from dangerous female influences. For Bly, a boy must be ready to "cut his soul away from his mother-bound soul" and move "from the mother's realm to the father's realm." He must steal the key to the wild man's cage from under his mother's pillow. (This is Bly's imagery, I hasten to assure you, not mine.) Bly's Legend of Iron John is based on a Brothers Grimm fairy tale published in the early nineteenth century about a prince and a wild man. Freud might have started something by looking to mythology as a guide to the contemporary male psyche.

Bly and others who have followed him also make the simple assumption that a father's presence in a son's life is by definition a good thing, and a mother's presence is by definition a bad thing, regardless of the individuals and their parenting skills. This argument doesn't address another obvious question, which speaks even more directly to the psychological health of our sons. If a father is indeed absent and the mother withdraws from her son so that she doesn't in some way compromise the boy's masculinity, where does that leave the boy? Completely alone, a result of both parents having withdrawn from him at a tender age. Certainly this cannot be a prescription for a boy's physical and mental well-being. One study that followed adolescent boys whose fathers were absent from the home found that boys who had stronger bonds with their mothers had an easier time making the transition from boyhood to manhood.

Bly and others have set up the false competition that mothers and fathers are in some kind of war over their boys' very souls, and that mothers have a dark, secret, vested interest in impeding their sons' development and masculinity. In truth, my research reveals that mothers and fathers have a shared interest in raising happy, healthy, well-adjusted boys, not a rivalry over who will have the prevailing influence.

Nonetheless, the idea of the emasculating mother still holds currency. Take therapist Dr. Kenneth M. Adams's recent book *When He's Married to Mom: How to Help Mother-Enmeshed Men Open Their Hearts to True Love and Commitment.* Adams, who is based in Michigan and specializes in sex addiction, claims to have successfully treated hundreds of MEM—that's his term for "mother-enmeshed men," an acronym he uses with abandon. According to Adams, men who are enmeshed with their mothers suffer from commitment phobia, addictions, and sexual problems, including something he calls "sexual anorexia," meaning men who fear and suppress their sexuality. They also shoplift, have low self-worth, suffer from guilt, and are indecisive. Adams estimates that one in ten American males is enmeshed with his mother; he says this "conservative figure" is based on data of sexually abused children, sex addicts, and adult children of alcoholics, where he claims "estimates of MEM can be made." Mothers of these men kept them too close in childhood, Adams says, and he recommends such men take a "healing journey" that limits their relationship with their mothers and increases time spent with their fathers.

I'm tempted to come up with my own acronym for authors of this genre: PAM—that's patronizing and misogynist. These portraits of emasculating mothers are very offensive to women. They bear little resemblance to reality and seem to be coming out of both extreme anxiety about being male and hostility toward women.

Michael Gurian, who is yet another popular champion of boys, argues that mothers' apron strings are strangling the manhood out of boys. In his book *Mothers, Sons & Lovers*, Gurian, a well-known therapist, writes that he has seen men who have all sorts of problems with women. They can't live with them, but they need them desperately. They are angry with women. They feel childlike when their mothers visit. They have trouble at work. They have difficulty as fathers. All of these problems seem unrelated, but Gurian says he has found the link. The problem, he believes, is that these men are still dangerously entwined with their mothers. Fathers are often "absent, distant, abusive or passive in 80 to 90 percent of families," Gurian writes, and therefore mothers have become far too great an influence on their sons. (This is a statistic that is difficult to verify, given the subjectivity of terms like "distant" or "passive.")

Gurian's prescription for all "confused and conflicted men" and "the painful wounds we have received in our mother's world" is that they must confront their mothers. This, it unfolds, involves a few steps. Sons need an "initiation rite" to separate. (True to form, Gurian is also fond of Native American ritual and myth.) "Separating from our mothers is a primordial door we must walk through if we are to learn about huge and deep parts of ourselves that our mothers have not been able to show us." Mothers of sons, he writes, consider it their job to "hold back the coming of manhood."

Where does he get these ideas? What mother wants to hold back her son's manhood? Granted, it could be a matter of interpretation. Certainly today's mothers are committed to raising boys who are more in touch with their emotions. Plenty of moms disregard the "be a little man" and "big boys don't cry" versions of masculinity. But retarding their son's development? Compromising his masculinity? That's not on the job description of any woman I know or any mothers I have interviewed. Yet listen to how Gurian describes the mother-son relationship:

> It is as if we are naked over a gorge, one foot still on the side
> of the gorge where Mother lives, the other on the side of the

gorge where lover/mate lives, the two sides of the earth gradually moving farther away from each other so that our psychic body is being split in two. As our legs are stretched apart more and more, our genitals hang less and less protected. Our manhood, year by year, becomes more and more vulnerable.

After this depiction of mothers who evidently would rather castrate their sons than let them grow up, it's not surprising that Gurian's other chapters talk about "consuming," "enmeshed," "dangerous," and "smothering" mothers. "Our mothers have devoured, or eaten away, parts of our masculine psyche," he warns. When fathers are withdrawn or absent, and mothers are angry about it, the son perceives that "manhood has been devoured by the Goddess, found lacking, spit out."

After Gurian is finished with this critique of mothers, he goes on to explain how men can free themselves from the damage mothers have inflicted, which involves some self-examination (there are lots of little quizzes), writing in a journal, getting therapy and joining men's groups, and writing one's mother a series of letters about hurt feelings, only the last of which he should actually mail. Men with dead mothers are asked to do an exercise in which they imagine this confrontation.

Gurian's theories would almost be amusing if they were not so profoundly insulting and insidious in the way they perpetuate the myths of the emasculating mother who wreaks lifelong damage on her son. They could also be more easily dismissed if the therapist didn't wield considerable influence in some educational circles. Gurian now runs an institute he named after himself and says he has trained more than fifty thousand teachers in more than 5,200 districts. He has written more than twenty-five books on boys and girls, focusing particularly on what he believes to be the intrinsic differences between them. He is a frequent speaker at schools and, as mentioned earlier, a strong advocate for single-sex education. In 2010 he reissued his guide for teachers and parents, *Boys and Girls Learn Differently!* That exclamation point is part of the title.

It's not surprising that a man who believes that mothers present such potential danger to their sons' well-being would also conclude that boys would perform better in the classroom if they were separated from girls. Gurian believes that boys and girls have different brain wiring. Girls, he has written, "are less able to separate emotion from reason" and would thrive in a more comfortable, unthreatening environment. Boys' higher level of testosterone gives them an advantage in math and spatial reasoning, he argues. Gurian advocates what he calls "gender-based learning" to help close the achievement gap between boys and girls. When complete segregation isn't feasible, Gurian recommends gender-tailored approaches to boys' and girls' education within the classroom.

Several scientists have challenged the studies on which Gurian's theories about male and female brains are based. "His claims are bogus," Barnett, the scientist at Brandeis, told me bluntly. In their book *Same Difference: How Gender Myths Are Hurting Our Relationships, Our Children, and Our Jobs*, Barnett and coauthor Caryl Rivers systematically reviewed the studies on gendered learning differences and conclude they are based on biased reasoning and sloppy science. Neuroscientist Lise Eliot also takes on Gurian and other "difference" theorists, concluding in her review, "The argument that boys and girls need different educational experiences because 'their brains are different' is patently absurd. The same goes for arguments based on cognitive abilities, which differ far more within groups of boys or girls than between the average boy and girl." Arizona State University recently launched the American Council for Coeducational Schooling, not only to counteract the gender-based education argument, but also to promote the many cognitive, psychological, and emotional benefits of boys and girls learning side by side. Single-sex schooling, they argue, promotes gender stereotyping and is unwelcoming to children who don't conform to traditional roles.

Nonetheless, the popularity of single-sex education is on the rise, even in public schools. In 2002, only about a dozen public schools offered single-sex classrooms. As of January 2011, at least 524 public schools in the United States had some single-sex offerings, according to the National Association for Single-Sex Public Education. Roughly 103 are single-sex schools.

Gurian's sway on the difference between boys and girls is

widespread and not only in single-sex educational settings. Alexandra, a psychology professor at a well-known university, ran into Gurian's influence when she visited her son's coed school to express concern about her nine-year-old son being bullied.

"I dealt with the principal and the school counselor and asked them to take the bullying seriously and not just give me 'boys will be boys,'" she said. "I wanted the whole thing to stop, but the counselor starts quoting me from Gurian's book and telling me about his work on boys and that boys are just different from girls. There are twelve hundred kids in this school and they're all being shaped by that damn Gurian. Meanwhile, I get painted as a hysterical mother who is freaking out."

If you do buy the idea that boys and girls learn differently, that also excludes a mother from helping her son with his classroom difficulties. She might be able to guide her daughter in learning—after all, their brains work in similar ways—but her son's method of grasping algebra or understanding the central theme of a book will remain a mystery to his mother, inaccessible to her. How can she possibly understand the workings of a boy's brain? This is nonsense. It might be true that men and women have been socialized to approach problems differently, but if that is so, it makes a mother's additional perspective all the more valuable. What's more, think about the logical extension to Gurian's theories. Men and women would eventually bring their dramatically different brains to the workplace. Should they be segregated there as well?

✌ Moms, Boys, and Masculinity

Just as we are living with an outdated narrative about the mother-son relationship, so, too, are we hanging on to old stories about how masculinity is formed and what it should look like. And clearly, these two topics are related. "Masculinity," like "femininity," is a cultural concept that changes over time. In his book *Manhood in America*, sociologist Michael Kimmel traces masculine ideals through history. George Washington, certainly "the man" of his day, wore a powdered wig and was aristocratic in his manner and tastes. The wigs, silk scarves, and even more foppish European attire were soon cast off by American men, and the manly man came to be seen more as a rugged individualist, a more rough-hewn type who worked with his hands. Given different cultural, political, economic, and technological conditions, different masculine ideals emerged—the self-made man, the blue-collar hero, the white-collar conformist, the playboy (swinging like Hugh Hefner), the cutthroat capitalist (think Master of the Universe Gordon Gekko), and the New Age man. Kimmel's point is that the concept of manhood is malleable and must be viewed within the context of history and popular culture. Today's "new macho" increasingly embraces men's more nurturing side. You wouldn't catch Clint Eastwood wearing a Snugli, one of those wraparound baby carriers, but no one blinks an eye when Brad

Pitt is photographed schlepping through airports, baby secured on his chest and a toddler dangling off each arm.

Academic fields like gender studies and male studies, following the earlier example of women's studies, are gaining popularity on college campuses. Scholars debate the influence of nature and nurture in the formation of gender roles, positing that traits that we tend to think of as inherently male or female are in fact shaped by cultural expectations, not anatomy or chromosomes. It's hard to imagine that this issue will ever be fully resolved. No doubt boys and girls are different and testosterone plays some role in that difference. The point is not to insist that males and females are exactly alike but simply to examine our assumptions about the distinctions.

As we have seen, the traditional view spouted by Bly, Gurian and company (and derived from the Oedipal theory) is that establishing a masculine identity is all about breaking away from your mother and embracing a traditional "wild man" identity as a male. Becoming a man requires defining oneself in opposition to one's mother. It presumes the necessity of male role models for boys. Masculine is simply defined as "not feminine."

But this is just not true. A wealth of new research has taken a much more expansive view of what healthy masculinity is and how it is established. Most of these theories put the question of masculinity into a broader cultural context, disputing Freud's famous assertion that "anatomy is destiny." Even traditional analysts believe that masculinity is far more complicated and ambiguous than simple maleness. Dr. Michael J. Diamond, a clinical psychologist and psychoanalyst who writes about the father-son relationship, disputes the traditional Freudian theory that only by identifying himself in opposition to his mother does a boy form a masculine identity. Optimally, he sees separation as a far more progressive—not oppositional—process, with boys identifying with both parents on their way to a healthy gender identity. "It is, therefore, *not* the boy's disavowal of his maternal identifications that is crucial to establishing his masculinity. . . . The underpinning for a boy's achievement of 'healthy' masculinity, instead, is founded upon a secure and involved attachment to both mother and father (or surrogate)," he concludes. In fact, Diamond believes that boys who violently repudiate their identification with their moms have a more fragile, rigid sense of what it means to be a man and often, having internalized a contemptuous, devaluing attitude toward all things female, develop difficulties in relationships with women. Diamond emphasizes that our culture plays a pivotal role in gender identity, and that masculinity is reworked throughout a man's life.

Ken Corbett, a psychology professor at New York University, argues that traditional psychoanalysis has ignored the complexity of masculinity. Any behavior that is outside the margins of what is culturally accepted is viewed as pathology. So a boy who is less traditionally "all boy" is seen as maladjusted. He argues for a wider acceptance of what constitutes "normal" boy behavior. Instead of emphasizing how boys are different from girls, Corbett focuses on how much boys differ from one another. (Any mother of more than one son knows that each boy has his own level of emotional sensitivity, athleticism, intellectual capacity, and every other human strength and weakness. The same parents produce children of vastly different natures.) Corbett, the author of *Boyhoods: Rethinking Masculinities*, not only focuses on the range within boys but also disputes the idea that boys are in crisis or are a homogenous group with problems to be solved.

Kimmel points to the psychological damage wrought by the perpetuation of the traditional Freudian view of masculinity on boys. Girls, he says, have a more seamless path to becoming women because they get to hold on to their bond with their mothers. "But boys not only have to separate from their mothers, they have to repudiate her," Kimmel said. "Boys are asked to pretend they don't need their mother way too early, when they are three or four years old, and this is done in the name of masculinity." Kimmel believes that boys are asked to develop an allegiance with an abstract concept—the idea of being a man—instead of with a concrete relationship with a real person. "Just when a boy learns how much he needs and loves this woman, she will push him away and reject him, and tell him no, you need to be autonomous and independent, you should identify with this idea and not me. And what boys learn is that women will betray them," Kimmel says. He added that boys will later bring a fear of closeness and betrayal into their adult relationships with women.

One recent study examined "healthy" masculinity in a

literal way, revealing that male adolescents who have a rigid, traditional view of what it means to be a man—agreeing or disagreeing on a scale to statements such as "Men are always ready for sex" and "It is essential for a guy to get respect from others"—tended to have poorer physical health than teenagers with a more nuanced view of what constitutes masculinity. Researchers believe this was in part because traditional beliefs include the idea that seeking help is a sign of weakness. (This parallels the idea that boys don't need their moms.) The über-masculine adolescents pay for their "toughness" with higher rates of substance abuse, HIV infection, and truancy in school. This research also echoes the study done by Carlos Santos, mentioned earlier, showing that middle school boys who embrace more traditional definitions of masculinity have poorer mental health and are less academically engaged than those who have a more expansive view of what it means to be a man.

Dr. Ronald F. Levant, a psychology professor at the University of Akron who has written extensively about masculinity, said that in his clinical practice and research, he has worked with men who are so out of touch with how they feel that they are only able to recognize the physical components of an emotion. For instance, these men might experience what feels like a tight band around their chest, or a pit in their stomach, but do not recognize it as anxiety. "They feel bad inside but they can't say why they feel bad," Levant explained. "As a result they are more likely to use less healthy ways of dealing with it, like numbing themselves with alcohol and drugs, or getting aggressive."

Levant's academic research focuses on how boys are socialized into traditional views of masculinity that discourage emotional expression. He calls this "normative male alexithymia." At its extreme, this type of socialization can prevent men from getting the help they might desperately need. Levant recently designed an intervention program for male combat veterans who suffer from post-traumatic stress disorder. Some of these men cannot benefit from psychotherapy to treat their trauma until their severe alexithymia is addressed. Many of these veterans, particularly of more recent wars in the Middle East, typically come from backgrounds where very strong, traditional views of masculinity were embraced, Levant said. In the program, these men are taught to recognize their emotions and to develop a vocabulary for them, as well as to be able to read other people's faces, tones of voices, and body language. Once they master these skills, they are then better able to go on to other therapies, like cognitive reprocessing or exposure treatment, to help them process their traumatic combat experiences.

"Real" men might appear tough, but they are often in quiet pain. And mothers can play a role in alleviating that suffering by helping theirs sons break through the code of silence early on.

⤳ Male Role Models

Expanding our view of how boys become healthy men, and particularly questioning the absolute necessity of male role models in a boy's life, is especially pertinent to single mothers and lesbian moms of sons. If we accept the traditional view about how developing masculinity requires rejecting Mom and identifying with Dad—these female-headed families are by definition a threat to boys' healthy development. Currently there are roughly 9.8 million single mothers in the United States living with children age eighteen and younger. The number of single mothers is at a new-time high. In 2008, a record four in ten births (41 percent) were to unmarried women, up from 28 percent in 1990, according to the "New Demography of Motherhood" study by the Pew Research Center. Back in 1960, only 5 percent of births were to unmarried women.

Between 8 and 10 million children in the United States are being raised in gay and lesbian families. In 2009, the Census Bureau estimated that there were 581,000 same-sex couples in the United States. Roughly one-third of lesbians are parents and about one-fifth of gay men are parents.

All the second-guessing that surrounds single and lesbian mothers keeping their sons too close is similar to what heterosexual married mothers get but on steroids. Straight single moms are accused of looking to their sons for emotional sustenance and for treating their sons as substitute husbands or male confidants. Lesbian mothers are suspected of creating gender confusion by not providing their sons with a heterosexual male role model. It's as if there is some secret code to imparting masculinity, one that mothers can't possibly know.

Underlying this critique is a deep uneasiness about a woman raising a boy on her own.

"I have definitely been told that I really have to get some male role models around my son so he knows what it is to be a man," said Deborah, a lesbian mother of a fourteen-year-old boy. "And my response is, 'What is it about being a man that is so complicated, and who is the person that he needs to show him?'" Deborah said that she did not want a model of extreme macho masculinity, but rather men in her son's life who were a loving presence. "My own father was not a hyper-masculine man but a nice nurturing person. Our president is not a hyper-masculine butch guy but a thoughtful, emotionally intelligent person. Those are the models I want for my son."

That said, Deborah still feels the criticism and sometimes wonders if she is shortchanging her son. She recently observed him working out with his soccer team and how much he seemed to enjoy "these two great coach dads." She worried that her son hungered for such men, but later discovered he didn't even know his coaches' names. Deborah says she hasn't determined if she is projecting her own fears about his lack of a father, or if her son has needs that he won't express because he doesn't want to hurt her feelings.

Carla and Andrea, the mothers of Max, sixteen, and Piper, fourteen, used an anonymous sperm donor to conceive their children. Before they started a family-, both women had concerns about what it would mean for their children not to have a dad. But Carla, a therapist, had seen situations where the donor had been known and involved as a father, and while it had worked for some families, for others it was "a disaster." They decided against a "male for male's sake." Both mothers were always honest with their kids about their conception. "We'd say, 'You have a donor; he's not your dad.' We didn't want them to feel that someone was missing or had left or abandoned them," Carla explained.

Max and Piper do have men in their lives who take them on outings and hang out with them—mostly their mothers' friends and family. But the couple continues to get pressure to provide male role models for their son, especially from Carla's father. "When Max was born, my father thought I should move back to my hometown because he'd be around. Now he is constantly saying to my son every time he sees him, 'Call me if you ever want to talk about girls.' Of course Max thinks this is ridiculous since my dad is five foot four and ninety years old." Still, it took Carla some time to make peace with the male role model issue. "I had to struggle to get to the point where I could think about my family as just another kind of family, not a family that was missing something." She admits she remains wary of other people's judgments. "My son happens to be a typical boy who loves sports and all that, but I have to say if I had a kid who was gay or more effeminate, I would be really uncomfortable; same if I had a masculine daughter. I would really be worried about what people were thinking about them being raised by two mothers."

Nathalie, who is raising her eighteen-year-old son with her

partner, has a different take on providing her son with a male role model. She believes our culture has lost sight of the more positive traits of traditional manhood, like honor, loyalty, and responsibility. She believes post–World War II fathers modeled self-sacrifice and a code of behavior that seems to be disappearing in a contemporary culture that tolerates—and sometimes celebrates—male immaturity and irresponsibility. Nathalie, a West Coast neurologist, talks to her son about how to keep promises, how to conduct himself with women, and the commitment of fathering children, topics that were once the province of father-son talks but which she is addressing as a mother.

"From my point of view, the values that I bring to my son come out of respect for those ideals that to me have no gender," she said.

Straight single women are not immune from the pressure to provide male role models. Ellen, a single mom, was warned against imposing her own emotional needs on her son. By the time James was born, Ellen's husband had left her and had no involvement in their child's life. She had been living abroad, but moved back home to Boston when James was two years old. On a routine visit to the pediatrician, the doctor asked Ellen if she would like to attend a support group for women with fatherless sons. She agreed.

"It was run by a man, and the first question was, 'Does your son sleep in the same bed with you?'" Ellen recalled. "I thought, my God, no, he's been in a crib for two years. I was exhausted from raising him alone and the last thing I wanted was to sleep with him. But this guy went on and on about the emotional needs of the mother that weren't being met. This 'big expert' scared the hell out of me."

Ellen didn't return to the group, but she laughingly recounted how she started tuning the television set to football games in front of her toddler. "He could barely walk, and I'm yelling out 'Defense!' 'Offense!' I didn't know anything about football, but that guy made me crazy."

Interestingly, divorce rates in this country might reflect our cultural assumptions that sons, more than daughters, need their fathers while growing up. The divorce rate has been lower for mothers of sons than for mothers of daughters in every decade since the 1940s. Two economists who reviewed census data from the last sixty years found that parents with an only child who was a girl were 5 percent more likely to divorce than parents of an only boy. The gap rose to 8 percent for parents of two girls versus two boys and 10 percent for families of three of the same sex. What's more, when the economists reviewed records of unmarried pregnant women having ultrasounds, they found that those carrying boys were slightly more likely to marry the father than those carrying girls.

The economists Gordon Dahl, then at the University of Rochester, and Enrico Moretti, at the University of California in Berkeley, focused on the economic and social effects of divorce and single parenthood. But their research raises the question of why "boys hold marriages together, and girls break them up," as Steven E. Landsburg, an economics professor, described the research in *Slate* magazine. Landsburg speculated that the numbers reveal a parental preference for boys. But other factors are likely at play, including the belief on the part of parents that boys need their fathers more than girls do. Mothers of sons might be hesitant to end unhappy relationships because they are convinced their boys need male role models.

"I've had women in my practice express that they are reluctant to break off the relationship because there is the commonly held idea that sons need their fathers," says Dr. Christine Nicholson, a psychologist with a private practice in Washington State, the mother of an adult son and daughter whom she raised as a single mother. "They say they don't know how to raise a son alone. Having done it myself, I think it was rough. At times I wished there was somebody a little stronger. You had to go toe-to-toe."

Monique, a California mother, reached a crossroads on this issue when her sons moved into adolescence. One night she took Deshawn, fourteen, and Marcus, twelve, out for Chinese food. Deshawn, who was already almost six feet tall, began to get upset during dinner.

"Mom, that woman over there is looking at me like I'm going to steal something," he told Monique, as he kept glancing at a nearby table. Monique looked over at the table and didn't pick up any particular vibe. But Deshawn had perceived hostility and fear from an older white woman sitting at a nearby table.

The moment crystallized an anxiety that Monique had been struggling with for some time. She had been divorced from her sons' father for eight years. She had a strong, close relationship with her boys. But for the first time, she wasn't sure that as a single woman she could help her teenagers navigate the road to manhood safely.

"What I experienced as an African-American woman wasn't the same as what they were experiencing as African-American young men," Monique explained. "I saw that Deshawn was getting angry and felt that I couldn't show him a good way to express his anger. I thought he needed that modeled for him."

She reluctantly decided that it would be best for her older son to live with his father during Deshawn's transition into adulthood. Her ex-husband agreed. No sooner had the teenager moved than Monique began to have regrets. She was no longer involved in her older son's day-to-day life, his schoolwork, and, most of all, keeping tabs on his emotional life. Phone calls and weekends couldn't take the place of their everyday life together. Her ex-husband, meanwhile, was providing little discipline at home for Deshawn and discouraged his son from pursuing a college education. For Monique, a PhD candidate, the belief that her son needed a male role model was ultimately trumped by a difference in values and parenting style. After a year, Deshawn returned to live under his mother's roof.

"Deshawn just needed a responsible adult to look up to,"

Monique says. "If I could do it over again I would have found other men in my community, coworkers of mine, where they could have been role models where it didn't have to mean separation from me. But then again, maybe I was enough."

Monique would be heartened to know that according to the new research, she very likely was enough. Many of today's scholars say that the quality of parenting is far more significant than the gender of the parent. Michael Kimmel puts it this way: "Single moms get a lot of pressure about male role models. I think it's a classic example of mistaking form for content. Here's what we know—children need a boatload of love and support, and all things being equal, it's better to have two parents giving it than one. But we also know that children of single moms, single dads, heterosexual, gay, can all thrive if given enough support and love. The form is much less important than the content."

The argument that children need both a mother and a father presumes that mothers and fathers bring separate gender-based skills to parenting, according to Timothy J. Biblarz, an associate professor of sociology at the University of Southern California, and Judith Stacey, a sociology professor at New York University, in a recently published study. Dads are presumed to be good at discipline, problem solving, and roughhousing; moms to excel in nurturing and caretaking.

But the researchers argue that past studies have spuriously associated parental strengths with gender. They compared two-parent families with different-sex and same-sex parents and found that the strengths typically associated with traditional mother-and-father families appeared just as frequently in families with two mothers. Less research has been done on two-father families, but initial studies point to a similar conclusion: gay parents on average are no better or worse than straight parents.

Nanette Gartrelle, a researcher at the University of California at San Francisco, also concluded that being raised by a same-sex couple proves no hindrance to children's psychological development. Her study of children raised by lesbian mothers found that on measures of development and social behavior, they scored similarly to children raised by heterosexual parents. This was true whether the lesbian mother had a partner or not. What's more, the kids in these homes scored higher than children in straight families on some psychological measures of self-esteem and confidence, did better academically, and were less likely to have behavioral problems.

Critics have also argued that children who grow up with single mothers are economically and socially disadvantaged. But in a study published in the *American Journal of Sociology*, which reviewed thirty years of academic studies, researchers came up with some surprising findings. The two groups of children who had the highest achievement were those who grew up in two-biological-parent families *and* those who grew up in single-mother-headed families. Kids who grew up with single fathers or in families with a mother and stepfather or with a father and a stepmother had consistently lower attainments. Once you allow for the parent's job, there is no ill effect from growing up in a single-mother family. Sons who live only with their father, or with their mother and stepfather, did no better than those from single-mother families, and in some cases they did worse, even when those fathers had a socioeconomic advantage over the single moms.

The point of all this is not to put down dads or to say that fathers are expendable—far from it—but to emphasize that children can thrive with a diversity of different parental combinations. Which is good news, given the reality that children today live in a wide variety of family arrangements. Marriage rates in this country continue to decline. More than one in four fathers with children eighteen and under now live apart from their children, according to a 2011 Pew Research Center Study. (In 1960, only 11 percent of children in the United States lived apart from their fathers; today the figure is 27 percent.) What's more, the vast majority of the public does not view marriage as the only way to form a family. In a nationwide survey conducted in 2010 by both Pew and *Time* magazine, 86 percent of people say that a single parent and a child constitute a family; 80 percent say an unmarried couple living together with a child is a family; and 63 percent say a gay or lesbian couple raising a child is a family. It seems the public is a little further along in accepting the reality of family circumstances than are some "boy experts" and social scientists.

✢ The Emotional Crisis

Another theory about what's causing the "crisis" focuses on
the psychic price that boys pay by being pressured to fit cultural stereotypes of traditional masculinity. This is the flip side
of idea that boys are suffering from too much female influence. Our poor sons seem to be either not masculine enough
or too masculine for their own good. In *Raising Cain: Protecting the Emotional Life of Boys*, the authors Dan Kindlon and
Michael Thompson argue that boys in this culture are steadily
directed away from their emotional lives and toward behaviors of stoicism and silence. Boys, they say, lack the ability to
read and understand their own emotions and the emotions of
others. The only "manly" emotions they learn are anger and
aggression, responses that will limit and damage them as they
grow up.

These therapists are far more tolerant of the idea that
mothers have a valuable and positive role to play in helping
their sons reach manhood. Kindlon and Thompson would
also like to see fathers help their sons become more attuned
to their emotional lives in part by demonstrating these skills
themselves. "Most important, a boy needs male modeling of
a rich emotional life. He needs to learn emotional literacy as
much from his father and other men as from his mother and

other women, because he must create a life and language for himself that speak with male identity. A boy must see and believe that emotions belong to the life of a man," they write.

But how equipped are most men to do this kind of emotional work? The generation of fathers of the current crop of older boys and teenagers generally weren't raised to be in touch with their emotions, let alone to express them. As the authors themselves write, "Fathers tend to fall back on what they have been taught to do with other men—namely compete, control and criticize."

Mothers know this. After all they are or have been intimate with these men. And they know their sons need help in learning broader emotional skills so that they don't suffer in the same way that their fathers did. In fact, many of today's mothers work hard to teach their sons precisely the emotional skills and range that Kindlon and Thompson say that boys lack. Not only do they do precisely what these authors recommend, mothers frequently do so in the face of criticism from their sons' fathers.

Take Patricia, a Massachusetts social worker and the mother of two sons. One night Patricia could see that Chris, her nine-year-old, was upset. The normally outgoing boy had been quiet all day after school and during dinner. A little later, she asked Chris what was wrong, but the boy just shook his head. When she walked over to the couch and put her arm around Chris, her husband gave her a sharp, disapproving look.

"My husband always does this—'Patty, Patty, he's fine, leave it alone.' It's like I'm hounding my sons."

Jeff, her husband, said he was worried that Patricia was interfering with Chris's need to grow up. "He should be able to handle his feelings," he said. "You just work through it. Someone has a little setback because they lost a game or their friend called them a name. You don't make a federal case out of it. You have to learn to deal with the world."

But Patricia didn't think a nine-year-old should be left alone to work out what was upsetting him. Nor did she believe that this approach had been the greatest thing for her husband's emotional development. She often feels that Jeff is remote and closed off from his feelings, and she believes it interferes with their intimacy as a couple.

A little while later she went up to Chris's bedroom. At first he was quiet. Patricia played a game in which she pretended to be able to peer into his ear and peek into his head. "Whoa," she said, "it's dark in there. What's this I see? Did something happen in school?" Eventually her son told Patricia about the fight he had with his best friend. What had started out as lighthearted teasing had spiraled into something more. His friend had called him an "asshole" and shoved him into a locker in front of some other boys. Chris was ashamed, angry, and uncertain about what to do. He didn't want to hit his friend and he didn't want to "look like a wuss." At school, the fourth grader had acted like it was no big deal, but he was actually quite upset about it. Patricia listened to Chris, helping him sort out his feelings about what had happened and talking about some options on how to handle it.

Like many mothers of her generation, Patricia was building on the foundation of emotional intelligence that began when she comforted and talked to her sons as toddlers. As her boys grew older, they would sometimes struggle to communicate, then verbally shut down. But Patricia continues to help both of her sons identify and talk about what they are feeling, despite the backlash that sometimes comes her way. Her husband remains ambivalent about her approach. Jeff acknowledges that it might be good for their sons, but only as long as it is done in moderation. "Part of the image of a man is that you're able to take care of things, even if they're hard," he said. "You're physically strong; you're emotionally strong. He should be able to work through his feelings. But I guess it's possible to go too far with that. It wasn't easy for me when I was a kid."

The call for men to model emotional intelligence is certainly a welcome one, but that transition is not going to happen overnight. Meanwhile, what is so frustrating for mothers is that while fathers are now encouraged to do this kind of emotional work with their sons—whether or not they are any good at it—mothers are still often harshly criticized for babying their boys. Patricia is representative of many mothers who described being urged to leave their boys alone to work things out for themselves. It would be ideal if both parents could model emotional literacy, but in many families that is not happening.

Why should the behavior seen as empowering and helpful when displayed by fathers be viewed as coddling and feminizing when exhibited by mothers? Even *Raising Cain* inadvertently captures this disparagement that mothers who are emotionally close to their sons still face. In the readers' guide conversation with the authors in the paperback edition of the book, Thompson relates this anecdote: "When I shared the subtitle [*Protecting the Emotional Life of Boys*] with a school administrator, she said, 'My God, you're going to license all of those smothering mothers.' We had a good laugh before agreeing that boys in fact did need protection in our culture."

The authors Kindlon and Thompson are not mother bashers. They each give tribute to their own mothers in an introduction. Thompson describes his mother as "a person of deep feeling and great sadness to whom I owe my capacity for empathy." Kindlon wrote, "War and baseball—it's almost a cliché of boyhood passions. But thanks to my close connection with my mother, I got to explore beyond the confines of the classic male mold. I have many happy memories of cooking with my mother and of her teaching me to sew (I still like to cook but never got the hang of sewing). Perhaps most valuable of all, because I spent time with my mother in these casual domestic pursuits, I have always felt relaxed and at home in the presence of women. Beginning with those hours in the kitchen, I learned how to talk to them and how to listen."

There you go—both men grew up to be as empathetic as they clearly are today at least in part because of their relationship with their mothers. And Kindlon and Thompson see an important role for mothers to play with their sons. They write about mothers and sons achieving a "synchronous" balance in the relationship, in which a mother understands and responds to what her son needs at different stages of his life. This, of course, is how in a perfect world we raise both our sons and our daughters. And these psychologists are among a handful who say that part of the "crisis" facing boys is that they are asked to prematurely separate from their mothers, a break from which they might never fully emotionally recover.

✧ Premature Separation

Olga Silverstein calls the way mothers separate from their sons "the great maternal betrayal." In *The Courage to Raise Good Men*, Silverstein, a psychiatrist, writes heartbreakingly about the ways in which mothers in past generations were complicit in pushing their sons away because they had bought into the theory that a boy would somehow be contaminated by a close relationship with his mother. Silverstein describes the many reasons mothers withdrew from their sons—ranging from the desire to protect their boys from becoming sissies to worrying that they were emasculating their sons by exercising control over them. Some mothers pushed their sons away to avoid the grief of projected loss. They assumed that they would not have a close relationship with their sons as adults and tried to cut themselves off from that anticipated pain. Most of these mothers loved their sons deeply and had good intentions. But ultimately, she argues, the separation—done in the name of masculine development—is actually a form of abandonment.

This estrangement caused enormous suffering for both mother and son. Sons experienced it as a withdrawal of maternal love. Silverstein described her therapy practice as full of emotionally disconnected adult men, who had long ago been cut off from their most tender feelings. Many of these men were angry with their mothers. The women she treated also suffered about the relationship, and complained of feeling abandoned by their adult sons.

Silverstein, who described herself as a post–World War II mother, recalled pushing her own son away in the name of allowing him to grow up and become a man. When Michael turned thirteen, she and her husband proudly moved him into a room in the third-floor attic space of their house, believing it would acknowledge the independence of their newly bar mitzvahed son, and give him the space that he needed to do his homework away from his younger siblings and the noise of the family. Michael was a high-achieving student and his parents assumed he would be thrilled with his new status and his privacy. Silverstein writes that it wasn't until three and a half decades later that Michael admitted to his mother that he perceived this "gift" as enormous pressure to succeed. She later recognized this period as Michael's "exile from our family life," noting "the picture I keep seeing in my mind's eye is Michael lying on his bed, eavesdropping enviously on the sounds of his siblings and parents downstairs."

Silverstein, who died in 2008, was born in 1923. Though her book was published less than twenty years ago, the mothers and grown sons she uses as examples are from her own generation. Her insights into the mother-son relationship were fresh when she wrote them, but they were also based on a lifetime of her own experience, not the current generation of mothers who are rejecting the idea of withdrawing from their sons.

Babette Smith, an Australian author and journalist who also wrote about post–World War II mothers and sons, echoed some of Silverstein's observations. In *Mothers and Sons*, she argued that mothers of earlier generations often misunderstood masculinity. When boys and men defensively hid their vulnerability and need for closeness, these mothers mistook it for "male strength." They withdrew from their sons defensively, feeling rebuffed and unneeded. Their sons, she wrote, came to view their mothers as uncaring and cold.

William Pollack also speaks compellingly about the disconnection that boys feel because they have been pushed prematurely to separate from their mothers. In *Real Boys*, Pollack argued that boys get the first shove as early as age five, when they are encouraged and expected to be independent and urged into situations at camp or school for which they might not be ready. The second push toward separation comes in adolescence, when boys are introduced to dating, new schools, rougher sports competition, and more. At this point, the pressure for a son to break from his mother becomes even more pronounced. The problem, Pollack says, is not that we encourage independence in our sons, it's that we introduce them to the world with too little emotional support. Not only do boys not have enough opportunity to express their feelings but they are given little room to regroup and change course if they are not ready to move on. Pollack describes this separation as "normative trauma"—that is, a harsh emotional disconnection that is expected for a boy to become a man. Girls, he notes, are not required to undergo this wrenching break. "I do go out on a limb with that term and I've gotten some blow back from it," Pollack said in an interview. "But most boys are traumatized into this separation psychology, while for girls we consider remaining connected to be a positive, normal, and even superior thing. Although boys and girls may connect in different ways, we are one species, and boys need connection as much as girls do." Pollack describes forcing boys to separate prematurely from their mothers as a "lose-lose-lose" situation. Boys yearn for connection, and either they follow society's dictates and suffer trauma from the separation, or they stay connected with their mothers and have a sense that they are not "real boys." The third loss is the societal cost—boys who are disconnected later tend to act out with aggression and struggle to feel empathy. "We wonder what is wrong with them, when we've socialized them to act exactly that way," Pollack says.

⨯ Turning Points

In 1998, when Pollack published his book, a new project was launched at the Jean Baker Miller Training Institute at the Wellesley Centers for Women. This was the "Mothers-Sons Project," mentioned earlier, codirected by Dr. Nicolina Fedele, a psychologist, and Cate Dooley, a social worker. Their goal was to examine the mother-son relationship by turning conventional wisdom on its head. Instead of viewing separation as the natural course of development between mother and son, the two women decided instead to empha-size strengthening the connection. They, too, believed that mothers and sons both suffered from the prevailing cultural injunction to disconnect from each other. Fedele and Dooley held workshops for mothers in the Boston area, in which they encouraged women to open up about their experiences of rais-ing sons. "The moms of older sons were in pain, and the moms with little boys as young as five or six were starting to feel the pressure to disconnect," Dooley remembers. "Their hus-bands were saying, 'Don't kiss him, don't baby him.'" Boys who are prematurely pushed toward independence are more fragile than they appear, she told mothers. "When you shut that connection down, he's on his own," Dooley says. "A boy doesn't understand why a mother who had been so loving and physical, pulling him in her lap and kissing him, is suddenly reserved. The kid has no clue. He just thinks concretely, 'Mom is leaving me now, she doesn't kiss me anymore.' No one is disavowing him of that, or naming it, or reassuring him. It just happens."

Fedele and Dooley make a distinction between separation and differentiation. In other words, they argue that boys can grow up to be healthy adults without severing the emotional bonds with their mothers. Their work was based on the relational/cultural theory of development introduced by Jean Baker Miller, which maintains that relationship connections are essential to healthy development. As Dooley and Fedele continued their workshops, they began to notice one overwhelming reaction from mothers: relief. At last someone was validating their maternal instincts. The mothers in the workshops wanted to keep their sons close, but were feeling enough cultural pressure to second-guess themselves. Moms would describe listening to their sons crying through the bedroom door but hesitating to go in, even though they were yearning to provide comfort. Now they were getting permission to open that door. "I began to start every workshop by saying, 'You are here to be reempowered to trust your instincts,'" Dooley told me.

In the years that have passed—well over a decade—since Silverstein and Pollack sounded the alarm about premature separation, and Dooley and Fedele conducted their workshops, mothers have come a long way. Most no longer feel they need permission to push back against those old admonitions to separate from their sons. Many of today's moms are not only keeping their sons close when they are younger, but also continuing to do so as their sons move into their teenage years and even beyond. Despite the heavy load of cultural and psychological pressure to do otherwise—along with the mixed messages from some "boy experts"—mothers work hard to stay emotionally connected to their sons. They intuitively know boys need their mothers and can benefit from their influence, and what's more, they now have the confidence to follow their instincts.

Maybe we moms haven't been talking about it much, because we get sick of battling the same old mythologies about mothers and sons. But that doesn't mean we fully bought into those dated theories. I know I never did. It wasn't as if I had some big pre-existing plan to raise my son differently than I had been told. It was more likely a combination of the arrival of a sweet and sensitive son and the naturally growing bond between us, backed up by several generations of feminism, which had taught me that the roles of men and women weren't nearly as set in stone as they were once presumed to be. We mothers were raising our daughters differently, with every expectation that they would take their place in the professional world. Why wouldn't we raise our sons differently, as boys with whom we could experience deeper emotional closeness and tenderness?

What I have discovered is that mothers are doing just

that. Every day, in kitchens and cars—and everywhere else that domestic life plays out—mothers are relating to their boys in a new way that reflects a more contemporary view of our culture. In doing so, moms are forging close bonds with their boys that they believe will help their sons to become strong men and strong human beings, less likely to fall prey to male "crises" of any sort.

5

Car Talk

Relationships are made of talk—and talk is for girls and women.
—DEBORAH TANNEN,
AUTHOR OF *YOU JUST DON'T UNDERSTAND:*
WOMEN AND MEN IN CONVERSATION

SHARON IS A FAN of what she calls "car talk" with her sons. Many mothers of boys are familiar with this method of communication. The two of you are engaged in an activity—tossing a ball, playing a board game, sitting side by side in a car—and that distraction allows a boy to open up about topics that, as Sharon puts it, would "normally send him running from the room." She doesn't always use a moving vehicle for the approach. She and her younger son watch basketball on television together and their best talks about life come from issues unfolding on the court.

"Basketball is his passion; it's his turf," she says. "I can start by asking him questions. What was that call about? Why do you think he's doing that? Or if one of the players did something bad in his life, I use it as a teachable moment. You find your opening with boys. It's always there if you look hard enough."

Sharon, who lives in North Carolina and has been involved in several successful computer start-ups, says it wasn't until she had sons that she understood the depth of emotion that males could have.

"My younger one has a lot more of the macho veneer, but both of my sons have a tremendous well of sensitivity," she said. "I think it's there in men, but I think there is so much cultural overlay that kind of straitjackets men. You get to see it much more as the mother of sons. They are younger and they are vulnerable with me in a way that an adult man would never be."

Marlene, a New Jersey realtor, wanted to talk with her son about a case of date rape that had taken place at the thirteen-year-old's school. She, too, chose a car as the place to hold this sensitive and potentially embarrassing talk.

"I knew he'd go running from the conversation, so I got him in the car and bought him a pizza and put it on his lap," she explained. "He couldn't get up and leave and he couldn't put his hands over his ears. Meanwhile, I was stopping to do errands, so when I was in and out of the car, he could sit there and have some time to regroup. Eventually, in bits and pieces, we were able to talk about it."

Mothers do not have to hold their sons captive in vehicles for conversation, of course, though it is a popular option. But whatever the venue, what we discover is that the more we talk with our boys, the more they will be able to talk to us. Reading to our sons, speaking to our sons, pulling the plug on their nonstop computer and video games, all can improve a boy's ability to communicate. We know that our boys are perfectly capable of expressing themselves if handled with patience and given some encouragement.

And this is something we want for them. Our mothers' and grandmothers' generations might have idealized a man who was "the strong silent type," but today that guy is no longer considered a desirable catch. Stoic and restrained men are seen as frustrating and irritating precisely because they are so incommunicative. It can be difficult to create emotional intimacy with them. We don't want our sons to retreat behind a similar wall of silence. And just because they are sometimes difficult to reach and reluctant to talk doesn't mean we shouldn't try to connect with our sons.

✎ "Boys Don't Talk"

One of the many myths surrounding the mother-son relationship is that boys don't talk. Expressive language is a "girl thing" and talkfests are part of the traditional mother-daughter bond. Since boys are constitutionally inarticulate, the theory goes, mothers and sons cannot bond on the same emotional level as mothers and daughters. After all, we can barely communicate across the sexes as adults. The entertainment media delights in reinforcing images of the grunting, monosyllabic male, rolling his eyes as his female partner talks on and on. In movies and on television, the emotions of a "real man" play out only across his face. How does a sensitive guy on television express himself when he's deeply upset? Usually by punching a wall. If a woman or girl were portrayed with these kinds of limited communication skills, she'd be seen as either stupid or psycho.

Moreover, those grunting guys are likely unhappier than those who can put their feelings into words. An academic study done at the University of Arizona published in 2010 made a connection between talking deeply and happiness. People who have substantive and meaningful conversations reported more satisfaction with life than those who engaged in superficial chats. It's good for our sons to be able to converse at a deeper level than "How 'bout those Yankees?"

Mothers who are close to their sons don't accept the idea that boys are incapable of conveying their thoughts. Not only do they know better, but many mothers work hard to see that their sons don't fall into this dated, degrading typecasting. They simply won't let them get away with it.

Does this mean that these mothers sit their boys down at the kitchen table, hand them a mug of steaming cocoa, gaze intently into their eyes, and say, "Let's talk about what's going on in your life"? No. That's a nonstarter for most boys, who—like many of their fathers—will squirm, look sideways, and anticipate their release from what for them is an uncomfortable and awkward situation. After all, boys are growing up in a culture that bombards them with constant messages about what it means to be male, and that includes balking at a direct inquiry into their feelings.

Nevertheless, there are opportunities for mothers to counteract these cultural stereotypes and engage in meaningful conversation with their sons. Despite the societal messages about boys' limited communication skills, many mothers of boys find that, when given the right opportunity, their sons can be much more emotionally expressive than expected.

"I don't think boys don't have words for feelings, I think they have just as many words and feelings as girls do, but they are repressed from speaking because they are shamed out of the capacity they have," says William Pollack, the author and psychology professor at Harvard Medical School. "If you give them the right environment, the words start to come."

Why boys often need distraction to open up—a kind of indirect approach to communication—is not clear. Research shows that by the time they are school age, boys' conversational styles are very different from those of girls. Girls talk directly about their feelings; boys tend to talk more about "stuff"—concrete topics. In addition, they are more likely to demonstrate love and friendship through actions than words.

Scholars have established that girls generally learn expressive language and develop more extensive vocabularies earlier in life than boys do, and that baby boys show higher activity levels. Again, it remains difficult to tease out how much these differences are due to the way parents interact with their babies and how much are attributable to biological predisposition. Studies have shown that mothers encourage baby girls' talking more than they do baby boys', and use more words about emotions, like "happy" and "sad," when speaking to their daughters. Fathers also use more words about feelings when talking to their daughters than they do to their sons. So from the beginning, little girls are being encouraged not only to talk but also to verbalize emotions more than little boys are. It follows, then, that once they are toddlers, girls talk more to others than boys do, further enriching the girls' verbal abilities.

Scientists have extensively studied how men and women process language in the brain. Subtle differences do exist in the way that the two hemispheres organize speech in men and women. But those neurological distinctions are not great enough to validate the fashionable notion that males and females are practically two different species when it comes to talking.

The idea that enormous psychological and physiological differences exist between men and women and account for their difficulty in communicating with each other has a strong grip on the popular imagination. *Men Are from Mars, Women Are from Venus* by John Gray has sold over 30 million copies since it was published in 1992. Deborah Tannen's book *You Just Don't Understand: Women and Men in Conversation*, published in 1990, argued that men's and women's conversational styles are so different that they are basically from two different linguistic cultures. It also attracted enormous attention and was a best seller for nearly four years. The arguments in both books were based on the theory that males and females are vastly different in the way they are wired to think and communicate.

But those books are based on research that is more than twenty years old. More recent studies show that the two sexes are more alike than they are different. With respect to communication skills, the new scientific literature reveals that biological sex doesn't play nearly as big a role in verbal skills as environment does. One study of four-and-a-half-year-old twins showed that verbal fluency is about 40 percent genetic. When researchers compared boys to girls, they found that the child's sex accounted for less than 3 percent of the total variance in language skills.

Here's a very telling part of the study—at the age of two, little boys who had a twin sister had better verbal skills than the boys who had a twin brother. Female twins had the highest verbal abilities of all. This means that who you spend your time talking to—or in the case of toddlers, babbling to—can influence how well you develop verbally. Even as babies, girls are socialized to have better verbal skills, and boys' abilities can improve simply by exposure to girls' language.

It also turns out that having a sister can be good for your emotional health, and it may be related to girls' verbal skills. A study of 395 families conducted by Brigham Young University discovered that having a sister prevents depression more than having a brother. Author Laura Padilla-Walker speculated that this might be because girls are better at talking with their siblings about problems, something they have been socialized to do.

Those brain scans and neurological studies back up what mothers already know intuitively: that a language-rich environment can improve a boy's verbal skills, so mothers can have a deep influence on their sons' ability to communicate.

The back-and-forth conversations between mothers and sons don't have to be on subjects of earth-shattering importance. It's as much about how to talk as what you talk about. It begins when mothers remind wailing toddlers to "use your words" to express their frustration and continues through adolescence when mothers refuse to let their teenage boys retreat behind a wall of silence. Jean, a physical therapist, remembers trying to teach her third-grade son, Robby, to verbalize his impatience. When Robby was hungry, he got cranky. And the eight-year-old, who never stopped moving, was hungry a lot. One day he was irritable because he didn't want to wait any longer for a waffle his mother was preparing. Jean simply handed him a frozen waffle.

"He said, 'Hey, this is frozen,' and I explained that everything has to be cooked or prepared and you have to have a little patience. He says, 'Okay, but I'm hungry.' I told him, 'Okay, we have to talk about this.' He sort of wiggled out of his chair and curled up and said, 'Oh, do we have to do that?

I hate talking.' And I said, 'Yeah, we have to talk about it.' Then he got used to it, that Mom had to talk about things. He struggled with it, but he learned a little about how to work through his frustration by putting it into words."

Jean said dealing with her son this way was deliberate. Even when he was younger, she tried to help him identify his feelings. "I could see Robby was sensitive and intuitive. When we were watching an animated movie, we'd look at expressions and I'd say, 'Oh, he's angry,' or 'He's upset.'" She didn't view this as coddling or intrusive, in fact just the opposite. Jean believes she was giving him the skills her son needed to cope with his world. When Robby was a few years older, he came home from school one day angry with his teacher, calling her an "idiot." Jean's reaction was not to talk him out of it or even, as I would have been more inclined to do, to tell him to respect his teacher. Instead, she acknowledged his anger and then tried to help him figure out how to deal with it.

"I'd say, 'You may be exactly right, the teacher may be an idiot, but so what? You still have to go to school, you still have to do the assignment, and you're learning a little bit about life. That's how life is. You meet a lot of idiots. I meet a lot of idiots in my job, but I still have to do my job. And your job is school.'" The two of them then talked about what the teacher had done to anger Robby—it turned out she had forced the boy to miss part of recess in order for him to redo a sloppily written class essay. They then discussed how he might handle the situation better in the future.

Jean persevered in trying to help her son sort out and articulate his feelings, whether they were about his ability to wait for waffles to cook or more serious problems in school. This is exactly the kind of maternal guidance that can help a boy like Robby prevent potential problems in school as well as emotional withdrawal later in life.

Erica, a consumer affairs advocate, describes herself as an anxious and critical mother, though as she talks about her sons it is clear that she is deeply devoted to both of them. "When they were younger and I was at work, I'd feel this longing for them. It can almost make me cry now thinking about it. I love them so much and I couldn't wait to get home and see them. Then I'd get home, and David would be lying in front of the TV and he hadn't done his homework, and I'd start to nag," she says. Erica still berates herself for badgering her young sons as much as she did, and like so many other mothers, wishes she had handled certain things differently. But as she talks about some of the "mistakes" she made, Erica also reveals that without being conscious of it, she was modeling emotional intelligence for her sons. For instance, she remembers tucking in her older son one night when he was about ten. She had nagged him at length about schoolwork while he was lying in bed. Afterward, Erica felt terrible just thinking about her son huddled under his blanket, wearing his favorite dinosaur pajamas. She told her husband she was going to apologize. He advised her not to do so because it would undermine her authority. But Erica thought it was important that

David know she was sorry, and she went back into her son's bedroom. She said she didn't get overly emotional but still expressed regret. "I said, 'David, I'm really sorry. I'm sure I'll start nagging again, but I apologize. Even when I'm criticizing, I love you. I know it was wrong.' It just felt really important that I do this, and when I apologized for my behavior, he was almost teary-eyed and it meant a lot to him."

These kinds of interchanges are neither philosophical discussions nor dramatic breakthroughs, but rather an ongoing series of seemingly mundane and sometimes exasperating exchanges that build emotional and social intelligence, as well as closeness between mother and son. They are so woven into everyday life, so unremarkable, that the significance of what is going on tends to go unnoticed. But each one of these conversations between mother and son is helping to nurture a boy who can better understand and articulate what he feels. Mothers not only encourage sons to try to express their own thoughts and feelings clearly, but also work to model the behavior themselves.

ᴠ Enmeshment

Many mothers find their school-age boys to be surprisingly vulnerable and sensitive. They anticipate discovering these traits in their daughters but not in their sons. Sometimes, mothers find themselves emotionally identifying with their boys in unexpected ways. "It's like osmosis. It goes from my cells to his cells or his to mine, with no space in between. He's as attuned to me as I am to him," said Tracy, describing her relationship with her ten-year-old son, Michael. "Like me, he's insecure, he wears his heart on his sleeve, and he's really mushy and emotional. He is also consistently affectionate, expressive, and completely delicious." When Michael was in third grade, he was clumsy and sometimes teased by other kids. "It just ripped my heart out," Tracy said. "This bond, I believe, is physical. When he hurts, I hurt. I really believe there's some DNA or brain structure similarities or something." Tracy says she has never discussed these feelings with anyone, because she suspects she'll be criticized for being "enmeshed" with her son. But she also hasn't pushed her sensitive son away, believing that having his mother available as a sounding board is helpful, not hurtful, to Michael.

"Enmeshed" is a term used frequently in psychology. To be enmeshed is to be entangled or ensnared, but when therapists use the term it refers to relationships in which there are no appropriate boundaries. In extreme cases someone who is deeply enmeshed with another doesn't know where he ends and the other person begins. It can apply to any kind of relationship, but it is most often mothers who are labeled as "enmeshed" with their children. One psychologist, on being asked about the mother-son relationship, didn't waste a second before he shot back with, "Oh, it's okay for a mother and son to be close, as long as they're not enmeshed." Certainly it's unhealthy for a mother to have no boundaries with her child, either a son or a daughter. You wouldn't want to see it in a father, either. But it is curious that the label comes up so often about mothers and sons, implying that an empathic closeness between the two might very well have pathology associated with it.

Of course there are mothers who really do overidentify with their sons. Being close in a healthy way is one thing; trying to create a child in your own image and having an emotionally symbiotic relationship is another. In fact, Tracy does sound as if she might have a problem with boundaries. And if she has so much trouble separating herself from Michael, she is not in much of a position to guide him emotionally. Witnessing this kind of mother-son relationship can cause others to react with alarm, if not contempt. Linda, a radio producer in Chicago, remembers the mother-son book group she started when her son, Peter, was ten years old. Years earlier, she had been in a mother-daughter book group with her older child, Samantha, and Linda was committed to treating her son and daughter similarly. The group dynamic was different with the boys than it had been with the girls. The boys were more competitive with their answers (for instance, calling each other "idiots" for their opinions) and tended to talk more about the action in the books, while the girls focused on the relationships. But what stands out in Linda's memory most about the whole experience is one of the mothers in the group, who joined with twin boys. The twins' mother, Missy, obviously favored one son over the other and in the eyes of the rest of the women was clearly overattached. "She molded him in her image, he even played the same instrument she had—the flute—and the two of them had all the same mannerisms. She was so identified with his success. It was like a cautionary tale right in front of us. It set up a situation where you watched their closeness and people thought, *'Ewwwww.'* Occasionally other moms would remark, 'You can go just so far with your son and you can go no further.'"

Most likely all of us can point to a mother-son relationship that we think is "too close," like the one Linda describes. Linda considers herself very close to her son, in a manner she believes to be normal and wholesome. But note that she used the example of Missy and her son as "a cautionary tale," as if being emotionally attuned and supportive of your son is just one step on a road that will lead to this kind of stereotypical "mama's boy" enmeshed outcome. That assumption is wrongheaded. The kind of healthy closeness where a mother supports her son for who he is as an individual is very different from one in which a mother is controlling and has over-identified with her son. It's not a slippery slope but rather two very different dynamics. The two are often mistakenly conflated, and almost always with mothers and sons. Even as she acknowledged the clear inappropriateness of Missy's behavior, Linda also observed, "No one ever made any judgments about closeness in the mother-daughter book group."

The cultural anxiety about the overly identified or "smothering" mother casts a long shadow over normal mother-son relationships. Take Barbara, a Connecticut stay-at-home mother who was called into the psychologist's office at her son's private school because John, her fifth grader, was unhappy in class. The therapist's interpretation of John's troubles: he was overly attached to his mother. "She said, 'You know, he's very attached to you.' She didn't exactly say that this was unhealthy, but she did make me aware I was his security blanket," Barbara explained. "I was quiet and this psychologist could obviously see that I was processing this, and then she told me I couldn't pull away all of a sudden and kind of pull the rug out from under him. I had to do it gradually. But I still had to do it."

Her husband, Alan, was also asked to meet with the school psychologist. His response to John's unhappiness was simple: he told the school to "fix it." It was at Alan's behest that Barbara had enrolled both of their sons at this all-boys school. He traveled frequently on business, and believed that the boys needed greater male influence in light of his recurrent absences. Barbara noted that, ironically, the younger grades in the school were entirely taught by women and that her sons probably got far more female attention and influence than they would have at a coeducational public school. After she gave some thought to her meeting with the school psychologist, Barbara decided not to change her parenting style or to push her son away. "It didn't seem unusual to me that John was so attached to me," she said. "I didn't change a damn thing and continued to do what I always did. I knew he was happy at home." In fact, it turned out that what John disliked about school was the intensely strict environment and scrutiny that went with it. As he got into the upper grades and had more freedom, he began to enjoy school more, and the "mother problem" ceased to be an issue. Because, of course, it had never been a mother issue at all. In fact, John's close bond with his mother likely helped him get through the difficult times he did have at his very rigidly structured school.

ᠵ Moms in Boyland

Many mothers feel the need to counteract some of the commercial messages about masculinity that bombard their young sons. In *Packaging Boyhood: Saving Our Sons from Superheroes, Slackers, and Other Media Stereotypes*, the authors review cartoons, movies, video games, toys, and other products that market certain images of what it means to be a boy. They argue that boys are sold the message that guys are supposed to be cool, independent, athletic, and stoic. Traits like warmth or empathy, let alone feelings of vulnerability or dependence, are rarely to be found in media depictions of boys.

Parents are largely absent in the world marketed to boys, the research revealed. On those rare occasions they are represented, fathers are often depicted as clueless or childlike and mothers as nags or worrywarts. Mark Tappan, a professor of education and human development at Colby College and a coauthor of the book, told me that out of all the marketing material he and his fellow researchers had reviewed, examples that show a "really close, healthy, positive relationship with a boy and his mom in childhood and adolescence are very rare." In reality, many boys have intimate, loving relationships with their mothers, but seeing the distorted images on television sitcoms, in videos, or in commercials "might cause boys to think, 'Maybe my relationship with my mom is wrong somehow,'" Tappan says.

There is profit to be made out of exploiting boys' fears of being called a "wuss" or a "faggot" for not complying with these limited descriptions of what it means to be male. Marketers hook boys by creating anxiety: presenting hyper-masculine men as models, and then selling a product that will help them measure up to the ideal, the book argues. As if that isn't enough, research shows that boys also get media messages that it is cool to be a slacker in school, and that they should be wanting sex all the time. These are certainly not lessons that most mothers or fathers want their sons to be absorbing. When boys grow up constantly exposed to these kinds of sexualized and exploitative messages, is it any wonder that mothers feel the need to provide an intervening voice and alternative view to help them grow into decent, compassionate young men?

"This is an ongoing conversation I've had with both my son and my daughter, and I've tried to keep it age-appropriate," said Helen, a Rhode Island mother of two. "When I would watch a movie with Jonah, I would say, 'This is someone who treats women well,' or 'That is a man who doesn't treat women well.' Or as my daughter got older I would point out images of women that had been Photoshopped. I constantly try to make my kids aware of images. It all started when Laura was watching *Aladdin* and turned to me and asked why Princess Jasmine's tummy was always showing." (Helen's daughter was on to something when she picked up on the scantily clad heroine. Disney has come under repeated criticism for perpetuating sexual stereotypes, though at least Jasmine, Pocahontas, and Ariel show considerably more spunk than Sleeping Beauty or Snow White ever did. The male heroes in Disney have a body type few little boys can aspire to as adults in real life—chiseled abs, impossibly broad chests and shoulders, and swashbuckling strength.)

Pollack says that his research revealed that it was most often "empathic, active, undaunted" mothers who were in the best position to help boys sort through the conflicting messages they receive about how they should behave and who they should become. Boys today are growing up in an often-harsh culture, where they are constantly asked to measure up, to be cool, and to be strong. The level of homophobia in many middle and high schools is staggering—"gay" has become a pejorative adjective, as in "that's so gay," if a boy likes a certain song or shirt, or even if he expresses too much feeling about something. Often it is only with their mothers that sons can safely express emotions without feeling scared or ashamed, since she is the one who is most likely to provide a nurturing environment full of love and support. Far from creating dependency, that secure home base with his mother provides a growing son with the confidence and courage to explore the world, just as she did when he was a toddler.

Betsy remembers when her son, Eric, was trying out for a travel soccer team in his Connecticut town. Looking back, she is bemused by how high the stakes seemed for a ten-year-old to make a select team, but at the time it felt all-important, especially to Eric. It was a two-day tryout, and on the first day Eric didn't play as well as he thought he should have. Betsy watched him walk off the field, still joking with his friends, delivering a few high fives and even appearing a little cocky. But when he got into the car her son was silent, and when he got home he burst into tears. He was distraught, and sobbed about how all his friends would make the team and he would be left behind. He was ashamed of what he called his "crap play." Betsy was struck by the different face Eric had shown on the field and how broken up he was at home. "He just got it all out and then we cuddled for a while," Betsy said. "The next day of tryouts he had his confidence back and looked like a different kid. It was like he needed to recharge his emotional battery."

Mothers who want to keep their sons in touch with and talking about their feelings often experience ambivalence. They know that the world can be harsh on sensitive boys in grade school and even tougher on boys as they get older. The peer pressure to conform is intense. No mother wants her son teased because he is perceived as a wimp. And many fathers would agree. Men tell me that they remember their own days on the playground a generation ago. Fathers sometimes see raising their sons to be tough as a way to protect them. "I don't want him to have the crap beat out of him because he's crying over a baseball game," said the father of a seven-year-old.

Martin, now an adult, recalls how differently his parents reacted to his childhood football injuries. "I remember when I was in junior high playing wide receiver on the offense. The defensive back has the ball and I come up and tackle the guy, and his helmet is in my stomach and I got the wind knocked out of me. I'm on the ground, but a few minutes later I get up, I get to the sidelines, and one of my teammates says, 'You should have heard your parents. Your mother was going on, "He's hurt! Marty's hurt!" and your father was saying, "No he's not—it's good for the boy."'"

Just about any mother of a son who plays sports learns early on that it is socially unacceptable to run out on the field if her boy is down with an injury. When I saw Paul take a bad hit in soccer and lay on the ground for a minute before limping off to the sidelines, I had to struggle to keep myself glued to the bleachers. I stayed put because I understood that it would shame my son if I ran to comfort him in public. Later, at home, if Paul was still hurting, I would give him some extra loving care.

The truth is, after he was a certain age, I didn't want my son to run, crying, off a field after a sports injury or falling apart in his classroom if he had a problem. This might seem to conflict with some of what I'm advocating in this book. Yet being the mother of a son requires a balancing act. We do want to support our boys' emotional growth and develop their sensitive side, but rejecting some of the worst elements of the boy culture doesn't mean throwing out all of it. We do not want to isolate our sons from their peers or set them up for torment. Of course, a great deal of how we react to our son's setbacks is age related. It's one thing to wipe away a five-year-old's tears on the sidelines; it's quite another for a mother to come bounding into the middle of a varsity high school game. You also parent a sixteen-year-old daughter differently than you do a six-year-old little girl.

The larger issue for mothers of sons is teaching boys to explore and articulate their feelings in a way that will help them to better cope with the current culture instead of being victimized by it. At the same time that mothers are transforming our understanding of masculinity by keeping their sons more emotionally open and available, they also know that our sons will be vulnerable if they are social outliers who completely reject traditional male standards.

Pioneering feminist Adrienne Rich wrote in 1976, "The fear of alienating a male child from 'his' culture seems to go deep, even among women who reject that culture for themselves every day of their lives." More than thirty-five years later, contemporary feminist scholars remain conflicted. "Feminism was obviously about challenging patriarchs, but it becomes so complicated when you're talking about sons because you're talking about taking away male privilege, and as a mother you want to give them the best of everything," Dr. Andrea O'Reilly, professor of Women's Studies at York University and the founder and director of the Association for Research on Mothering, told me. "We want to raise strong girls, but do we want to raise weak boys? No. A lot of mothers want to walk away from this. As much as they want to raise a feminist, they are happy if their boys look at porn and become captain of the football team. They're proud of their daughters for being tough, but moms are far more ambivalent about their sons being feminine. A lot of it is homophobic and a lot of it is sexist, but we know the penalty for a boy stepping out of traditional gender is far higher than a girl stepping out."

Much of this conflict comes down to defining femininity and masculinity. In teaching our sons emotional intelligence and rejecting some of the stricter gender stereotypes, mothers don't have to view themselves as taking something away from their sons but as giving them valuable skills—a little more comfort in being who they are and an opportunity for a broader human experience. But talking theoretically about humanity and having a kid tormented on the playground for being different are two very different things. At the end of the day, we want to safeguard our sons. We know they haven't been well served by old models of masculinity, since it cuts them off from so much emotional potential. But we also don't want to put our boys in any danger by pushing them to a place where their own peers will reject them.

⁓ Confusion in the Ranks

In straddling these two sometimes conflicting goals, mothers can give their sons shaded, and occasionally mixed, messages. For instance, it might be all right to cry about something at home with Mom, but it's not a good idea to do it in school. Mothers can continue to provide a safe haven to which boys can return after coping with the more callous environments of school and competitive sports.

"I think I've respected that there are times when they needed to go out into the outside world and show a different side of themselves, and I'm not interested in taking that away from them," said Margo, a Rhode Island mother of two sons. "First, you have a child aware of what they're feeling, and then given the culture that they live in, what's an acceptable response. But if they don't know what they're feeling first, they're going to be off target."

Mothers are often conflicted about how to advise their sons. When a boy who had once been a good friend started bullying her son Marcus in the second grade, Grace wasn't sure how to handle it. She didn't want to undermine Marcus's self-confidence, but she also wasn't sure the eight-year-old could sort out the situation himself. Eventually she called the school, and the boys were put in different sections of the class. "I was torn because I knew Marcus had to become more self-reliant during those years, but I also didn't want him floating out there in the wind. In the end, I thought it was good for him to know that there were people behind him who would take actions to protect him."

But mothers who want to protect their sons from bullying are often discouraged from doing so, told that they should let boys work it out among themselves or that their sons should "man up." Marie's son was in the ninth grade when he became the victim of cyberbullying. In a story reported in *The New York Times*, the single mother from Massachusetts discovered that someone had set up a fake Facebook page using her son's name and photo. The site had nasty running commentary about her son's classmates and was designed to look as if he was writing it. Her son was ostracized at school and miserable.

Marie decided to intervene, but it wasn't easy to do so. School officials told her the harassment was going on off school grounds so it wasn't their responsibility. Cyberbullying is a relatively new phenomenon and Marie had a hard time navigating through the authorities that might be able to help her and her son. When she finally discovered the culprits and they were prosecuted, word leaked out in her community and Marie began to receive anonymous phone calls in the middle of the night.

"They told me my son should just suck it up," she told the

Times. "They said he would be a mama's boy. They would rant and then they would hang up."

It's hard to imagine that a mother who attempted to stop her daughter from being harassed would be told the child should "suck it up," or that helping her out would make her a "mama's girl," or whatever the equivalent would be.

Still, many mothers remain ambivalent. Judith, a doctor, said she felt uncertain about how to advise her son about fighting. "You know, I have all these ideas, but the reality is I also have a small kid who wears glasses," she says. "I tell him in a conflict to walk away, be the stronger one, and all my other ideas. But it's the real world out there, and he's going to have to learn how to deal with it. My big secret is that I'm thrilled when I see him act aggressively, because I feel like he's not going to be cowed."

Alone Together Time

Many mothers talk about how much they cherish their time alone with their sons and how it is during this one-on-one time that their boys open up emotionally. These moms are not necessarily describing formal outings or mother-son "dates." More commonly, it is the drive to soccer practice or music lessons, walking the dog, tossing a ball, or simply a trip to do routine errands. Sometimes it is just hanging out together in the kitchen. For me, it was going to the grocery store with my son. Like many mothers, I discovered that it was during the time spent away from the rest of the family, even in a setting as mundane as a supermarket, that my son would most often reveal his innermost thoughts and feelings to me. As we wandered the aisles or sat side by side in the car on the way to and from the store, Paul's feelings about school, soccer tryouts, or situations going on in the family were likely to come out. Not that it was always some big drama. Mostly, we just had a good time together because we were so companionable and our outings so low-key. We still have a running joke about never buying produce out of season, the result of a long-ago grocery trip when he was hankering for fresh peaches in February.

Some mothers actually are able to carve out the time to go away on mini-vacations with their sons. "I started doing these mother-son trips with each of my sons every summer, just one-on-one time with each of them," Katie said. "We'd take a bike trip. I started doing that when they were eight or ten. We'd go for an overnight on Martha's Vineyard; we'd bike around. It was wonderful. It was so fun. And we'd talk about everything. Things would come up that we hadn't talked about all year."

For others, even a meal out represented a kind of intimacy and opportunity for connection that their own mothers and brothers hadn't been able to share. "One of the ways my mother set the tone in the family was that mommies and daughters do things together and daddies and sons do things together," Jennifer said. "That was a family rule I wanted to change and I did. It's okay to go out with my son. I love going out to dinner with Jeremy. I think he's the funniest person around. He's also an extremely sensitive boy, and when we're out just the two of us, I'm really getting to see that."

Ruth and her son, Anthony, began their tradition on a rainy day when her then seven-year-old was bored. Ruth took her son over to the piano and taught him to play the duet "Heart and Soul." "By the end of the afternoon, he was able to play both parts, and he looked at me and said, 'Mom, that is the best time we ever had,'" Ruth said. "Years later, we still play those duets together and there's just a special feeling to it."

Sometimes, these traditions of mother-son time, which usually begin during the school-age years, are based on an effort to support a boy's interests. It can be particularly helpful for boys whose passions don't run toward sports or other more typical male pursuits. Vivian's son, Alec, was intellectually precocious as a child. He would get keenly interested in a topic—George Washington's crossing of the Delaware, say, or the Temple of Dendur—and Vivian would take him to museums, historical societies, any place that would nourish Alec's curiosity for whatever topic he was obsessing over. "Those trips were wonderful, in part to see things through his eyes, to help him understand more, to try to feed someone who was that intellectually hungry. It was a great thing to be part of," Vivian said.

It was also a time when Alec would open up about his experience in school and with his friends. Over time, Vivian intuited that when the two of them were out together, she should leave part of her mothering at home. Mostly, she would just listen. When Alec talked about the things that were bothering him, Vivian was careful not to advise too much. "I think it's sort of a facet of our particular relationship that I will sit back and listen longer without offering, 'You should do that.' That's one of the reasons my son talks to me at greater length. He will get the opportunity to lay everything out on the table without getting unwanted advice."

Jane's son, Dylan, couldn't have been more different in temperament than Alec. Dylan, a redhead with a spray of freckles across his nose, was one of those boys who hung upside down on the jungle gym shouting "Look at me!" and bounced off the living room furniture. Emergency-room trips for stitches were not infrequent. To channel his energy, Jane got him involved with sports. But she wasn't a mere spectator. She learned to connect with her son through activity—enjoying more rough-and-tumble play when Dylan was younger and playing sports with him until he finished middle school.

"Playing catch, I would say, 'Burn it in, give me your hardest,'" she remembered. "And we would play tennis. In the beginning, I could beat him and then we were about the same. I can remember one time, we were playing, he was maybe eleven, and I wasn't playing my hardest, thinking—eh, let him win. What do I care? Then he caught on that I was not playing my game. And he said, 'Mom, if you are not going to play competitively, I'm not playing. Don't mess around with me. Play for real.'"

Jane picked up her game, but Dylan won and was gratified. I remember my own son being infuriated when he perceived I was giving him what he called "pity points" in a game. He wanted a challenge and did not want to be patronized by his mother. At the same time, the competition was real without being cutthroat. The point—at least for mothers—was not victory; it was time spent together doing what the son enjoyed. Over time, Dylan could dominate Jane consistently in tennis as my son can now beat me rather consistently in anything but word games. (In my defense, he is thirty years younger, eight inches taller, and ambidextrous. Okay, maybe I'm more competitive than I like to admit.) Most important, when mothers and sons play games together, whether on a court or a game board, a companionship develops and it opens up a safe zone where they can talk about what's going on in other areas of both of their lives.

As he has gotten older, Dylan has been able to articulate how important it was for him to have his mother come to his high school games. His older sister, Emily, is involved in theater and often performing. "He said to me, 'My soccer and my baseball are as important to me as when Emily is in a show. It needs to have the same family importance.' He likes my being a spectator, but especially my being interested in what he's interested in," Jane said. And it's only when she is driving him home from games, when the two of them are alone in the car, that Dylan pours out his emotions about how he could have played better or his frustration with a coach or teammate. As the trip continues, other issues—like his worries about his grandparents' health—also unfold. Jane said she mostly listens, but also tries to help him sort out his feelings.

Whether it's a trip to the museum or the ride home from an away game, it's in these moments of being together and away from the family that a different relationship develops between mothers and sons. In some very real sense, it is much more a relationship of companions, one in which the son's feelings, ideas, and thoughts are treated with respect. This is also a crucial time when the mother-son relationship can develop naturally and blossom outside the criticism and second-guessing that so often surrounds it. It is as if a protected zone is established, where both mother and son are free from judgment and can simply enjoy each other as two people who love each other dearly. If there was anyone around to witness it, they would see that ease, companionship, and tender closeness. But because of the stigma around moms and sons, it often remains a mother's secret pleasure, rarely discussed with the rest of the family.

For instance, when Vivian and Alec got home from their trips to the city, the mother-son relationship would often quickly revert to "Alec, go pick up your room." They didn't talk about what was going on in Alec's emotional life in front of his father or two sisters. If asked how the trip to the museum was, Alec would most likely simply answer, "Fine." But there remained something different about the time alone together that Alec and Vivian shared, and the tone of companionship was immediately picked up again the next time the two of them were alone together.

Jim, now forty, grew up in the Tennessee countryside, far from the world of museum trips or organized soccer. What he remembers most is his mother teaching him how to shoot a rifle. She grew up as one of eleven siblings on a farm in Canada, he said, and could handle a gun better than anyone he knows to this day. When the two of them were out bird hunting, mother and son would talk about what was going on in the family and in Jim's life in ways that were impossible in the larger family setting. "My dad was in the navy and he was a man's man, very stoic, very type A, very critical," Jim said. "Mom made up for it by teaching us compassion and that not everything is as it seems or is black and white, no matter what Dad says. Those hunting trips and those talks made life bearable for me and my brother."

For Shelly, it was a Christmas shopping tradition that began when her son, David, was a young boy.

"Maybe you're thinking, why didn't I ask my husband to join me?" Shelly, a New York magazine editor, says. "Do I really have to explain? Even when I'm shopping for his family, it's my problem to find everything because all he really wants to do is get out of the store as fast as possible. My daughter probably would have agreed to go with me, but within fifteen minutes either she would have been telling me what to buy or I would have been exploding at her for something she did or said."

Shopping with David was tension-free, though, and provided that one-on-one opportunity away from the rest of the family for her son to open up about his life. "When the morning arrived, we had our routine down pat. We would drive to the deli and order the sandwich we both loved but ate only on these Christmas shopping jaunts—a crisp bacon and egg sandwich—two for him, one for me, followed by coffee for me and hot chocolate for him. Then we would sit in the car in the deli parking lot and enjoy breakfast, gabbing away. It really didn't matter to me which store we shopped at or what we actually bought. It was the day itself that was so special. He would tell me all about his life, what he was thinking about, what he wanted to be thinking about, and I couldn't get enough."

When her son was younger, Shelly would do most of the listening and her son would do most of the talking. But as David got older, Shelly began to talk to him about her life as well: her dreams and how well her life reflected them. This was a common theme among mothers of sons. Boys were not only opening up about their worlds; mothers were also sharing their everyday experiences and ups and downs. And often that meant discussing what was going on at work.

↩ Moms, Boys, and the Workplace

My survey revealed that as their boys start to get older, around eleven or twelve, mothers begin to bring more of their own lives—most particularly their professional lives—into the relationship. They do not consider themselves to be abandoning their parental role or believe they are becoming confidantes instead of mothers. Rather they feel it gives their sons a fuller picture of who their mothers are as people. It seems a naturally developing part of the relationship.

Carole loves to talk business with her son. Over the last eighteen years, she has turned what had begun as a math-tutoring job into a highly successful college preparation company, with offices in major cities on the East Coast. Business is booming, but lately Carole has found herself getting restless, and she's beginning to look around for a new venture. She enjoys discussing this with her thirteen-year-old son, Brian, who she feels understands her. Entrepreneurial genes run in the family. Her son began his first business at the age of ten.

When Brian was in the fifth grade, the South Beach Diet became popular. With his mother's encouragement, Brian decided to start a catering business in the development where the family lived. He drew up a menu of dishes for seven days and put flyers in his neighbors' mailboxes. Carole helped him shop for ingredients and cook the meals. She taught Brian to subtract his expenses from his income and increase profit by buying generic food in bulk. The time together was special on two levels, Carole said. First, it was while they were cooking together in the kitchen that Brian would open up about what was going on at school, his frustration with his basketball coach, and some of the intrigue among his friends. "My son is very expressive and he feels like no one understands him like I do," Carole said. Second, cooking time with her son was meaningful to Carole because she loves that Brian is following in her entrepreneurial footsteps.

"He's just good at making money and he got it from me," Carole says. "He loves to do it. My daughter says she wants to do these things, but she doesn't have the patience. With my son, it's the most fun we have together. I feel like we totally get each other."

Carole often discusses situations she's handling at work at the dinner table, and doesn't apologize for bringing home some of what she's dealing with at the office. "I've told them that the whole world is not about you, and I'm a real person, and I'm going to bring you some of my issues, too," she says.

This is not a generation of frustrated mothers who grew up with limited professional opportunities and who now live vicariously through the accomplishments of their sons and husbands. I recall the autobiography of journalist Russell Baker, who was born in 1923, and wrote, "My mother had a passion for improving the male of the species, which in my case took the form of forcing me to 'make something of myself.' She would spend her middle years turning me into the man who would redeem her failed youth." Today, few mothers are looking to their sons to live out their own thwarted dreams. The majority of mothers are in the workforce, and it's only natural that their professional life plays a role in how they relate to their sons.

Mothers' conversations with their children about work

seem to differ in certain ways from how fathers discuss what goes on at the office, in the store, or at the job site. Fathers tend to report more of what happened in a fact-based way, whereas mothers' anecdotes tend to center on relationship dynamics, the issues they create, and how they handle them.

Laurie and her husband, Richard, ran a production company together for many years. The films they were making were often a dinner-table topic, but they brought very different perspectives when they described their work lives. "Rich was always talking about the product and I talked about the process," Laurie said. "I'd talk about the relationships, the guy who was doing the animation, and you know he has a daughter, and how many kids the cameraman had. Whereas Rich was more, 'We are entering this movie in this festival,' and 'The movie will be on Disney.'"

When Sharon began her career in the early days of information technology companies, she was often the only woman on the staff. She felt it was important to discuss workplace dynamics with her sons. "I made a point when my sons were younger of bringing home stories or problems from the workplace—'What would you do, how do you feel about that?'" Sharon said. "I thought a lot of that was part of my job as a mother. A lot of it was ethical or people dynamics. A lot of those stories lead to the kinds of conversations we had when they got older and would talk to me about what was going on in their lives. They've got their trials and tribulations.

We have the kind of relationship that's still mother-son and there's a lot of respect and I'm a valued mentor."

Mothers also use their own work experience to teach their sons about handling their emotions in their day-to-day lives. When a boy is struggling with something that is upsetting him in school or with friends, many mothers do not believe their sons should "suck it up" and put on a macho front of aggressive bravado. But, as mentioned earlier, mothers also do not want their boys to emote all over the place, leaving them open to teasing. They search for a middle ground. Finding this balance is not foreign territory for working women.

Women of my generation have learned some hard lessons about exposing their emotional vulnerability in the professional sphere. We've probably all had times when we were driven to tears at work—certainly I've had editors who made me want to cry. But we've learned not to go to pieces when criticized on the job or to express inappropriate emotions in front of our colleagues. One young woman learned this the hard way on national television. Her team had lost a flower-selling contest on an episode of NBC's *The Apprentice: Martha Stewart*. The disappointed contestant made the mistake of telling the diva of domesticity that she felt like crying. Stewart, her prospective employer, was not moved. "Cry and you are out of here," she said. "Women in business don't cry, my dear."

"Emotional intelligence" doesn't mean being emotional. It means being attuned to the dynamics around us, as well as our own feelings, a skill that is as critical for little boys on the playground as it is for big boys at work and out in the world. It means knowing what you feel and understanding how to react appropriately. These are adaptive human social skills, not male or female traits. Today's boys are not entering a work-force in which dominance and aggression are the most highly prized professional attributes. Being able to negotiate, to work collaboratively, and to be a team player are far more valued skills. In some ways, women are uniquely qualified to impart these to sons who are growing up in a changing culture. Moth-ers who are pushing back and encouraging their boys to break through the silence and learn to connect aren't just forging a special bond of closeness between mother and son. They are equipping their boys with skills that will serve them for the rest of their personal and professional lives.

Sons also directly witness mothers balancing their work lives with their family lives. They are on the front lines observing both the tension and rewards of combining a career with family. Watching their mothers navigate the sometimes competing demands of home and work gives boys a broader perspective than they would get by only watching how their fathers combine career and family. And mothers tend to talk more about the kind of juggling they are doing, and enlist their children in making it work, by drawing up family sched-ules and organizing chores.

Robin travels constantly in her job as vice president of

advertising for Microsoft. She worries about the strain it has put on the household, and says that her son, Lucas, often sees her stressed. Still, they talk about the pros and cons of her demanding job.

"He'll say, 'Why don't you change jobs?' and I'll say, 'Lucas, it's a really big job, you don't just quit.' But then I'll say, 'It's just killing me, I feel I can't handle it and I'm sorry I'm so stressed,' and he'll say, 'But you're the boss, you know how to run a company. You wouldn't be able to do that if you weren't smart.' He's just a little boy and I've sat around and been so upset and so tired, and he'll put his arm around me. It's amazing the things he'll talk to me about, and how deep we can go in terms of emotional conversations. There's this bond of security that comes from that."

Because the majority of mothers work outside of the home, one might assume that they inevitably spend less time with their children than mothers of past generations did. But a 2006 study found that despite the surge of women in the workforce, mothers are spending at least as much time with their children today as mothers did forty years ago. In 1965, 60 percent of children lived in families with a breadwinner father and a stay-at-home mother. Today that figure is roughly 30 percent. Despite our fantasies about that golden age of family togetherness, a national study of thousands of married and single parents revealed that mothers and fathers today spend more time reading to, playing with, and caring for their children than parents did forty years ago. That didn't happen magically. Parents reported strategies to maintain the time they spend with both sons and daughters, and not surprisingly, some things had to give. The number of hours spent on housework declined for mothers and increased for married fathers. Parents have also cut back on free time and personal care, and have become proficient at multitasking. The culture has also changed considerably since 1965: families are smaller, and society has become more child-centric. But the conclusion of the report was counterintuitive to the popular wisdom that mothers in the labor force are shortchanging their children on one-on-one time. And now the grown children of working mothers are weighing in. In a survey conducted by the Families and Work Institute, men who had mothers who worked all or most of the time while they were growing up were significantly more likely to strongly agree that working mothers can have just as good a relationship with their children as mothers who stay at home.

These realities—the time spent together and the conversations between mother and sons about their lives—have fostered a new level of companionship. Rather than raising a boy who will be entering "a man's world," mothers today are bringing up sons who will be part of their world and who will ultimately be working with, and for, women, as well as with and for men. Sons are not entering a separate sphere that is alien to their mothers.

Kathy, a Presbyterian minister in Washington, D.C., still laughs when she remembers introducing her six-year-old to a well-known pastor who led an extremely large urban congregation. "Mom," her son told her in a stage whisper, "I didn't know men were allowed to run churches!"

Certainly my own son was often aware of issues I was dealing with at work. He knows about difficult assignments, cutthroat colleagues, and deadlines. He has also witnessed the excitement I experience when I achieve recognition and success. At times he has offered surprisingly clearheaded feedback. When my son became sports editor of his school newspaper, we could compare notes on how to write the best lead paragraph for an article and commiserate about sources that don't get back to you before deadlines.

Naturally, I also talked about work with my daughter when she was growing up, and I still do, especially now that she's in the workforce herself. I love comparing professional notes with her, and we give each other a great deal of support and feedback about work, not to mention many other parts of our lives. But the assumption that daughters and mothers will be close and sons and mothers won't is based on the idea that daughters will identify and relate only to their mothers and sons only to their fathers. In generations past, this usually meant that girls would be following their mothers into the realm of home and hearth and boys would follow their fathers to work. Today, women and their boys are no longer on separate paths, and this reality is reflected in their everyday conversations and interactions.

"The fact that I worked, the fact that I was a partner with

his father, the fact that he knew I had a career before children, the fact that I was a feminist—that changes things," said Laurie. "I think Andrew has always respected me." Researchers have shown that adolescents consider their mothers, in particular, to be an important influence in their career choice. In one study, scholars set out to look at the differences in the ways that mothers talked to their twelve-to-fourteen-year-old daughters and sons about their career goals. The researchers began with the assumption that gender would significantly influence the way a mother would talk to her children about their future. They were surprised to find that the guidance mothers gave their sons differed little from what they gave their daughters. The only distinctions were that mothers tended to be a little more specific about vocational goals with sons and tended to have slightly more conflict with daughters.

Mothers have not only joined fathers in serving as professional role models for their sons, but they have also modeled a somewhat different perspective on working life. What's more, because these boys are growing up to see their mothers as equal and contributing partners in the household, they are getting a completely different view of manhood than the generations of boys that preceded them. Think back to the post–World War II and baby boomer generations, when it wasn't uncommon for a father who was leaving on a business trip to turn to his school-age son and say something along the lines of "Take good care of Mommy. Remember, you're the man of the house now." The boy, who might have still been in elementary school, was already being given status as head of the household, superseding his adult mother. Mothers of earlier generations were complicit in this, reminding their young sons that they were "mommy's little man." These boys were being raised to see themselves in the future both as caretakers and as the dominant sex.

Sons today see their mothers leaving for business trips. Imagine a mother turning to her daughter and saying, "Remember, you're Daddy's little woman now!" Today's sons are not growing up with the message that a woman cannot take care of herself. Nor are they raised with the belief that one day they will necessarily be more important than women. How could all this not have a huge impact on the way mothers and sons relate to each other?

By the time sons are ready to enter their teenage years, the mother-son relationship has already been transformed from what it was in generations past. Mothers who never bought into the idea that four-year-olds should "man up" continue to encourage emotional expression in their older school-age sons. When they are getting the message to leave their sons alone so they can emotionally toughen up, mothers push back. At this stage, too, mothers carve out time alone with their sons. They try to help their boys identify and articulate their feelings. Many mothers also begin to share with their sons another part of their own lives, an adult world of work that these boys will ultimately share with women. The result is a growing sense of camaraderie and mutual respect along with the special love and tenderness that have always been a part of the mother-son bond. This combination of respect and tenderness will prove to be crucial as sons move into adolescence and begin to establish their independence as well as develop their own burgeoning romantic lives.

6

Moms and Teenage Boys

Strong emotional contact with his mother is
especially upsetting to any teenage boy.
—ANTHONY E. WOLF, PhD, AUTHOR OF *GET OUT OF MY LIFE, BUT
FIRST COULD YOU DRIVE ME AND CHERYL TO THE MALL*

·

A FEW YEARS BACK, a psychologist who had written a best-selling book about how to deal with teenagers came to speak at a PTA meeting at my children's school. As he described the often-epic battles between mothers and daughters, mothers in the audience started chuckling in recognition. They whispered that it was as if the speaker had been sitting in their kitchen the night before, witnessing the latest family skirmish. Much of what this author said about teenage girls certainly rang true to me—their wild swings between contemptuous rejection of parents and desperate need for parental approval, the drama, the door slamming, the rapid mood shifts, a teenage girl's ability to nurse a grudge for days on end. Then the speaker switched gears to discuss teenage boys. He had surprisingly little to say on the topic. Teenage boys, he said, just go up to their rooms, close the door, and come down four years later, no worse for wear. What's more, this was completely normal. Like many other experts on parenting, this psychologist believed that the best way to raise teenage boys was to leave them alone. Just don't bother them and they'll be fine. Daughters need careful guidance, supervision, and support, not to mention a mountain of patience from their mothers. But the last thing a boy needs when he is trying to grow up is his mother. A loving mother's best approach, then, is to let her son retreat behind that closed bedroom door and wait until he's ready to emerge, presumably fully formed as an emotionally healthy adult.

Really? Many mothers don't agree with this advice any more than they accepted the counsel to stop cuddling their toddler boys or to disengage from their school-age sons. Most of the mothers I surveyed and interviewed have largely rejected the belief that remaining emotionally close to their teenage sons prevents them from developing normally. In fact, these women believe they play an important role in the process of helping their sons navigate the bumpy road from adolescence to adulthood. Far from thinking they are stifling their sons' emotional growth, many mothers believe they are helping to develop it. And because of the groundwork they have already laid, these mothers have been delighted to discover that, if they continue to make themselves available, teenage boys will continue to open up about their feelings just as they did when they were younger.

That's not to say it is easy. At no time is a mother's tenderness and understanding needed as much as during adolescence, the most delicate phase in the mother-son relationship, when sons are developing sexually.

~ Boys and Puberty

I really struggled with how to open this section, because every time I began to write, the words seemed laden with sexual innuendo. Here are a few examples of sentences that quickly met the delete button: "Puberty is when things really come to a head." "This is when things really get hard." And worst of all: "This is where the rubber hits the road." Get the problem? If you are talking about mothers and their sons' emergent sexuality, using words like "head" or "rubber" or "hard" immediately jump out as wildly inappropriate double entendres. I kept cracking myself up at the computer. This actually is tricky territory. But let's try to look at this issue without the usual prurient smirking.

Conventional wisdom holds that mothers must back off from their sons when they are going through puberty. Teenage boys are so overwhelmed by their constant sexual urges and fantasies that the love and attention of their mother confuses them, according to this view. Mothers must withdraw both their physical affection and their loving tenderness from their adolescent sons, because any gesture might be misconstrued as seductive. Boys, and perhaps their mothers, won't be able to control their thoughts or themselves. Here is a typical example of this kind of counsel from *Get Out of My Life, but First Could You Drive Me and Cheryl to the Mall?* by Anthony E. Wolf, an advice book that was very popular when my son was entering his teens. The following can be found under the section titled "The Problem of Mommy":

> Most adolescent boys are attracted to women. For most boys there has already been one particular woman in their life whom they have loved deeply. *Unfortunately, that woman is their mother* [my emphasis]. Hence, until they get their new and fairly amorphous sexuality firmly focused on females outside the home, their mother becomes a problem. The possibility always exists that strong feelings in connection with a boy's mother might be tinged with sexuality and might therefore become really unacceptable. In fact, because everything with adolescent boys is so sexualized, strong feelings toward anybody are a problem until that sexuality is better focused.

The take-home message I got from Wolf was that as the mother of a teenage boy, I had become a problem. A problem that could interfere with my son's developing sexuality, no less. Worse news followed: that a son's "strong feelings toward anybody"—and by that I presume Wolf means to include his love for his mother—are so problematic that she must be altogether avoided until the son can handle his sexuality (a process that takes years, by the way). I might add there is no corollary "Daddy Problem" mentioned for girls.

It is true that many mothers struggle with the intensity of their feelings as their sons start to grow from boys to men. The issue is not that they have a greater love for their sons when they are teenagers—indeed many adolescents are even difficult to like at times. It's just that mothers begin to worry that their maternal love for a physically maturing son is wrong. "Why do we feel so embarrassed?" asked Catherine, the mother of a sixteen-year-old son. "Is it that society told us that there's something sick or pathological about loving your son so much because he's the opposite sex, and that there's some sexualization that we just can't admit to ourselves?" She sat quietly for a moment sipping coffee and then mused, "Maybe there's an element in Freud that isn't totally off."

It's time to return to Freud and his Oedipal theory. Freud believed that the final Oedipal phase takes place during the teenage years. During a long period of latency, roughly from the ages of six through eleven, the sexual feelings of children lie dormant, according to the theory. During puberty those feelings are reawakened. By this point, boys and girls have developed a superego, having internalized society's morality and solidly identified with their same-sex parent. (This theory presumes that heterosexuality is "normal" development.)

When all goes well, the final phase of the Oedipal drama is "resolved." The parent of the opposite sex is conclusively abandoned in favor of a more suitable object of passion, and mature sexuality develops. Just as in the early stages of psychosexual development, Freud was not talking about emotional closeness between parent and child, but about unconscious sexual desires. Again, normal maternal love, tenderness, and caring have been conflated with seduction and sexuality as if they are one and the same instead of very distinct feelings.

∿ Don't Touch!

Caitlin, who volunteers at a hospital in Minnesota, continues to hug and kiss her two teenage sons, even though they have grown so tall that they have to lean down so she can reach their faces. To her, it has always felt natural, and she recently found herself envied by a friend who has withdrawn from touching her own son. "I grew up in a household where you kissed everyone good morning and good night," Caitlin says. "My sons are both over six feet tall now, and I still give and get those kisses. My friend told me she had made the mistake of backing off physically. She did this mental notation when her son turned thirteen and she initiated the whole no-more-touch thing. Now she doesn't know how to get it back. She told me all this after she watched my son give me a big hug. When I was listening to my friend bemoan the fact that she made this error, what fascinated me was that even though she was sad, she didn't feel she could say, 'I would like a hug and kiss.'"

Most mothers are not blind to their sons' emergent sexuality and the onset of puberty. When a teenage boy stumbles out of bed with an erection, when the bedroom sheets are sticky, when a boy spends a lot of time in his bedroom with the door locked, many mothers are neither shocked nor overwhelmingly confused about how to act. They generally understand that their adolescent sons have frequent sexual thoughts and fantasies. They can recognize the need to respect their sons' privacy as they go through this normal transition. Stephanie, the Kansas mother of a seventeen-year-old, intuitively knew she had to pull back from being as physically demonstrative as she had been before her son began puberty. "When he grew so, so, so big on me, it kind of changed things. We were incredibly affectionate when he was growing up. He was loved and hugged and touched and kissed so, so much and it's definitely different now. I try to be respectful of the fact that he's a young man and he doesn't need his mother smothering him with kisses and saying, 'I love you, honey.'"

Mothers like Caitlin and Stephanie do not believe they need to take an all-or-nothing approach to physical affection when it comes to their teenage sons. Like many other mothers I spoke with, they recognize that their sons are not babies or little boys anymore, and that the days of pulling him onto their lap for a cuddle or planting big, wet kisses all over his face have gone. But they still feel comfortable showing maternal affection, just a kind that is more age-appropriate. Mothers told me that they try to take cues from their sons as to what works and what doesn't. Casey, a Chicago mother, says she wraps her arms around her boy and hugs him from the side. "I can still embrace him, but he's more comfortable with that than he is with a full frontal," she says. "Actually, so am I," she added, smiling a bit awkwardly. Another mother described stroking her teenage son's forehead when he watched television. "It's tender but not weird, and I can feel him relax," she said. "Tender but not weird" seemed to epitomize how many mothers feel about staying—literally—in touch with their teenage sons. But some experts don't seem to find this as dangerous and misguided as Wolf and others do.

"Do mothers and sons sometimes tread on something that feels sexual?" asks author and psychology professor William Pollack. "Yes, but it is also almost always true that it's not sexual at all. We're still a very puritanical society and we worry about any kind of sexuality. But that doesn't mean that during the time the son is developing, the mother and son can't feel close in a way that's nonromantic. In fact, the model of platonic love is helpful as boys grows older, because it gives them a much broader experience in how to deal with women." Pollack added that mothers and sons can find what he called "that snuggle zone." A son might be comfortable with physical affection at home but not in public—and this is something that can be talked about between them. He notes that as long as the relationship is healthy, physical affection is not only benign but also can be a comfort to a young man.

Mothers are also capable of viewing their sons as sexual beings without being overly aroused by their teenage chests or towering height. "We confuse sex and sexuality," says Lynn, the mother of two sons in their twenties. "My sons are incredibly beautiful and incredibly sexy. I can see objectively they have sexy bodies. There's this narcissistic extension of pride— Oh, I made that. Did that really come out of me? I can admire the beauty of them, of their bodies, and feel sensually connected but not at all have a sexual experience with them."

Of course, boys do not morph into full-grown men overnight. Emotionally they ricochet back and forth between being boys who need a comforting hug and being young men who want their privacy and their physical space. Young teenage boys are surrounded by media images of hyper-masculine, fully developed men when their early adolescent reality is closer to dark fuzz above upper lips, bad skin, and funky smells. Boys can feel so unattractive and unlovable during this period that it seems an especially poor time for mothers to suddenly start withholding affectionate hugs and physical comfort. It might seem to some boys that they repulse even their own mothers.

Another reason for "keeping in touch"—literally—is the evidence that hugs and maternal tenderness can mitigate violent and aggressive impulses in boys and teenagers. Research examining risk factors for adolescent violence reveals that cultures where a warm, physical affection toward young children is customary have significantly lower rates of adult violence, and vice versa. Angry, risk-taking adolescents lack experience in both emotional and physical intimacy, researchers found. In one study that focused particularly on mothers and sons, boys who displayed more aggression had mothers who were less nurturing and physically affectionate than the mothers of calmer boys. The aggressive boys were also less liked by their peers, and responded to this rejection with yet more aggressive behavior.

Some mothers approach the onset of puberty as a time of sadness, almost mourning, for the little boy who seems to be disappearing day by day. They experience a sense of loss for the sweet, uncomplicated relationship they once had with their preadolescent sons. "He was this chatty, loving, affectionate boy," says Bonnie, a Philadelphia mother describing her son, Billy. "Until he was fifteen, he was hugging and dancing with me. In those pubescent years, everything stopped. Suddenly, he didn't even want to be seen with his mommy. When his sister went to college, he wouldn't go out to a movie or dinner alone with me. He'd go with his dad and me, but he refused to be alone in public with me."

Rebecca's sons were only sixteen months apart, and they entered puberty almost simultaneously. She ached for the little boys that they once were. "Suddenly their voices changed, their faces changed, they got hair on their legs, a different kind of hair, more wiry and less silky. The sense of loss I felt was huge," she said. "I remember sobbing on my way to work. The little boys that I had were inaccessible to me."

Lisa's son, Jordan, is about to turn fourteen and he is already several inches taller than she is. Jordan used to invite her into his room; now he doesn't want her in there at all. When they watch television together, Jordan flinches if their legs brush accidentally. Her daughter, who is eleven, "still hangs all over her father," but Lisa is careful with her physical affection with her son.

"You know how in the past, you went out with these guys, and the most interesting boyfriends were the most unattainable?" she asks. "So here you have a son, and he gives me a little morsel of attention, and it kind of reminds me of those challenging guys I was really into. I feel like I went out with two kinds of guys—those that were wonderful, sweet, and a little boring. And then there were the other boys who were more of struggle, who paid less attention to me. The thing with the teenage son is more like the second kind. As they get older, they start to reject you, so any little piece of affection is so wonderful. This is so embarrassing, but it's like, 'Wow, he really loves me, he put his arm around me.' And you just stand there and don't want to move."

ᨒ A Love Affair

The way Lisa and some other mothers describe their emotions at this stage can sound a bit like the early stages of a love affair. Between the mother-son outings and the emotional closeness they foster, the intimacy that develops really can seem to have a haze of romance. Diane described time alone with her son, Zach, a high school junior, as "heaven on earth." Last year, the family planned a vacation at the beach. Because of everyone's busy schedule, mother and son arrived at the rental condo a few days ahead of Zach's father and two sisters. She described their dinners together at fancy restaurants and walks on the sand in a way that practically sounded like a honeymoon. "It was perfect," she said, smiling wistfully. She went on, at first defensively, to describe how much she loved her husband, and how, despite their battles, she was very close to and proud of her daughters. But when she talked about Zach, there was a particular tender dreaminess in her voice.

"I think that mothers and sons with good relationships often have that magical feeling of when they first fall in love," said Stacy, a psychologist and the mother of two sons and a daughter. "It's kind of being a little bit under a spell, of sometimes not seeing the facts that clearly because that love affair is so strong and so everlasting, whereas with your husband, it comes and it goes, it waxes and wanes."

Thrilled as they might be by the emotional closeness with their teenage sons, these mothers are quick to tell you that their feelings are not sexual but a form of deep parental tenderness. Lisa puts it bluntly: "It's like romance without the sex." While the talk and feel of romance might be innocent, it inevitably produces anxiety and distaste because of the implied eroticism. There is no worse accusation to lob at the mother of a teenage son than to call her seductive. Of course we know that if a mother's love really is eroticized, it will almost certainly interfere with a boy's normal psychological development, and if she ever acts on those feelings, the results will be disastrous as well as criminal. The horror of incest is so huge that it makes every physical aspect of mother-son love suspect. But statistics show that sexual abuse is much more prevalent in father-daughter relationships than it is between mothers and sons. Studies have shown that adult males abusing young females make up the majority of child abuse cases, followed by adult males abusing boys. Less than 5 percent of reported sexual abuse is between women and boys, with almost none between mother and son.

In fact, sexual abuse by adult women is apparently extremely rare. The percentage of sexual abuse by female perpetrators reported to law enforcement is between 1 and 4 percent of all sex abuse cases. Some experts argue that sexual abuse of boys is underreported because of the stigma attached to it. Further, the boys might not recognize it as abuse until years later. This could hinder reporting and distort the statistics. Regardless, our society continues to disproportionately tolerate physical affection between fathers and daughters while condemning it between mothers and sons. For instance, father-daughter dances are hallowed traditions in many schools and organizations ranging from the Girl Scouts to church groups. The registration form for the Triangle Father-Daughter Dance in Raleigh, North Carolina, reads: "Every father needs to 'date' their daughter, and every daughter needs an example of how a young lady is to be treated by a man." A high school mother-son dance? It would never fly. Imagine the reaction to this flyer: "Every mother needs to 'date' her son, and every son needs an example of how a young gentleman is to be treated by a woman." It would be greeted with profound distaste, if not outright alarm. I'm not suggesting that mother-son dances are a great idea whose time has come; rather, I am pointing out the double standard that exists when it comes to father-daughter as opposed to mother-son relationships.

No matter how benign the gesture, the criticism mothers get for touching their sons ramps up considerably during the teenage years. An engineer at IBM described hugging her fourteen-year-old son during a family event, and having a cousin ask in a withering voice, "How old is he again?" One mother described stroking her son's head when he was upset about something. "My husband snapped at me, 'Why don't you two just get a room?'" Another was sitting on the couch with her teenage son's feet in her lap. She was massaging his feet and she and her son were giggling about something. "My husband was trying to discuss something with me and I was distracted," this New York mother related. "And suddenly after an exchange of 'Are you listening to what I'm saying?' and 'Yes, I'm listening,' he says, 'Well, you are sitting there making out with my son.'" One of the assumptions behind these disturbed reactions is the belief that there cannot be either affectionate gestures or emotional intimacy between a man and woman, even if they are a son and his mother, without sexual tension. There is no distinction between a maternal hug and a seductive embrace, or between maternal devotion and romantic, sexualized love. Any kind of closeness revealed in a tender touch or tender feelings raises alarm, followed by a quick admonition to mothers to let go of their sons both physically and emotionally.

Compounding these fears are the old worries about mothers feminizing their boys by being too influential. Heather described her husband's "teasing but not teasing" banter with their strapping, athletic sixteen-year-old son, Jed. "He says, 'Oh, Sissy Boy has to tell Mommy how his soccer game was,' or 'Oh, Sissy Boy's Mommy has to feed him chicken soup before he goes out.' The funny thing is my husband is very affectionate with his son, but this 'Sissy Boy' teasing comes from that guy place." Heather views these kinds of comments as a reflection of her husband's own experience, and for the most part she shrugs them off. So does Maria, whose husband grew up in Mexico.

"When Pablo calls Caesar 'you big mama's boy,' I think it is the whole Latino culture and the guy thing, but it's particularly hard on Caesar. He's the kind of kid who you know there's a problem when there's just one tear right here," said Maria, pointing to the corner of her eye. "When my husband says stuff like that to Caesar, I think, Okay, Caesar's going to be sensitive, he's going to be a very good husband, he's going to be kind, and he's not going to kick the dog. And I really do believe that is because he is a little closer and a little more aligned with his mother."

↜ "Son-ectomies"

Even without the social pressure on mothers to withdraw from their sons, maintaining a close relationship with a teenage boy is a particular challenge. Adolescents, sons and daughters alike, are working hard to gain autonomy from their parents. They demand their privacy and independence. They experiment and push limits. That darling little boy who worshiped his mother morphs into a large creature who mumbles, rolls his eyes, questions her values, criticizes her musical taste, and begins that same kind of "get away from me but stay close, I need you" relationship that teenage girls have with their mothers. I remember feeling blue when my old routine of waking up my son by gently rubbing his back was replaced with an alarm clock that blared rap music, followed by my son's watching ESPN's SportsCenter in a glazed stupor. There's a very real sadness when your children begin to move, and not always gracefully, toward greater independence.

Mothers of teenage boys know they need to negotiate these tricky shoals carefully. And while they do understand the need to pull back bodily in some ways from their physically developing sons, it doesn't follow that mothers also think they should simply go "cold turkey," leaving sons to struggle alone with their often volatile emotions. No one expects mothers to sever their emotional closeness with teenage daughters to allow girls to grow up. Why should sons be suddenly cut off from their mother's warmth, support, and hugs? As one Vermont writer put it, "I didn't think I needed to do a 'son-ectomy' on my kid."

Many mothers I interviewed report being able to sustain their bond with their sons while at the same time acknowledging their sons' increasing maturity and independence. Stephanie says she was the kind of mother who once "ran after the summer camp bus, banging on the window and acting like a moron," but has since learned to pull back. "I adore that boy and my relationship with him is still incredibly close, but he has his limits and I respect them. He doesn't need long drawn-out conversations all the time. But when something is up, he'll still come to me." Certainly I wasn't going to insist that Paul needed his mommy to wake him up every day for high school. He was old enough to get himself up, and his new routine reflected his growing autonomy, not a drifting away from emotional closeness. Likewise, many mothers I spoke to believe that the job of parenting teenage boys should not be one of benign neglect. Some of the contemporary researchers on masculinity would agree.

"Mothers are no less necessary in the lives of their teenage boys than they were when he was in diapers," says sociologist Michael Kimmel, whose most recent book, *Guyland*, describes a world where male teenagers and young adults often feel isolated and confused, unable to commit to their relationships, work, or lives. In interviews of more than four hundred boys and men ranging in age from sixteen to twenty-six, Kimmel describes a culture that pressures young men to couch their insecurity in bravado and bluster and to avoid adult responsibilities such as completing an education, starting work, becoming financially independent, committing to a partner, and becoming a parent. Instead, these young men resort to behaviors like bullying, sexual conquest, and violence to mask their own anxiety and sense of fraudulence. Kimmel argues that parents who stay close to their sons can prevent some of the worst elements of this period. Mothers, he argues, often represent compassion, empathy, and nurturance, qualities young men in their teens and twenties desperately need.

It is reassuring to see male experts like Kimmel and Pollack champion a mother's role in guiding her son. But they are the exception rather than the rule. More often, mothers are told to back off from their sons. At the same time, teenage boys get the message that they should not reveal their vulnerability and neediness to anyone, let alone depend on their mothers. Between the cultural pressure on both mother and son to push each other away and the natural tendency for adolescents to withdraw, maintaining an emotional connection during these years is a challenge.

"No matter how much you try to keep the lines of communication open, boys absorb the culture that as a man you have to stand on your own two feet," said Angie, the mother of sixteen-year-old Jack. "My son is affectionate and a basically good kid, but at this point he doesn't tell me what's going on in his life, except under extreme duress. The culture tells him that because he's a man, he shouldn't tell his mother anything, whereas my daughter can tell me everything, and that's supposed to be Okay."

Audrey, a teacher in New Hampshire, has a son who is often angry. Kyle, a skateboarder, is rarely without his iPod and not easy to connect with, even when he takes out his ear buds. No matter what emotion Kyle is experiencing—sadness, disappointment, or frustration—he usually ends up slamming doors and yelling, Audrey says. She has learned not to engage him when he is fuming but to wait until he is able to calm down. Even then, it takes a while to get him to open up.

"He'll go up to his room and slam the door," Audrey says about her sixteen-year-old. "Then I wait a while. When I knock on the door, I say, 'Maybe not now, but when you're ready, I do want to talk about this.' Eventually he reaches a point where he cries because he breaks through the anger. Then he goes through these moments where he talks about the pain. I've learned not to fight his anger but just to say, 'You tell me when you feel like you can talk.'"

Audrey believes this approach is good for her son, because Kyle appears relieved once these outbursts are over and he has been able to put into words some of what is bothering him. She tries to find a balance between giving him the time and independence to learn to manage his anger, and not leaving him alone to cope with the aftermath—the flood of other emotions that usually follow the eruption.

Julie, an Ohio consultant, has four sons and described each one as going "radio silent" for periods as a teenager. In telecommunications, radio silence is a status in which all radio stations in an area stop transmitting. Sometimes, the boys in Julie's family seem similarly shut down. At other times, the household is full of static. Julie remembers when her third son, Ben, was preparing for his bar mitzvah. The year had not been one characterized by family harmony. Ben had a severe learning disability and every night Julie spent two hours at the kitchen table trying to help him with his homework. It always ended in a fight. He didn't want to do it. She insisted that he complete the assignments. His attention span was short. She was tired after a full day of work, trying to help him, and often losing patience. But Julie was determined that he succeed in school and persevered, trying to keep him focused.

Meanwhile, she and her husband had to stand in front of the congregation and talk with glowing pride about their son. "We were really struggling to come up with something, anything, nice," Julie said. They racked their brains for positive qualities and settled on his sense of humor. Even in the midst of this obnoxious phase, Ben was funny, Julie recounted. "I'd be furious about something he'd done, and he'd say, 'Don't get so hyped up about this, Mom. I'm just going through a phase.' It would always crack me up." Julie worked to stay connected with Ben through his silences and volatile moods, and by the time he was in tenth grade, things were easier between mother and son. "By the time he was fifteen, I adored him," she says. Today, of her four boys, it is Ben who shares the most with her.

"We speak constantly," Julie says. "Even at the age of nineteen, I'm his great confidante. He shared every single thing that went on in his life. I knew in high school all the problems he had with girls and figuring out where he fit in the social hierarchy. He's a very emotional kid and feels things extremely deeply. He's also very verbal and he can share. He'll tell me, 'I'm feeling crappy, and it was so bad, and can you believe she did this to me?' He's my extreme, in terms of what and how much he shares. But he's independent, living in New York City, trying to make it as a comedian, dealing with auditions and rejections. That requires a certain toughness."

Julie believes that the closeness with her boys, now twenty-three, twenty-one, nineteen, and seventeen, was influenced not only by her efforts, but also by personality and birth order, and that the relationships shift over time. "I'm the same mother, though certainly I've spent more time alone with the youngest. But my boys have different temperaments," Julie says. Still, she says the emotional connections with her teenage sons came as an unexpected but delightful surprise.

Not all efforts at maintaining closeness during the teenage years are achieved through talk. Mothers can be a comforting emotional presence, a safe harbor during periods of adolescent angst, simply by offering quiet companionship. "I have a very close relationship with my son, but he's not very articulate," said Joanne, whose pale, lanky, dark-haired son bears a close physical resemblance to her. "We don't talk a lot but we have a similar sensibility. I make breakfast for him every morning even though he's eighteen. We may not talk, but if someone comes in the mood is broken." What kind of mood did Joanne mean? "It's like a calm and quiet place," she explained. "I am not a big talker, either. My son and I like to be together, but we don't have to fill all the space with noise and commentary."

✎ Risky Business

The tradition of a more open exchange during mother-son outings away from the family can continue during the teenage years. It is sometimes as if a judgment-free zone opens up, where even the more volatile topics of the adolescence can be addressed calmly. One New Jersey mother drove her seventeen-year-old son to buy new glasses, and as they were waiting for the lenses, she turned to him casually and said, "So, how long have you been smoking pot?" He looked at her in amazement and asked how she knew.

"I framed my face with my hands, and said, 'Look at this, this is not stupidity.' And then we just had this completely honest discussion." She told him the truth—she had found rolling papers in the pocket of some jeans her son had put in the laundry hamper. He talked about how he found getting high relaxing. She was angry, but calmly told him why she objected. What was talked about at LensCrafters stayed at LensCrafters, this mother said. She didn't raise the topic in the larger family context, because she believed it would have been explosive and lead to a lot of yelling from her husband. "It wouldn't have been helpful and it sure wouldn't have made my son stop getting high," she says. But when she was alone with her son on other occasions, this mother continued to discuss his pot smoking and her disapproval. She believes her ongoing concern helped mitigate his use.

Her maternal instincts are backed by science. A multitude of studies have shown that teenagers who have good communication with their parents are more likely to resist negative peer pressure and less likely to become involved in drugs in the first place. But interestingly, it is a boy's mother who is the most influential when it comes to risky behaviors, according to recent research. One study of inner-city teenagers reveals that boys reported feeling closest to their mothers and more comfortable talking to them than talking to their fathers or any other adult about important and potentially controversial topics. These feelings of safety and closeness held true across the spectrum of race and class.

The nature of such communication was especially revealing. Mothers tended not to have one "big talk" about drugs and alcohol with their teenagers, but rather gave them intermittent messages about risky behavior during the ongoing natural dialogue of family life. This day-to-day interaction was more effective than the sit-down drug talks encouraged by the media, the report said. In fact, mothers are so influential and effective in the way they talk to their teenagers, the study concluded that mothers should be the logical targets for drug education and intervention programs.

It does seem rational. By the time many boys reach adolescence, a deep emotional foundation has been set, making mothers a safe place to go with confused and intense feelings. All those years of mother-son outings, the hours spent on developing emotional intelligence, mothers' continuous efforts at staying close to their sons when society is telling them to retreat, have a cumulative effect. And it is revealed in the trust that teenage sons place in their mothers. Nearly nine out of ten women in my survey said their sons shared with them most of what was going on in their lives, including hopes, dreams, and concerns. Mothers reported that their sons came to them with a great many emotional issues that they did not bring to their fathers.

↵ The Division of Emotional Labor

"Emotional stuff? Charlie has to come to his mother," Marianna said. "His father is a lawyer. He isn't going to spend fifteen minutes going through this scenario or that scenario. His father is going to be much more, 'Okay, do this, do that.' So if he really wants to talk and needs emotional support, he knows he has to come to me."

It might be because fathers of most young men now in their late teens, twenties, and older generally were raised by fathers who were not themselves encouraged to speak about their emotions. But the way mothers and sons communicate remains markedly different from the way fathers and sons do. One mother tagged it "a division of emotional labor."

Certainly that has been my experience. My son has a close relationship with both his father and me. Both of us talk with him frequently, but the tenor and content of those conversations couldn't be more different. I remember a typical phone call home from my son at college in which we spoke for twenty minutes. Then I passed the phone over to my husband, and they spoke for about the same amount of time. Later, when my husband and I sat down for dinner, we compared notes. Among other things, my son and I had discussed his feelings about his tryout for the jazz band, the courses he had signed up for next semester, a frustrating conflict he had worked out with a professor, how he was managing his time between sports and academics, and the sensitive question of what gift he was considering getting his girlfriend for her birthday.

I filled him in on my anxieties about work and my concerns about my father's driving abilities, and updated him on the state of everyone else in the family, right down to the health and adventures of our two cats. What did my husband have to report after his twenty-minute conversation? The entire time they had discussed the New York Rangers, the Washington Redskins, college football, and ski conditions in the Northeast. I'm not saying that the kind of male socialization and bonding my son does with my husband isn't important or meaningful. The two of them are very close. But it is an entirely different method of communication. (In fact, some psychologists have argued that sports provide the safest way for men to express their emotions in our current social climate—men can jump up and down in excitement, they can get tearful in victory and defeat, not to mention have permission to hug, smack each other's butts, jump in piles on each other, and otherwise physically and emotionally connect with other men in ways that would be totally unacceptable outside the realm of a sporting event.) Heaven knows that even those men who "don't talk" can become amazingly articulate when it comes to the finer points of their teams' strengths and weaknesses. And for some fathers who grew up in the 1950s and 1960s, this is the best way they know how to communicate and connect with their teenage sons.

Janine, who is in advertising sales, talked about how much her conversations with her son, Ryan, now a college freshman, differ from those her husband, Henry, has. Her experience is similar to mine.

"Henry will go, 'Did you see the Yankees last night? Why did he miss that ball?' Or 'I played golf yesterday. I played like crap.' There's something in between them—there's a distance.

It can't be too intimate," Janine says. "Sometimes Ryan will try to pull that with me. Like if I go, 'How was school?' and he goes, 'Good.' Or 'Who did you take to the dance?' and he goes, 'You don't know her anyway.' And I say, 'Look Ryan, I'm not going to stop until you give me more.'" Janine says she can get Ryan to talk about his feelings for the girl and what is actually going on in his classes, not to mention extracting a report on how well he is sleeping and eating.

Most mothers of adolescents tend to be more attuned to the details of their teenagers' lives than fathers, according to a 1997 National Longitudinal Survey of Youth, though the study also indicates that significant numbers of both parents of this generation are involved in their children's activities. For instance, 57 percent of mothers and 34 percent of fathers knew "almost everything or everything" about their teen's close friends, as reported by the adolescents themselves. Seventy percent of mothers and 49 percent of fathers knew about teachers and school activities, and 73 percent of mothers and 55 percent of fathers knew whom their teen was with when not at home. Not only did the analysis measure parental monitoring, but it also drew connections between that kind of closeness and adolescent outcomes—namely, that the greater the parental involvement, the lower the risk of suspension from school, delinquent behavior, substance use, and high levels of behavioral and emotional problems.

Knowing the facts of what's going on in a teenager's life, whom he is hanging out with, and what he is doing is one thing. Having access to his feelings about what's going on is another. In my survey, seven out of ten mothers said their sons share their emotional life more with them than they do with their fathers. Teenage sons particularly come to their mothers to talk about intimate relationship issues.

"I intuitively can get when Matt needs to talk," says Jody, a voice-over actress. "When he broke up with Anna, he seemed fine and cool, but he was pretty devastated. For a while he would say things to me like, 'It's hard, she was totally a source of comfort for me,' or 'She was close to the dog and misses him.' When Mark [Matt's father] would hear that, he'd say, 'She's just working you over.' But I would say, 'Yeah, those things are really hard, but you have to balance what was working in the relationship with what wasn't. Remember, you were pretty unhappy a lot of the time when you were going out.'"

Helping to steer their sons through breakups seemed to routinely fall to mothers. With their friends, teenage boys are more likely to resort to bravado, claiming the end of the relationship was not a big deal. And if they can admit they are upset by a breakup, they don't always get the support from their friends they are looking for. "When I told one of my guy friends that Becca had ended it, all he said was, 'Yeah, well she's a bitch,'" said Teddy, seventeen. "After that I didn't want to get into it with him." Teenage girls are more likely to have girlfriends who will talk at length about the ups, downs, and demise of a relationship, but boys have fewer outlets, which might be why mothers are often the ones to provide much-needed comfort and counsel.

"My son had a particularly heart-wrenching breakup with his girlfriend," Evelyn said. "He called and said, 'I need to talk to you alone.' He told me he was feeling out of control psychologically, sad, and distraught." Her son, Jared, had planned to drive across the country with his girlfriend. After they broke up, he bought the girlfriend a plane ticket and then asked his mother if she would make the trip with him instead. "He didn't ask his father, he asked me. That's where he comes to when he feels really vulnerable."

Evelyn and Jared made the trip, taking turns with the driving, sometimes talking about what had happened, other times listening to music. There were also many miles during which they rode quietly and without conversation. But even in the silences, Evelyn was glad she was present and that her son was not alone during what was an extremely painful time for him.

It is not always easy for a mother to listen to her son talk about his problems with his girlfriend, and not, as is commonly assumed, because she is jealous, but because she wants to protect and shield him from pain. "I felt terrible when his girlfriend broke up with him because he really loves her and she really hurt him," said one mom. Another described herself as feeling like "a lioness protecting her cub," but she restrained from making any negative comments about the girlfriend, "lest they get back together." Denise said she started getting anxious about girls before her son even noticed them. "I'm just worried some girl is going to steamroll over him. He is so easygoing and such a nice guy."

On the other hand, not every mother feels that no girl will ever be good enough for her son. "I remember at my son's school, another mother saying, 'When Sam was born, I took one look at him and I couldn't imagine that any woman would be good enough for him.' I thought, 'Are you kidding?' For me it was, 'Is my son ever going to find someone who can love him?'" remembers Connie.

Let's Talk About Sex

Many mothers are the ones who talk to their sons about sex. Jan, who works in corporate public relations and describes herself as "a proud feminist," believes that her two sons need to hear about sex from a woman's perspective. "I brought the tampon out and said, 'This is what a tampon is.' I explained this is what prostitution is, this is what sex is. Part of my agenda was for them to have a healthy respect for women, not to fall into the trap of degrading women." Steffi, the mother of a son who is a three-hundred-pound offensive lineman for a Division I university football team, agreed with Jan's approach. "It's so much more effective for me to have the sex talk than for his dad to do it. It means more coming from a woman to explain that no means no, and yes sometimes means no, and about being sensitive to women and protecting yourself." Mothers of boys also told me that they worried about their sons' vulnerability, especially about getting a girl pregnant. "What if some girl is lying about using birth control?" Janet asked. "I've told my son over and over again, if he gets a girl pregnant, that will be a responsibility he will carry for the rest of his life. I worry about it a lot." Mothers also counsel their sons about not putting themselves in situations where they could be seen as perpetrators, or worse, actually turn into one. "One of my friend's sons was accused of date rape when he believed it was truly consensual," said Beth Anne, the mother of two teenage sons. "I am very specific with my boys about the dangers they can face as young men. The whole Duke University scandal about the rape accusation brought on a lot of discussions in my house. They have to be really careful in situations with young women, particularly when there is drinking and pot smoking involved."

Dan, now twenty-three and a law student, has been on the receiving end of counsel about women from his mother since the beginning of high school. "Most of my adult life I've had a girlfriend, and my mom has always been very adamant about how to treat them," he says. "She taught me to treat girls well, but she also wants me to be wary of them because she doesn't want me to make any bad decisions just because I'm infatuated with some girl. Be nice but be careful. She's like that with every girl I've brought home."

Dan said the angriest he's ever seen his mother was when,

just before heading to work, she discovered a girl she had never met sleeping in Dan's bed. This was during a summer he was living at home to save money. "We'd had the condom talk a long time before, but she was still not cool with me sleeping with girls in her house."

Mothers are certainly influential with their children on the subject of sex. Studies have shown that teenagers—both boys and girls—are more likely to talk to their mothers than their fathers about their romantic relationships. Moreover, teenagers who report high levels of closeness to their mothers and are aware of their mothers' strong disapproval of early sexual activity tend to delay their first sexual experience, according to investigators at the University of Minnesota, who analyzed data from the National Longitudinal Study of Adolescent Health, the largest research ever undertaken on teenagers in the United States. Researchers measured closeness and connectedness by asking teens how much they felt their mothers cared about them, how warm and loving they perceived their mothers to be, how the quality of communication was between mother and teen, and finally how satisfied teens felt with their relationships with their mother. They found that younger teens and older teenage boys who reported a strong sense of connectedness with their mothers tended to postpone early sex. Interestingly, the effect was not seen among older teenage daughters.

A study that focused on inner-city black teenagers between the ages of fourteen and seventeen echoed the national report's findings. Teens who were close to their mothers and who perceived her disapproval of early sexual activity stayed virgins longer, and those teens that did engage in sex were more likely to use birth control. In this study, researchers used a scale to measure teens' relationships with their mothers, which included statements such as "I am satisfied with the love and affection my mother shows me," "I am satisfied with the emotional support my mother gives me," "I am satisfied with how many things my mother and I have in common," "I am satisfied with the amount of time my mother and I spend together," and "I am satisfied with the fun my mother and I have together."

Emotional support, common interests, fun activities, time together—all those measures of evaluation seem to echo just what so many mothers told me they are doing to keep close and connected with their sons.

A study that looked at mothers' influence on the timing of their teens' first sexual experience revealed that mothers are nearly twice as likely to recommend a specific form of birth control to their fourteen- and fifteen-year-old sons as they are to their daughters. The authors of the study are not sure what accounts for the difference, but speculate that mothers try to control their daughters' sexual behavior, while with their sons, they focus their concerns on the risk of infection and early parenthood.

Many mothers I interviewed say they have an easier time talking about sex with their sons than with their daughters.

Claudia's face clouded with exasperation as she recalled dealing with her two teenagers. "I took my daughter to the gynecologist, and she got plan B, that emergency contraception pill that prevents implantation after sex. About a year into her relationship with her boyfriend she used the pill. When I replaced them as a favor, she screamed at me, 'I hate how you know everything.' With James, we talked about his being careful with sex and respectful with his girlfriend. The only time we argued was when I found a used condom by his bed. It was his senior year in high school and I told him this was not a motel by the hour."

Cathy, a Michigan accountant, had a similar experience. Her son had a steady girlfriend in high school and it was Cathy who addressed the question of birth control. "I felt close enough to him that I could ask if they were sexually active," she said, "and he said, 'Aw Mom, of course I am.' He answered it truthfully. He kind of rolled his eyes a little bit, but he didn't get annoyed or angry or anything. If I had talked to my daughter in the same way, she would have screamed and yelled and carried on, and told me to get the hell out of her room."

"Car talk" continues to be a venue of choice for conversation at this age and particularly when it comes to the topic of sex. Elaine had heard rumors that girls were performing oral sex at some of the high school parties taking place in her town. She wasn't sure how much her sons, ages sixteen and fourteen, knew about what was going on. She introduced the topic during a long drive on the Long Island Expressway.

"I got on at Exit 36 and we were going to Exit 70," Elaine says. "I turned the radio off and said, 'Who knows what a blow job is?' The sixteen-year-old slunk down in his seat, but the fourteen-year-old didn't know what it was. I explained and there was dead silence in the car. Then my younger son said, 'Can I ask you something? What do girls get out of it?' I thought, 'I don't know about your age but at my age they get really expensive jewelry.' But what I said was, 'Good question. I think they think that boys will like them.'"

Studies have shown that mothers are more likely than fathers to talk to both their sons and daughters about healthy sex. Moreover, mothers have a greater influence with sons than fathers on sexual behavior: the more talking with Mom, the physically healthier the adolescent boy. This is particularly important because adolescent males tend to become disconnected from the health care system as they get older, precisely at the time when they become at risk for sexually transmitted diseases as well as substance abuse, violence, and other health concerns. There are, of course, several factors that prevent teenage boys from visiting the doctor, including lack of insurance. But given that a key predictor of teenage boys accessing health care is parental communication, an ongoing conversation between a mother and son about what it means to be a man, how a young man should take care of himself, and how to ask for help could be lifesaving.

๛ Confronting Sexism

Another way that mothers are influential when it comes to educating their sons about sex is by addressing the more misogynistic aspects of culture that surround teenage boys. Our sons are growing up in a culture where guys engage in binge drinking, play increasingly violent video games, watch degrading pornography, and hear rallying cries like "Bros before hos," all in the name of manhood. They are the targets of marketing campaigns that encourage boys to objectify woman as well as feel an overwhelming sense of male entitlement. Women are either babes or bitches. Teenage boys are constantly barraged by images like the rock star surrounded by a bevy of buxom babes, or television shows and movies that pair overweight, clueless slackers with smart, sexy, ambitious, and devoted girlfriends. To sit through a nationally televised football game is to witness a parade of commercials that objectify and degrade women. Here are some advertising highlights from recent Super Bowls: Two gorgeous, sexy women on a "Go Daddy" ad announce they have exciting news—a new "girl"—"a hot Hollywood icon" who is "smart and business-savvy" will be joining their team. When Joan Rivers, who is pushing eighty, is revealed in a tight-fitting, black tank top, the camera pans to horrified men in the audience. The year before, "Go Daddy" featured a woman who whips off her shirt to show her large, perky breasts, while the commercial urges viewers to "See more now!" and directs them to the website. Neither the breast display nor the mockery of an older woman trying to look attractive has anything to do with selling Internet domain names, which is the company's business. In another commercial for Motorola, young actress Megan Fox is selling phones by sitting in a bubble bath, taking a picture of herself, and sending it out to her contacts, causing electricity overloads and spousal spats along the way. In a fourth spot, the E*TRADE "Jealous Girlfriend" commercial depicts a baby boy in a white T-shirt explaining the volatility of the stock market in a cool, male adult voice. Then we see a baby girl, bow taped on her head, who says in a whiney adult female voice, "I just don't understand why you didn't call." She then adds, "Was that milk-aholic Lindsay over?" Lindsay, an even more clueless-looking baby girl, comes on the screen saying, "Milk-a-what?" The commercial depicts a smart "player" juggling two dopey females trying to hook him—and they're babies!

These depictions of women undermine mothers who are trying to raise their sons to be good men. A new and equally troubling marketing angle is revealed in commercials that paint men as emasculated and oppressed by women. A Dodge Charger ad broadcast in one Super Bowl shows a montage of miserable-looking men on-screen while a depressed male monotone voice deadpans, "I will clean the sink after I shave. I will take your call. I will listen to your opinion of my friends. I will listen to your friends' opinions of my friends. I will be civil to your mother. I will carry your lip balm. I will put my underwear in the basket." After a long litany of the many distasteful things men are forced to do to please women, the voice finishes with, "And because I do this, I will drive a car I want to drive." Then the car zooms into view as a newly invigorated masculine voice proclaims: "Charger. Man's Last Stand."

Young men are the target audiences for most of these commercials, but many mothers do not sit silently on the couch as they witness underlying messages of sexism and misogyny play across television screens. Instead, they try to engage their sons in conversations about these depictions of women.

"I was watching some terrible video awards show with my son and my daughter, and I said, 'Look at this rapper and look at the women behind him,'" says Adrienne, the mother of a fourteen-year-old daughter and a sixteen-year-old son. "I asked, 'Why is Beyoncé dressed like that, why does she have to wear so little clothes? She is probably making more money than Kanye, but he has clothes on when he performs.' This is an important conversation for both boys and girls." Many mothers make an effort to point out the demeaning portrayals of women in movies and on television. "In just about every action movie that my guys love, the woman is the eye candy—skinny, big-boobed, falling out of her too-tight clothes, and usually in need of rescuing," says April, the mother of two teenage boys. "It makes me crazy. The thing is, you can't talk about it when they're in the middle of watching this crap, and by the time they're done, they've moved on. I still usually say something, though, because I just want them to register my perspective."

The most effective venue for these discussions between mother and son is not around friends or the rest of the family, let alone the second-half kickoff. But one-on-one, they can be effective. The issue can also be handled with humor, which most teenage boys appreciate. The truth is that the babies in the E*TRADE commercials are pretty funny and the less humorous sexism can be disarmed on the same level. For instance, Gretchen, a marketing researcher, sent her two teenage sons the link to a video spoof of the Dodge Charger commercial, called "Woman's Last Stand," which she found on YouTube. It shows a series of miserable-looking women on-screen while a depressed-sounding woman intones, "I will make seventy-five cents for every dollar you make doing the same job. I will assert myself and get called a bitch. I will put my career on hold to raise your children. I will diet, Botox, and wax—everything."

"They watched it, but I clearly found it funnier than they did," Gretchen sighed. "At least they got another view of reality, the female view."

The Barnard College a cappella group posted their rendition of hip-hop superstar Dr. Dre's song "Bitches Aren't Shit" on YouTube. Dressed in pink, the young women's angelic voices rise in harmony, gently singing the lyrics "Bitches ain't shit but hoes and tricks, lick on these nuts and suck the dick." Those are actually some of the milder verses, and the incongruity of hearing the incredibly misogynistic words coming sweetly out of these college students' mouths makes its point.

"What moms can say to their sons is, 'Hey, have you ever actually listened to that lyric?'" Michael Kimmel says. "'That's people like me they're talking about.' Moms can keep guys connected at the concrete level as opposed to the abstract."

☞ The Perfect Guy

A surprising number of mothers talk about having created a son who in their eyes is a near "perfect guy." Of course, ever since the first mother gave birth to the first boy, mothers have believed they have produced the perfect son. These mothers are so wrapped up in son adoration that they can see absolutely no wrong in him. This maternal blind spot can trigger all sorts of problematic family dynamics, including spousal resentment and sibling rivalry. It is a phenomenon that can drive daughters wild with irritation.

"I can't even tell you how my mother is with my brother," said Terry, who at forty-five is still struggling with the inequity. "It's astounding. I try not to take it personally. My mother loves me but there's something about my brother. I can do one hundred things right and it's nothing. My brother hooks up her cable and it's like he built her a shrine. All he has to do is give her the time of day."

Annie grew up in the Bronx in a traditional Chinese

family where her brother was constantly given preferential treatment. "The sun rises and sets on my brother," Annie says. "When my mother doles her stuff out, he gets the prime cut. Like, traditionally, the girl gets a beautiful, engraved carved chest. It was in my mother's family. I loved it when she opened it, the smell of cedar, the traditional Chinese dresses. I had wonderful memories of it. When it came time for her to move, I knew she couldn't take it. I asked her for it, but she said no, she would give it to my brother. My brother is very untraditional, he's not sentimental, and he couldn't care less." Annie, the mother of a teenage son and a daughter, said she has been committed to raising her children equally, adding, "I'm hard on both of them."

Such blindly devoted mothers risk raising irresponsible sons when they fail to hold them accountable for their behavior and then protect them from its consequences. "My sister favors her son to the point where it's doing the boy real damage, excessively complimenting him for small things while glossing over or ignoring really bad behavior," says one worried aunt. "I want my nephew to grow up to be a good guy, a strong man who takes responsibility for his actions, and I'm worried that he will not." (This kind of mothering can go to extremes. Teresa Capone, the mother of notorious gangster Al Capone, may hold the title for maternal denial. Until her death, she insisted, "Al's a good boy." Her son did take good care of her, building her a luxurious home and providing escorts to drive her around Chicago in a bulletproof Cadillac. She, in turn, brought homemade macaroni and cheese casseroles to him in prison. But Mama Capone turned a blind eye to the criminal activities that made her infamously violent son one of the most wanted men in his time.)

It goes without saying that when most mothers today refer to raising "a perfect guy," they don't mean they believe they have raised a flawless human being. Rather, part of the contemporary "perfect guy" notion is based on these mothers' beliefs that they are raising a new kind of man, one who can really connect with and respect women. With a son, a mother is given a chance to work from a fresh palate, creating her own sense of the ideal male. As Edie, a Manhattan artist, put it, "When you give birth to your boy it's a clean slate, and you think, 'I'm going to raise him to be a nice guy who actually likes women.'" Listen to Marianna, who was originally anxious about having a boy, talk about her son, Charlie, now twenty-four:

"This generation of boys is being raised by women who are part of the feminist movement. And you know we want to raise men who are better than the generation before, more understanding, more passionate, more involved with their children. And that's really kind of what we are supposed to be doing, breaking through some of these myths, some of these stereotypes. So you look at your son and you think, 'That's a wonderful man.'"

Of course, seeing one's son as a perfect guy is also partly rooted in narcissism. A mother's enchantment with her son is often based on the delightful recognition of her influence on this other—this male—creature. Claudia, who had reluctantly cleaned her newborn's testicles, said of her son, now twenty-three, "One of the things I love about James is that he is male in his tastes, but he is very female for me in his emotional life and in the way he thinks. He hasn't learned to be the hard-ass male that sort of repressed his emotions." Adele described her twenty-year-old son this way: "It's like seeing my own reflection but in a boy. He's perfect."

No wonder mothers find their sons to be such wonderful companions! There is something inherently familiar and sympathetic about these boys. They seem to be growing up into just the kind of men all women dream of having in their life.

"He just gets me" is a phrase I heard from mothers over and over again. Listen to Shelly, as she recalls shopping trips with her son, David. "We would come back exhausted, but those were some of the happiest days of my life," she said. "I know this sounds crazy, like I'm using my son for a substitute husband, but it wasn't like that at all. But I would be kidding myself—and you—if I also didn't admit that I loved the fact that this person, who seemed so in tune with me, was my son, my creation, a person who would be in my life forever and would, in a sense, click with me the way no one else in the world ever would."

Mothers want to raise good guys, men who will become loving partners, husbands, and parents. Part of that means pushing back against a culture that often encourages boys to keep their feelings to themselves, man up, and degrade women. Boys growing up today are often the confused recipients of these mixed messages. They are expected to keep up a tough, macho front while at the same time being emotionally aware and sensitive and treating women respectfully. It's a confusing time to be a young man. How do they feel about their mothers keeping them so close?

Let's hear it from the boys.

7

Let's Hear It from the Boys

"HOW DOES YOUR SON feel about your writing this book?" I've been asked repeatedly. I usually respond that both of my children are fairly used to suffering public exposure because they were frequently featured in my columns for *The New York Times*. But I know the people asking about my son are trying to get at something different—how does a *guy* feel about his mother speaking publicly about their relationship? Finally, I asked Paul, now in his early twenties, directly.

"Well, first of all," he said, "any time that Jeanie or I are featured in something you're writing, it's embarrassing, regardless of the topic, so that's not a gender thing. On the book about mothers and sons, I'm sort of embarrassed and a little flattered. We have a pretty special bond. So I guess it's both kind of great and kind of embarrassing because a guy's relationship with his mother is really not something you talk about."

For most men, when it comes to Mom, mum's the word. Despite the centrality of the relationship between mother and son, and how fundamentally significant it might be to them both, the subject of mother love remains taboo among teenage boys and young men. Many men told me they rarely discuss their mother with anyone, least of all their male friends. Privately, though, sons open up to reveal not only a deep attachment to the women who raised them, but also an ongoing sense of gratitude, friendship, guidance, and camaraderie well into their young adult lives.

"You want me to talk about my relationship with my mom?" asks Jeffrey, sounding a little anxious. "Hold on," he whispers into his cell phone. "Let me call you back from some place private, where I can admit out loud how much of a mama's boy I am without embarrassing myself too much." A few minutes later, out of earshot from his roommates, Jeffrey, a twenty-five-year-old management consultant in New York, describes how he finds time to call his mother four or five days a week, despite his long work hours and frequent business trips. He says that he relies on his mother for advice and feedback, talking to her about "everything—work, politics, and the girls I'm dating." Jeffrey explains the extent to which she has influenced his values and his tastes. He goes on to describe how much he admires his mother, especially her combination of toughness and compassion. Then he pauses and asks, "You're not going to use my full name, right?"

Jeffrey is not alone in his self-consciousness. Many young men qualify their attachment to their mothers with reassurances of their own independence and masculinity. The specter of being labeled a "mama's boy" still looms large, and the definitions of just what constitutes that pitiable creature seem to have grown increasingly harsh:

mama's boy: A usually polite or timid boy or man who is extremely close to and solicitous of his mother. First known use: 1850
—Merriam-Webster Dictionary

A male person, especially a young man or boy, who is overly attached to or influenced by his mother.
—Wiktionary

Wuss . . . Sissy . . . Pansy . . . Pussy . . . Wimp . . . Bitch.
—Urban Dictionary

This is powerful language. A great deal of emotion is packed behind the disgust and derision aimed at a man who is seen as overly attached to his mother. Contempt for women and implicit homophobia are no small part of it. "Are You Still a Mama's Boy?" asks a headline from an article in *Details* magazine. The subhead goes on: "If you have your mother on speed dial and seek her opinion about all your dates, you have more in common with guys who sleep on Spider-Man sheets than you'd probably care to admit." The illustration for the piece: a grown man at his mother's breast.

"Mama's boys" who show up in advertisements targeting men are a sorry lot. Take a series of television commercials for Degree deodorant. They star an "inaction hero" named Mama's Boy. The voice-over announces that Mama's Boy "never sweats because he doesn't risk leaving his Mama." Mama's Boy "comes with internal magnets that prevent separation." Scenes play out featuring Mama humiliating her adult son in public. The Mama doll has a string to pull that offers "six different guilt trips," like "You'll be sorry when I'm gone." Also available, the commercial announces, are "The Wuss" and "The Suck-Up."

A commercial for Miller Lite features a young man ordering a light beer without specifying a brand. The sexy young female bartender calls him a "mama's boy," and she is proved correct when a middle-aged woman suddenly shows up in the bar with a bottle opener, grabs her son's beer, and says, "Let me open that for you, sweetheart." (When I first saw this commercial I took it as general mother bashing, but an African-American mother of a teenager told me she saw it through a different lens, because the mother and son in the ad are black. "There's a black woman bossing around a black man," she pointed out. "It's sexist, but it is also part of the bigger mythology that black women are too strong, so they push men away. Not only is loving your son a lot wrong but then you get the message that you are pushing your son away because your personality is too strong as a black woman.") In the commercial, the young man is humiliated by his mother's overbearing presence. The take-home message for all sons—real men don't hang out with their mothers.

Since the contemptible "mama's boy" remains the prevailing mother-son stereotype in our culture, it is small wonder that guys are reluctant to openly discuss their true feelings of connection to their moms. No one wants to be seen as that guy—the one who doesn't want to separate, with the mommy who won't let him grow up.

"If you want to live up to your dad's expectations or be like your dad, that's cool. But if someone says something like that about his mom—you want to be like her, or you want her approval, and you get a bunch of dudes in a room, that guy is going to get crap," says Tyler, a twenty-year-old college student in Pennsylvania.

Brent, who attends community college in suburban Maryland, says he has a good relationship with his mother and enjoys spending time with her. When he was younger, the two used to have a great time taking long bike rides together. But now Brent is uncomfortable being alone with his mother in public. At home, he and his mother watch hockey games on television, sitting side by side on the family room couch and cheering wildly for their beloved Washington Capitols. But when it comes to attending games at the Verizon Center in

D.C., Brent will attend with his father or with the whole family, but refuses to go to the arena with just his mother.

"If you're with your friends and you said, 'Yeah, I went to a hockey game with my dad last night,' no one would say anything," says Brent. "But if you said, 'I went with my mom,' they'd think it's weird. At a certain age, you just shouldn't be going out in public with your mom." Brent pointed out that his father had taken his sister to hockey games, and no one had found it strange. And Brent's mother and sister regularly had a girls' night out. "Maybe it's a personal space thing," Brent mused, "or an age thing, or a sports thing, but it doesn't seem right for a son to be going out with his mother. If you were to hang out with your mom and be proud of it, you would be a joke."

This prohibition against mother-son closeness in late adolescence parallels a phenomenon between boys and their male friends, according to New York University psychology professor Dr. Niobe Way. In her research on boys' friendships, Way found that in early adolescence, when boys are thirteen, fourteen, and fifteen years old, male friendships are deep. What's more, boys often discuss their close friendships with a great deal of emotional sensitivity, describing the attachment, the pain of betrayal, and the support they get from one another. But by the time boys enter late adolescence, they no longer express themselves in such openly emotional language and begin to distance themselves from their male friends.

"By the time they're eighteen, if you ask them the same question about their friendships, they'll say, 'I'm not gay,'"

Way said in an interview. "They'll talk about the loss of the friendship and how they miss it, but right now they have to choose between isolation or having a girlfriend." Way's findings about boys' friendships are consistent among boys of all races and social classes. Why do older teen boys feel so much pressure to cut off emotional intimacy with their male friends? Way cites a culture she believes has become increasingly homophobic. "When it comes to the potential for more emotional expression, straight men have become more and more paranoid. As more gay people have come out, there is more implicit homophobia and more rigidity about male heterosexuality," she says.

Older teens particularly feel pressure to project a cooler, more macho image. Think about how friendships between young men in their twenties are depicted in popular culture. They drink together, get high, hit on women, go on harebrained adventures, and have conversations along the lines of "Dude!" or "Whoa, dude!" It's not as if young men have actually lost the capacity to articulate thoughts and feelings. It's just that the pressure is so intense not to do so. Emote to another guy? "Dude, that's so gay." And it is not just conveying affection, fear, or other "shameful" emotions that are prohibited. Even the expression of excitement can be taboo.

Jake, who grew up in Maine, remembers a particular poker game with a group of friends in high school. The stakes were getting high and the volume of chatter about who was going to win the pot was reaching a fever pitch. "One of the guys—we call him 'The Diesel'—holds up his hands and says, 'Ladies, ladies. Calm yourselves down,'" Jake recounted. "He made us feel like idiots for getting worked up." Even enthusiasm becomes a suspect emotion, one suitable only for females. The teenagers in this poker game had all known one another since elementary school, and had seen each other through some emotionally wrenching times—the divorce of one boy's parents, the serious illness of another boy's younger sister. But it seemed that by the time they were teenagers, cool detachment and a kind of kidding/insulting manner of addressing one another was the only acceptable way to communicate.

The pressure teenagers feel to appear distant and cool from both their mother and their friends puts them at double risk for emotional isolation. Young men get the cultural message that growing up means going it alone. Our sons are pushed to separate from those closest to them in ways that our daughters are not. Girls don't find it humiliating or shameful to be seen out in public alone with their fathers or their mothers. If a dad takes his teenage daughter to a ball game or out for a meal, it's no big deal—most would think her lucky to have an attentive father. Nor do daughters face pressure to withdraw from their girlfriends as they enter late adolescence, lest someone mistake the intensity of their emotional connection with other girls as lesbianism. In fact, that concern sounds ridiculous when we reverse the genders. But the unrelenting pressure that teenage boys and young men face to withdraw from those closest to them is heartbreaking, not least because a wealth of research shows that people who are emotionally and socially connected are far more mentally and physically healthy than those who are isolated. Suicide rates and other high-risk behavior begin to escalate in young men precisely at the time when they are encouraged to pull back from the people who provide their deepest emotional support. "The two most important relationships for boys are with their mothers and with their best friends," Way says. "The two are connected. We know that the emotional connection and attunement that mothers foster is associated with better adjustment for boys. But we live in a screwed-up, deeply homophobic culture. We're not in a 'boy crisis'; we're in a human crisis of disconnection."

Maintaining a warm, emotional connection between mother and son is further complicated because a close bond with Mom is often mistakenly confused with being unable to mature. Today, psychologists make a distinction between separation and individuation, arguing that becoming a self-reliant adult does not require becoming emotionally isolated. But that's not the message that most young men get in our culture. "There's this very harsh and ultimately negative idea that the whole marker of mental health for males is that they be independent," says author and Harvard Medical School psychology assistant professor William Pollack. "The problem with that is that we are both biologically and psychologically set up to be connected to each other. We get our sense of safety, of warmth, of caring, and we learn to give it to others by being connected, not disconnected."

Of course, sons do push back when they feel their mothers are treating them in ways they find babyish. Erica's son, David, a twenty-two-year-old law student, remembers his mother dropping him off at the dorm, and then calling out the car window to remind him to make a copy of his insurance card before a medical appointment. Several other students overheard and he was humiliated. "If my mom offers to do something for me, even if it's something as small as making a doctor's appointment or doing my laundry, I sort of feel incompetent," David says. "I know she's not trying to be overbearing and that she just cares about me. But she needs to recognize that I'm an adult. There's a stigma to being overly attached to your mother, that's sort of a symbol that you haven't grown up." The truth is that many daughters bristle over these kinds of nagging interchanges, too. But the conflicts don't threaten a daughter's sense of identity in the same way that it might threaten a son's "manhood." It is assumed that daughters can grow up to be mature women without making an emotional break with their mothers, and they are expected to stay connected while they navigate adulthood.

✐ The New Mama's Boys

Despite the broad societal pressures young men face, the culture is beginning to shift and sons are changing the way they relate to their mothers. Just as we see a generation of mothers quietly rejecting the messages to back off from their sons, so, too, have sons pushed back against the taboo of being too close to Mom. Like their mothers, sons often keep quiet about this deep bond, in large part to avoid the derision that comes their way if they admit to it. But as men mature, solidly establishing their own identity, many become more comfortable speaking openly about the closeness with their mother.

Will, twenty-six, who is finishing his fourth year of medical school in Virginia, says, "Now I feel more comfortable and confident talking about my relationship with my mom. It's not something that guys freely express—who our emotional supports are, the intricacies of our relationships with our family members and friends. But I think a lot of my friends in my age group feel like it's good and healthy to have a close relationship with your mom, and that it shows you're a grounded person." Will went on to talk earnestly about what his mother means to him. He calls his mother his "moral compass." His dad, Will said, is a "practical compass," whom he consults for "business or contractual decisions." Will says he looks to his mother for advice and guidance on "the tougher decisions" about how he wants to live his life. "Mom definitely understands me, even more than Dad," he says. "I don't have to explain my mind; she always kind of knows what's going through my head. I'm a pretty independent guy and I don't feel like I need to call home all the time, but Mom has always been my comfort zone."

A great many men I interviewed described their mothers

as an emotional refuge when they were younger and still available to help them sort out some of their feelings as they have grown into adulthood. "I was the kid who was always picked on in grade school, but as bad as it got, my home was always my safe haven because Mom was my safe haven," said Jonathan, a graphic designer in Illinois. "I think that was the start of our closeness." Jonathan, twenty, assumes that the emotional bond he has since developed with his mother is unique, and that he is an outlier among young men. "I've always had a certain amount of trust and understanding with my mom that I think goes beyond normal—well, not normal, but beyond average mother-son relationships," he says. "Actually, I don't know what average is, it's just that I can talk to my mom about almost everything, and I don't know if most guys can."

Jonathan might be surprised to learn that he is far from alone in his openness with and closeness to his mother. In my online survey of men eighteen and older, 40 percent report being equally close to both their mother and father, while 44 percent report being closer to their mother, and 8 percent say they are closer to their fathers. (The remainder of men either have a deceased parent or say they are not close to either parent.) When it came to sons opening up about their feelings, the numbers become more skewed. Fifty-three percent of sons say they share their emotional lives with their mothers more than with their fathers, while only 4 percent share their feelings with their fathers more than with their mothers. About 23 percent of men open up equally with both parents. (The rest don't discuss their feelings with either one or have lost a parent.)

Nick, an actor, is typical of young men who look to their mother for emotional guidance. "As much as I love my dad and feel close with him, we do not discuss the things I discuss with my mom, our thoughts, our lives," he says. "My dad doesn't even discuss his work with me much, it's mostly random stuff. We'll talk about movies or people he saw that I knew when I was growing up, or we'll joke. Where my mom and I are always in deep conversations about many things." Nick, who is thirty and grew up in Mississippi, said that he believes his father, who is sixty-seven, is part of a generation of men who were taught that talking about problems is a sign of weakness.

Academics who study masculinity use scales to measure men's perceptions of what it means to be a man. One end of the scale reflects traditional views of masculinity: men should be tough; men should strive to be respected, men should never show weakness. Some of these studies assess how much men agree with these interpretations of manhood, and then ask them to rate the stressfulness of certain situations in their lives. For men who identify themselves at the very traditional end of the masculinity scale, "Telling someone that you feel hurt by what they said" appears as an example of an anxiety-producing scenario, just as "Being unable to become sexually aroused" does. It's telling that a man might find articulating his feelings, particularly if they involve sadness or shame, just as stressful as being unable to function sexually. It's no wonder that sons growing up today might not feel comfortable sharing their innermost thoughts and worries with fathers who were brought up with these more traditional beliefs.

The older teenagers and younger men whom I interviewed are beginning to embrace a far broader interpretation of masculinity. They do not feel they have to entirely model their emotional lives after their fathers'. Rather, they appreciate their fathers' other strengths, but also feel comfortable going to their mother for emotional support long after they are supposed to have "separated" from her. What's more, they feel they can emulate their mothers, as well as their fathers, in their emotional lives. And they don't feel like they are compromising their masculinity in doing so.

Patrick, a twenty-seven-year-old in the hotel business, says he is close to both his parents. But when it comes to his emotional life, he says he tries to pattern himself after his mother more than his father. "My father has a quick fuse and is quick to resort to anger. He never showed weakness or broke down," he says. "The only time I saw him cry was when his mother died. I'm more like my mom with my emotions. I'm less the stereotypic guy in that way. I'm not as quick to anger as my dad, and I'm kind of proud of that. Not to critique my dad, it's just that I saw the way Mom handled things and how Dad handled things, and I try to be more like her."

Bill, thirty-eight, also made a conscious choice not to model himself completely after his father, whom he described as "my-way-or-the-highway, stoic, and angry." Now a step-father himself, Bill, who lives in West Virginia, says he does not want to repeat his father's mistakes. "My brother and I are committed to raising our kids differently."

Many men describe having a loving relationship with their fathers. The issue is not that their fathers are not good or loving men, but simply that sons go to their mothers for different kinds of guidance and support. Walt, a husky twenty-three-year-old, does not seem like the kind of guy who would call his mother his best friend. An outdoorsman, Walt's favorite place to be is in a tent in his native New Hampshire, deer hunting rifle at hand. He enjoys many traditionally male hobbies, which he mostly pursues with his father. Yet his mother, Walt says, is his "best friend by far."

"I guess the way I look at it, there's friends and there's family, but with her it's the best of both worlds," Walt says. "I can go to her with anything. With friends, I wouldn't go to them with lots of personal stuff. They are just the people I have fun with." Walt describes himself as "pretty inseparable" from his mother when he was growing up. He remembers the two of them playing with toy cars, dancing together to old Beach Boys songs in the kitchen, and going for long walks with the family dogs. Now, his mother works for a company that sells feed for cattle, and he often accompanies her on long drives out to farms. That's when the old "car talk" tradition continues. "I go to Mom for everyday life advice, what to do in this situation or that. For Dad, it's more outdoorsy stuff, camping, hunting, fishing. I am close to him, but he doesn't have the communication skills."

By being emotionally open with their mothers, these young men are developing a wider definition of their own masculinity. Pollack notes that research by early feminist scholars showed that fathers who were supportive of their daughters breaking out of the mold of traditional femininity provided them with greater security and a broader sense of their own possibilities as women. It stands to reason, Pollack said, that this also holds true for boys and their mothers. "If a son sees that a loving and mature woman really cares about him and about his sensitivity, his empathy, his love, his thoughtfulness, and admires him for that, and even better than that, a mother cares about a mature man, perhaps his father, that boy every day is absorbing, even unconsciously, a broader sense of what it means to be a man," Pollack said.

As I mentioned earlier, single mothers face unique pressures raising sons, and are often warned not to look to their sons for the emotional support they might be lacking in their own lives. But some sons of single mothers talk about the emotional strength their mothers modeled. Tremaine, for instance, grew up without a father. He was adopted at birth, but his parents divorced before his adoption was finalized. Early on, Tremaine became a companion to his mother, though "not in a way that was debilitating to my growth or in a way that I was bound to her or obligated to make sure she was emotionally okay," he says. Growing up with a single mother was not optimal, he believes. "There were certain things my mom couldn't teach me. She couldn't teach me to be a guy. I don't mean stereotypical guy things like the toolbox in the garage, but there are certain perspectives she couldn't provide. But I survived and thrived."

Tremaine, now twenty-five, says his mother did provide a safe haven for his emotional struggles, particularly as they moved to "increasingly whiter and more affluent communities," where as a young African-American he was in the minority. Most valuable, he said, was that his mother taught him a specific kind of emotional strength. "My mom is a rock," he explained. "A lot of people she has had to deal with haven't been very strong and have been very self-centered. I've learned from her a deep love of family, but also how to deal with family members who have bottomless emotional needs. She doesn't allow herself to emote; she's learned to be practical and a voice of reason, and I've learned that clarity of mind from her. She wasn't trying to give me a female perspective—she's not even an overly feminine person. She's a workhorse. My mom was trying to empower me to be ready for life."

ﾟ "Women's Work"

Tremaine's friends sometimes tease him about being the only guy they know who is in his twenties and already has a retirement fund. But Tremaine says that financial responsibility was one of his mother's key lessons. Even as a young boy he was aware of how much they owed for rent and how much grocer- ies cost. What's more, Tremaine's mother taught him how to cook, wash his own clothes, and clean the house. He is one of many young men of his generation who have been taught housekeeping skills; some because their mothers are devout feminists, others because their mothers are busy working full- time jobs and simply expect their sons to pick up the slack.

Many young men grew up with mothers who were part of the women's movement and received, as one son put it, "constant mini-lessons" on women's rights. One night at the dinner table, Luke, a Wisconsin high school student, made a snide comment about feminism, and his mother didn't take it lightly. "I had this history teacher who was very opinionated and we had just learned about the Equal Rights Amendment. Understand, I grew up with NOW writing pads all around the house. So that night, when I made some crack about Gloria Steinem, my mother was not happy. There ensued a half-hour lecture in defense of the women's movement and about this great person I had maligned."

But for others, their mothers served more as examples than as women with a political agenda. Ken, a computer secu- rity specialist from Georgia, described his mother, a nurse, as "a tough lady." She worked full-time, and Ken and his older brother pulled their load around the house. In fact, Ken learned many skills traditionally considered "women's work," not because his mother espoused political feminism—she had grown up on an isolated farm and was uninterested in politics—but simply because she had too much to do and expected her sons to help out. "I knew how to sew in fifth grade; I was allowed to use the sewing machine because we had to mend our own clothes," Ken explained. "We knew how to do dishes, and how to clean the house. I could use an iron when I was twelve years old." Ken says he was very close to his mother growing up, and remains so today. Now forty-three, Ken says that as he's gotten older, he has grown less defensive about the relationship. "When I was growing up, I got tagged the 'mama's boy' because I was the youngest and I would run to Mom," he says. "If someone who didn't know me well called me a mama's boy today and they meant it seriously—well, I don't fight anymore, I got all that out in the army. But I would have severe disdain for that person, because it shows their ignorance." While she was strict, his mother was also compassionate, Ken says. "To this day, she is the kind of person that I can pick up the phone and tell her just about anything."

Tremaine says his mother's training in housework was as valuable as her instruction on finance, stability, and self-respect, particularly as he looks at this generation of young women. His words would make feminists smile. "One of the key lessons I learned from my mom was self-reliance," he says. "I can't fit into the role of 'I'm gonna be bringing home the bacon'—that doesn't exist anymore. It's been really important to me to see that old distinctions don't exist anymore, especially now that I'm hearing how single females are making more money than young males. The world is just turning upside down. I'm fine with that and I'm glad she prepared me for that."

Experts say that mothers like Tremaine's are doing their sons a favor. "What we know about the children raised in traditional homes today is that they will live in untraditional homes tomorrow," says sociologist Michael Kimmel. "If moms do things like teach their sons how to cook, how to fold, they are teaching them what they need to know. In a less traditional but more contemporary family, the payoff is even greater. Your son is learning that mothers work and that is something that adults do, not just something that men do. He will be accustomed to women being committed to their careers, and much less shocked when his wife is the same way."

That's a lesson Charles learned long ago. His mother went back to work when he was old enough to take care of himself and his little brother after school. Today, Charles is married to a doctor with a demanding practice, and he has his own busy career as a prosecutor in a state attorney general's office. Speaking while cooking dinner for his three children, he said his mother taught him far more than culinary skills. "She influenced me in many ways, but one was her personal work ethic," he said. "When she started working, that helped us leave the projects and purchase our first home." Charles says he and his mother understood each other well, and that she was always an encouraging, positive force in his life. Another way she was influential? "Between my mother and the other women in my family, I've never been scared of strong-willed women."

᧡ Marrying Your Mom

The notion of marrying someone like your mom has been kicking around for at least a century. In 1911, "I Want a Girl (Just Like the Girl That Married Dear Old Dad)" was a hit song. It's not surprising that a man would be attracted to the kind of person with whom he is familiar and comfortable. As *Ebony* magazine put it in an article on mothers and sons, "The old adage 'like father, like son' needs correcting. More appropriate is 'like mother, like son.' For the mother-son connection determines to a great extent not only what sons think about themselves but also what they think about women in general." Of course, being attracted to what is familiar is not always a healthy thing; researchers have tracked multigenerational patterns of abuse and dysfunction. Those patterns can pan out in harmful ways—a son whose mother is always criticizing him might marry a woman who constantly finds fault, because that's what he's used to. Likewise, a daughter who perceives her father to have abandoned her might choose an emotionally unavailable husband. Conversely, a son who has had a warm, trusting, and loving bond with his mother will likely seek out an equally empathic relationship with a spouse. These scenarios are oversimplifications, of course; attraction to a potential mate remains a complex mix of the emotional and the physical.

Yet there is evidence that men tend to choose partners who resemble their mothers, not only emotionally but also physically and intellectually. In a 2008 study, David Perrett, a professor at the University of St. Andrews in Scotland, surveyed three hundred men and four hundred women who were in romantic relationships. He found that people tend to choose someone who has the same hair and eye color as the parent of the opposite sex; a person's own characteristics or that of the same-sex parent are far less significant. If a son has a brunette, brown-eyed mother, he is likely to choose a partner with the same coloring. Perrett also points to evidence that reveals facial resemblance between men's mothers and their own spouses or partners. Finally, Perrett makes the connection that men who reported having a good, close relationship with their mothers are more likely to be attracted to women who physically resemble them. "When people have a good relationship with the parent in question, it seems we want to replicate that good experience in our romantic relationships," Perrett says.

Or, as twenty-seven-year-old Craig put it, "Of course I want to marry someone who is very much like my mom. My mom possesses a lot of the qualities that I would like in a lifetime partner, both personality-wise and with emotional support. This is the first woman I ever loved, so it only follows I will love someone like her."

For years, conventional wisdom about searching for mates was that men were attracted to good looks and women were attracted to earning power. Supposedly, this was based on human evolution—an attractive woman would bear healthy children; the aggressive man would be good at hunting and gathering. But like so many other "givens," this notion was based on research that dates back many decades, and seems to be more a reflection of social mores than biological predispositions. Several new studies show that the old assumptions don't hold up. A recent in-depth study of romantic attraction conducted by two Northwestern University psychologists reveals that men and women are equally inspired by physical attraction and earning power and ambition. "The earning-power effect as well as the good-looks effect didn't differ for men and women," comments Eli Finkel, an associate professor of psychology at Northwestern.

Researchers at the University of Iowa found that men are increasingly interested in an educated woman who is a good financial prospect. Men rate education, intelligence, and ambition as "important characteristics" and a "good financial prospect" as equally desirable. (Women, by the way, are increasingly interested in finding a man who wants a family.) Both sexes consider mutual attraction and love, as well as emotional stability, "essential."

There is also a connection between a mother's academic and professional achievements and the partner her son seeks. It turns out that a man's choice of his ideal mate is influenced by whether his mother earned a college degree and if she worked outside the home while he was growing up. Sociologist Christine Whelan found that nationally 72 percent

of high-achieving men, defined as those who have a graduate degree and/or earn salaries in the top 10 percent of their
age group, had mothers who worked outside the home. High-
achieving men are highly likely to marry a woman whose education level mirrors that of their mother. Whelan analyzed data
from a survey of 3,700 Americans and found that 62 percent
of sons whose mothers have graduate degrees marry women
with graduate degrees. Among those men, three-quarters
agree, "Men are more attracted to women who are successful
in their careers." Whelan says that her findings demonstrate
that successful men in their twenties and thirties today are
the sons of a pioneering generation of high-achieving career
women who serve as role models for how a woman can be
nurturing and successful at the same time. "The baby boomer
mothers and the generation after that really provided strong
models for their sons," Whelan said in an interview. "When a
man thinks about what an attractive woman is, he may very
well think of his own mother, and he would want to pair up
with a woman who can be both assertive and nurturing, who
can close a multimillion-dollar deal and diaper a baby."

Still, most young men are not like Craig, who directly
admitted wanting to marry someone just like his mom. In fact,
for most men, that idea seems to call up the usual Oedipal
anxiety. Parker, a twenty-nine-year-old architect, took pains
to explain why the woman he married last year is nothing
like his mother. "Look, having a good relationship with your
mom is going to make any son have a better understanding

of women, but for me, every woman is so drastically different from my mom," explained Parker. "I just see my mom as so special and different, with all her strengths and foibles. I definitely know I didn't approach relationships with girls the same way I do my relationship with my mom." After Parker made that clear, he described his mother at length—her love of gardening, her amazing cooking, her pursuit of a master's degree later in life, her work for a nonprofit arts council, and her position as "emotional rock" in the family. He also grumbled about his mother's nitpicking and her way of making him do things repeatedly until he gets it right. Then Parker switched gears and began to highlight the many similarities between his mother and his wife, Allison. Both women are high-energy perfectionists. Both have graduate degrees. Both love to entertain. Both plan everything months in advance. As he thought about it, Parker was surprised to realize that his mom and his wife share a number of traits. But he insisted the differences are far greater than the similarities. Like many men, he had trouble making the connection.

Yet when asked how they think their relationship with their mother influences their choice of a girlfriend or partner, men's comments are revealing. Take Brad, who complains that his mother sometimes babies him. He also says that he has a great deal of respect for his mother intellectually and for the way she leads her life. Recently, Brad caught himself picking a fight with his girlfriend, Sophie, over something that seemed relatively minor at the time—her reading habits. On reflection, though, Brad realized he was unconsciously comparing Sophie to his mother. "The classic thing you hear is that every guy is looking for his mother," says Brad. "I always wonder if I am, and if the characteristics I like in my girlfriend are the characteristics I like in my mom. Like my girlfriend was not reading *The New York Times*, and my mom reads it every morning. That's not the only reason I want my girlfriend to read it, but I use my mom as an example of someone who is socially conscious and considers it important to know what's going on."

In my survey, 84 percent of sons said that their mothers are "very" or "extremely" influential in the development of their values. The survey also belied the Irish proverb that says "a son is a son 'til he takes a wife." Two out of three sons who are married or in a long-term relationship say that they are just as close to their mothers now as they were before. But surprisingly, an additional 10 percent say they have become closer to their mothers after getting married.

Jon, twenty-one, who grew up in a Korean family, says that having a steady girlfriend has strengthened his bond with his mother. "I was always very close to my mother, but since I've been with Elizabeth, I've grown even closer," he says. "I can really speak to my mom about emotional issues and things in the relationship in ways that I can't with other people, even with my oldest guy friends. It's easier to open up to a mom." Jon's father works in an import-export business and travels often, and Jon says he has always been strongly influenced by his two sisters and mother. "I guess I can relate to women very easily and I think it's played a big role in how easy it is for me to talk to Elizabeth," he speculated. Jon, speaking from his dorm room at Cornell University, adds, "Actually, Elizabeth is here right now listening to this, and she's nodding that she agrees. She likes that I'm close to my mom."

Sean, a college hockey player, says his girlfriend feels the same way. "Becky thinks the fact that I'm really close to my mom has really helped our relationship," he says. "I have been told that I'm a gentleman. Becky thinks that my closeness to Mom contributes to my treating women well." Sean goes on to say that he believes he has long been comfortable in the company of women. "It's funny, because although I hang out with a group of twenty-five guys at school, I prefer spending time with girls," he said. "I find them easier to talk to. I was talking to one of my friends last night who just started dating a guy, and one of the things she told me she likes about him is that he's emotional. That used to be a bad thing, but now, I know a lot of emotional guys, and no one looks at them as less masculine. Women like it."

Many young men told me that women are frequently interested in how well they get along with their mother. "I can't tell you the number of times this girl or that girl asked me about my mom," said Thomas, an aspiring writer. "I think it may be because girls like to see guys as emotionally vulnerable, or maybe it's the pop culture thing—let's see how he treats his mom. But I know this—girls are always really interested in your relationship with your mom."

Thomas is on target about the pop culture. Here are a few headlines from articles targeted to women on the topic: "When Mr. Right Is a 'Mama's Boy'" (*Ladies' Home Journal*); "Ladies, the Best Catch Is a Man Who Loves His Mum" (*The Times* of London); and my personal favorite: "Mummy's Boy = Best Husband" from the *Daily Mail* in England. These stories instruct women that men who respect and love their mothers will respect and love other women—"including you," says the *Ladies' Home Journal*.

This idea might seem self-evident, but sociologists at Ferrum College in Virginia decided to back up the assumption with research. Their study of thirty-three couples reveals a correlation between men who are close to their mothers and women who are satisfied with their partners. In a paper titled "Mama's Boy or Lady's Man?" the researchers reported to the American Psychological Association that men who described themselves as "understood" by their mothers tend to be viewed as "affectionate" by their partners. What's more, men who feel they communicate their feelings effectively to their mothers have partners who are happier with their romantic life. Also, men who express a strong love for their mothers tend to have girlfriends or wives who are described not only as lovers but also as "best friends." By teaching their sons to be more open, to articulate their feelings, and to be gentler, a mother also might well be affecting his attractiveness as a mate, Sarah Roberts, the study's lead researcher, suggested in an interview with Reuters. As for the "mama's boy" stereotype that claims a woman should avoid a guy who strives to please his mother? The researchers find that men who say they try to "make their mothers proud" ranked high on their ability to communicate with their female partners.

"When you think about it, if the relationship has been good, then who is the boy better to trust to get a first sense of how women should be treated in the world than his mother?" says Pollack.

✔ A Little Monkey Business

At this point let's take an enlightening primatological detour on our exploration of the mother-son relationship. Genetically, bonobos, and other chimpanzees, are the species most closely related to human beings. These primates have captured the public's imagination because they have been romanticized as the make-love-not-war hippies of the animal kingdom. Bonobo apes—males and females alike—employ sex as a kind of social currency, using it to defuse conflicts, acquire food, and ingratiate themselves to those higher up in a somewhat unbending social hierarchy. Bonobos are known for seeming to prefer sex as an overture, as an alternative to engaging in a violent confrontation with outsiders to their own community.

It turns out that the bonobos are also a society full of primate mama's boys. Male bonobos spend almost 90 percent of their time in the company of their mothers. Normally in bonobo society, the highest-ranking male in the group mates with the greatest frequency. But recently primatologists and biologists began to wonder if their strong mother-son bond might affect the mating hierarchy. To find out, researchers spent two and a half years observing a community of more than thirty wild bonobos in Salonga National Park in the Democratic Republic of Congo, particularly focusing on adult and adolescent males. They discovered that for a male bonobo, having his mother around actually increases his odds of mating. *Science* magazine reported that normally, when the primates split into small groups of males and fertile females, the highest-ranking male bonobo has by far the most sex with the most partners. But scientists observed that if the lower-ranking male bonobos have their mothers present, the top male mates with less frequency and with fewer partners, leaving more females available for the more subordinate apes. The very presence of the mothers leveled the playing field for their less dominant sons, biologist Martin Surbeck of the Max Planck Institute for Evolutionary Anthropologist in Leipzig, Germany, told *Science*.

I'm not suggesting that hanging out with Mom is going to help a human son's chance of hooking up, let alone that a guy wants his mother around when he's trying to mate. But this study does show that being a "mama's primate" gives you an edge, at least in the jungle. And there's an argument to be made that the social and emotional skills that human mothers impart to their sons help make them more attractive to females, too.

✣ Football, Sons, and Moms

How often have you seen this: a professional football player scores a touchdown, and, swarmed by cameras in the end zone, he beams, waves, and yells, "Hi, Mom!" In their moment of triumph, even the toughest athletes give a shout-out to Mom. Football-playing sons and their moms capture something universal about the relationship—no matter how big and strong he gets, a guy still wants his mom's love and approval. Campbell's Soup ran a six-year advertising campaign that featured NFL stars like John Elway and Terrell Davis with their mothers. In the early iterations of the ads, actresses were hired to play the men's mothers, until Wilma "Char" McNabb, the mother of football star Donovan McNabb, announced that she could play herself, thank you very much. After that, only real mothers appeared in the ads, which basically showed the moms feeding their enormous sons and their enormous teammates Chunky soup.

Men whose traditional masculinity is as firmly established as that of professional football players can safely afford to indulge nurturing moms who scold them to eat well and bundle up for the cold. There is something endearing about tough guys showing tenderness and deference to their mothers, and because of who they are, the "mama's boy" insult doesn't touch them. New York Giants quarterback Eli Manning, who marched his team to a Super Bowl victory in 2008, told reporters he would have been "lost and clueless" without the guidance of his mother, Olivia. When he was younger and struggled with reading, his mother patiently helped him work through his difficulties. Eli grew up in the shadow of his older brothers and father, all outstanding football players. Eli was dragged to dozens of athletic events and practices as a child. His father began to worry it would turn him off to sports. Eventually, instead of sitting through a string of his brothers' games or staying with a babysitter, Eli joined his mother on antiquing trips. At first he just went along because he had nothing else to do, but after a while, he started to enjoy the outings, he told *The New York Times*. During high school, mother and son grew especially close. With his dad traveling for weeks at a time and his older brothers in college, Eli and his mother began a ritual of just the two of them eating dinner out once a week. The one-on-one time gave both mother and son a chance to open up. "I got to know more about her," Eli said. "She told stories about growing up or about college. It kind of helped me get my stories out," he told *The Times*. The two are temperamentally alike—more reserved and quiet than the rest of the family. According to father Archie Manning, "Eli and Olivia are certainly very close. They have that special bond that you see between mamas and their baby boys."

Football moms have even organized to help support their sons as they navigate the ropes of the business. Mrs. McNabb, the president of the Professional Football Players Mothers

Association (PFPMA), explained the group's mission to me shortly after returning from the NFL draft, which she attended to meet new players and their mothers. "This is a new, overwhelming time in their lives," she said. "The sons have finally reached the ultimate level of the sport they chose to play. It's a different world for them, and we as moms need to know that—not to interfere in their situation, but to be a safety net for them." The mothers assist their sons with everything from understanding NFL benefit packages to helping their sons set up foundations and conduct charitable work. Just as important, the mothers support one another, especially when one of the sons gets injured. Mrs. McNabb especially remembers watching Donovan play through a game with a taped broken ankle. As she was on her way home, she got calls of sympathy from fellow players' moms, who understood what she was experiencing. "For mothers—our hearts are on the field," she said. "We say the men watch the game and we watch our sons. It's rough. You want them to do well in their position. My son happens to be the quarterback, and I'm like, 'Oh, please just protect him, hold your man, give him some time.' And when Donovan does throw the ball, I'm saying to the receiver, 'Please just catch it.' I do get to rest a little during the defense, but still I'm thinking, 'Could you please just keep the lead?' I'm just exhausted by the end of a game." Mrs. McNabb noted that some NFL mothers can't even stomach watching their sons play.

Of course most football-playing sons are not in the NFL

but in Pee-Wee and Midget leagues and on high school and college teams. Their mothers are usually very much a part of the process, whether it's driving back and forth to practice, cheering in the stands, or standing by in the emergency room after a nasty hit to their child. Mothers might have their hearts on the field, but their football-playing sons also have their mothers on their mind, at least during the opening huddle, where the "mama" jokes can fly. "You talkin' 'bout my mama?" quipped Mac, a doctor who led his high school football team to the New York State finals as captain. "I can tell you as an athlete this is fun only to a point. Mama jokes hurt so badly because a boy's love for his mother is special and he will defend her at all costs." Vince, a former Division I college player who now coaches high school football in Massachusetts, says that he does not tolerate any trash talk among his players. "To trash talk someone's mama, that's the worst transgression. A coach doesn't want to hear it, because we all love our mamas." In thinking about the relationship between football, an intensely male-dominated sport, and mothers, Vince says there is something primal about wanting to share your greatest triumphs on the field with your mother. "When you've just scored a touchdown, you're just full of joy. Who's the one person who is going to feel as good at this moment as you are—and maybe even better? Your mom."

Ray Rice, a running back for the Baltimore Ravens, told his hometown newspaper that he could somehow hear his mother's voice among the screaming fans of a packed stadium.

"I hear her at the games—seventy thousand people and she'll find ways for me to hear her." Mrs. McNabb said she believes athletes have a special appreciation for their mothers. "It's not just the big football players, it's the big basketball players, it's the big players period. A lot of moms did a lot of things to help raise these men to be the men they are. Whatever they needed to do to support them, cleaning houses or whatever, they did, and the boys remember that. And they've gotten to a level where they appreciate everything that their mom did, and they don't care who knows it and they don't care who sees it."

☞ Mothers and Others

Swimming superstar Michael Phelps seems to illustrate Mrs. McNabb's point. Deborah Phelps was a permanent fixture at her son's practices and races. She has spoken publicly about how she helped Michael through his childhood struggles with an attention disorder. When reporters crowded around the Olympic swimmer after he won his eighth gold medal and asked him how he felt, Phelps's response was simple: "I guess I just want to see my mom."

Nor are athletes the only celebrities to celebrate their mothers publicly. Hip-hop star and producer Kanye West was known to have a very close bond to his mother, Donda West, who died in 2007. She not only accompanied him to parties and award shows, but also played an important role in his growing business empire, serving as chief executive of his business enterprises and as chairwoman of his foundation. West composed a tribute to his mother while she was still alive, called "Hey Mama." Explaining the song, he told reporters, "My mama is my best friend. I talk to her every day." After the song became a hit, articles appeared with headlines like "Kanye: A Mama's Boy After All." At first Ms. West was offended by the term, but over time, she changed her perspective. In her book *Raising Kanye: Life Lessons from the Mother of a Hip-Hop Superstar*, she writes, "Now I think of the phrase in very positive ways. That you're a mama's boy doesn't mean you're not a man. Kanye is very much his own man. I recall him saying in an interview, 'I'm not tough, but I am strong.' He can love his mother and still be a strong man."

The 2011 Academy Awards was another showcase for moms and sons, one that revealed the ongoing disconnect between how the relationship is portrayed in our culture and how moms and sons actually relate to each other. Many of the year's nominated movies were an exercise in mom bashing. *The Fighter* showcased monstrous matriarch Alice Ward, played by Melissa Leo, an overbearing, vicious, manipulative mom to her sons. In *Black Swan* the crazy ballerina smother-mother, played by Barbara Hershey, gives Joan Crawford a run for her money as the worst Mommy Dearest of all time. In *The King's Speech*, the young stammering George had a cold and distant mother who neglected him as a child and who could barely tolerate a hug from weeping son Edward.

But in real life at the awards ceremony, mothers were getting multiple shout-outs from the stage. The term "mominees" was coined, because a notable number of nominees brought their mothers and grandmothers as their dates. And when Tom Hooper gave his acceptance speech for best director, he singled out his mother for being the person who first spotted the raw material that would eventually become the movie *The King's Speech*. His memorable comment, which lit up Twitter for days and was quoted repeatedly in the press as one of the highlights of the ceremony: "The moral of the story is, Listen to your mother."

8

Looking Forward

Youth fades, love droops, the leaves of friendship fall.
A mother's secret love outlives them all.
—OLIVER WENDELL HOLMES

～

SHORTLY AFTER I BEGAN researching the topic of mothers and sons, I discovered a conference that had been held in 1998 in Toronto called "Mothers and Sons: Challenges and Possibilities." Moments before the opening reception, a rare earthquake had shaken the Canadian city. On the final morning of presentations, a power failure shut down the auditorium lights. These occurrences were perfect metaphors for the academics attending, many of whom felt that they were both shaking things up as well as intellectually stumbling in the dark on the subject of mothers and sons, says Andrea O'Reilly, an associate professor at York University in Canada, who hosted the event. Rounding up papers and presenters on the topic was a challenge, she remembers. "Our conference the year before on mothers and daughters had been hugely successful. It was twice the size and there were too many keynotes to choose from," Reilly recalled in an interview. "We had the opposite problem with mothers and sons."

Although the Canadian group likely did not know it, across the border, in Portland, Maine, another group of concerned citizens had that same year founded an organization called "Boys to Men." Its mission: to reduce interpersonal violence. Boys to Men trains high school boys in leadership and also runs programs for fathers, encouraging them to be active and engaged in their sons' lives. That all sounded great, but by the time I found the organization—more than a decade later—I still did not see anything in the group's literature on whether they saw a role for mothers in raising boys to become healthy men.

"It's funny that you are asking me that now," Layne Gregory, then the executive director, responded when I called her. "We recently started a mothers' advisory committee for Boys to Men, to try to get more input from the mother angle. For the board, this feels like a big step—branching off into motherhood. There are some folks who are worried that bringing mothers in will dilute our focus on fatherhood."

The impetus for forming the mothers committee had come in part from the boys. During focus group sessions, the boys had described their relationships with their mothers as very important to them and had expressed "a hunger for connection," as she put. But—and here was a theme that I would later hear over and over again—these boys, especially as they became adolescents, were getting messages that it was not masculine to reveal their vulnerability and that rather than continue to enjoy the relationship they had with their mothers, they should start to tone it down. In other words, manhood and mother-son closeness did not go together.

Mothers, too, had expressed a need for support, Gregory told me, and the organization decided to set up the mothers' committee. These women wanted to talk about issues ranging from bullying to safe sex. Across all age ranges and socioeconomic backgrounds, mothers were also anxious about the "boy crisis." "We do these presentations all over the state, and it is primarily the moms who feel the highest level of urgency and alarm about what's going on with boys, why they are underachieving," she said.

Once these meetings were started, they had a consistent format. The first half was devoted to mothers talking about what was going on in their own lives with their own sons. In the second half, they would focus on specific topics, usually related to education. One spring afternoon a few months after I first spoke to Gregory, I drove up to Portland to meet with these women. They represented a range of different backgrounds, from psychiatrist to yoga instructor. Most worked at least part-time, many full-time. Some still had children at home, even babies; others were empty nesters. But they were all the mothers of sons.

We sat around a conference table, and the stories began to

pour out. It was here that I heard the tale of the woman who had bought the pink jelly sandals for her son and was later taken publicly to task for doing so. This was where a lawyer told me she was chided for kissing her one-year-old on the lips. One woman talked about her ambivalence in advising her son about bullies. Another worried about her son becoming a bully. A mother of an older son talked about watching him go through a painful breakup with his girlfriend. Freud and his Oedipus theory came up several times, from mothers of sons of all ages. For me, it was the beginning of what would be a fascinating exploration of the complex and intimate bond between mothers and sons.

A year later, I was invited back to be the keynote speaker at the group's first conference for mothers, called "Raising Boys to Men: Supporting Mothers." By then I had a much better handle on the research done in the twelve intervening years between Andrea O'Reilly's groundbreaking attempt to gather together experts on mothers and sons and the efforts of Boys to Men to bring mothers into the discussion of how to raise good men.

As I told the gathering, I was surprised by how little direct research had actually been done on mothers and sons through most of this period. It seemed sometimes as if a collective decision had been made that Freud already had figured out the relationship dynamic, so there was little need to revisit the subject. The new findings that did reveal the benefits of mother-son closeness were serendipitous—that is, they were peripheral to the original focus of the studies from which they emerged. For instance, it was only when Carlos Santos studied boys' attitudes toward masculinity that he made the connection that boys who had warm, secure attachments to their mothers also enjoyed better mental health. Similarly, attachment studies, studies on adolescent drug use, and related research that reveal the advantages of a strong mother-son bond have all made the connection tangentially.

That's not to say that no one had been looking at the mother-son relationship. It was the early modern feminists, while confronting patriarchy, who first began questioning the prevailing wisdom on how mothers should raise boys. They have been given very little credit for this work, and they deserve to be recognized. These scholars struggled with bringing up boys in a sexist society. Feminists argued that because women were so devalued, sons could neither respect nor value their mothers. Reading this literature now is a reminder of how dramatically things have changed. "We are creating and nurturing the agents of our own oppression; once we make them, their education as men in this misogynist society will pull them from our arms, set them above us and make them the source of our degradation," wrote Judith Arcana in *Every Mother's Son* in 1983. She argued that while mothers rejected traditional ideas of masculinity, they lacked the social clout and the confidence to raise their sons with a different set of values.

Gradually, as women's role in society changed, the scholarship began to shift to accommodate new realities. Instead of viewing motherhood as a kind of servitude that reinforced sexism, feminists began to embrace the power of motherhood as a way to initiate social change. In the 1990s mothers and sons got a small second wave of attention. Psychiatrist and author Olga Silverstein was among the first who challenged the idea that separation from their mothers was good for sons and to argue that much of the pain in men's lives stems from their early estrangement from their mothers. The Mothers-Sons Project began to put theory into practice. When Nicolina Fedele and Cate Dooley started working with mothers in groups, they discovered a great well of need. Mothers were sad about the distance they had put between themselves and their sons. It hurt to stand outside a bedroom door, listen to a boy crying, and feel uncertain about whether offering their sons comfort is appropriate. Mothers knew they missed the affection and the connection they had with their sons when they were younger. But now for the first time, mothers were starting to get the message that separation wasn't just about their own loss. Their sons were suffering, too. As Cate Dooley recalls, "I told mothers, 'You know the depth of your own pain. Your son feels that same pain, but he doesn't have the words.'"

Dan Kindlon and Michael Thompson, in *Raising Cain*, as well as William Pollack, in *Real Boys*, picked up the emotional suffering of boys. It was during this time, in the late 1990s, that the "boy crisis" rose to prominence. These two books were not about the mother-son relationship, but the authors did allude to the positive role mothers could play in helping sons combat limited definitions of masculinity. Pollack, in particular, championed mothers' potential, arguing not only that a strong connection with his mother makes a boy emotionally and psychologically healthier, but also that mothers are the key to resolving society's confusion about masculinity. Nonetheless, he said, mothers remained unsure of themselves when it came to raising boys.

Now, a decade and a half after Pollack first made these observations, mothers have taken the lead in this movement. More mothers are confident about keeping their sons close and defying those dated rules about raising boys. Fewer moms are mindlessly enforcing gender stereotypes.

Let's get back to the recent conference I addressed on mothers supporting their sons, hosted by Boys to Men. Unlike the 1998 Canadian conference held between an earthquake and a blackout, this gathering unfolded on a beautiful and serene spring day at the University of New England in Portland. Also different was that this conference was not geared to academics mulling over the feminist implications of raising boys, but rather to a wide range of moms who were in the midst of raising their sons and looking for support and guidance. The workshops included topics such as the latest brain science on boys' development, talking to adolescents about sex and sexuality, combating gender-stereotyped media images, and supporting single and lesbian mothers. The several hundred mothers who attended were enthusiastic participants. Just like the mothers I met around that first conference table, and just like the women from all over the country who answered my survey and spoke to me about their experiences, they, too, were longing to talk about raising their sons and looking for validation as they kept their boys close.

↝ A Broader Conversation

It's time to open up this conversation on a larger scale. Mothers are more than ready. It is clear that many moms have been quietly but systematically questioning a great many things they had been told about the right way to raise boys. These mothers are following their instincts by nurturing close mother-son bonds. And those instincts are backed by a growing number of scientific studies that prove a close mother-son relationship improves a boy's well-being. In fact, nearly every study on happiness points to communication and deep connection with other people as the key to emotional health.

This type of mothering couldn't be more different from the stereotypical images of "mama's boy" closeness, where a mother keeps hold of her son through domination or control and resents his happiness with another woman. Of course, there will always be mothers who dote on their sons, believing that the sun rises and the moon sets on their boys. There will also always be mothers who use their sons as a substitute for the emotional support they lack elsewhere. Some moms will continue to infantilize their sons, doing far too much for them and expecting little in return. And sometimes, even mothers who have healthy, close relationships with their sons will slip into unhealthy patterns, because we are all human. Likewise, you can find examples of damaging conduct in every other parent-child combination. Who hasn't heard about twisted mother-daughter relationships, abusive father-daughter relationships, or hostile, competitive father-son relationships?

Parenting is a challenge, and sometimes, especially as our children get older, we need to take our cues from them. When I was finishing this book, my son came home for a few days on a school break. He had papers to write and I had chapters to revise. I suggested that he bring his laptop to my office so we could at least hang out together, something I still refer to as "parallel play," a throwback reference to the days of toddler playdates. We were both quietly tapping away on our computers when I looked up and saw from my son's face that he was obviously upset. I surmised that he had gotten an e-mail that had distressed him, and suspected that it was from his long-term girlfriend, with whom he was working out some issues. He didn't say a word, but he looked so blue that I felt compelled to speak.

"Paul," I said. "You do appreciate the irony here, right? I am sitting just a few feet away from you, writing a book on the benefits of mother-son closeness. I can see you are suffering and I'm not sure what to do. On the one hand, I wish you would talk to me about whatever it is, so I could maybe help. On the other hand, you are a twenty-one-year-old man and I want to respect your privacy."

My son looked over at me with a small smile and said, "Yeah, Mom—go with the second thought." Message received. Respect his privacy. We both went back to our computers. I didn't ask him again about what was upsetting him, though later on I gave his back a gentle pat. The closeness between us doesn't mean I need to know every detail about his life or that I need to keep him as my baby. To me, it means simply that I'm a loving presence as he continues to find his way in life, much in the same way that I try to be for my daughter.

✒ Backlash

We are at a cultural crossroads. The roles of men and women have changed dramatically. As the ground shifts under our feet, we are witnessing a cultural backlash, as some seek to return to the days "when men were men and women were women." You see this in the hysteria over an advertisement featuring a five-year-old boy with painted toenails. You see it in the celebration of "man caves," guy-only spaces that one men's website described as "a sanctuary dedicated to masculine awesomeness, where bros can be bros like they were in college without the interference of domestic obligations like girlfriends, wives, and horribly tedious household chores." You see it in men's movements that accuse feminists of wanting to destroy men and take away their dignity.

"Men are reacting to the increased demands on them by

pushing back in a way that's misogynistic and violently anti-feminist," says Ronald Levant, the masculinity scholar. "I see it in the homophobia among boys and in the way porn is becoming more degrading and more violent. It's amazing what kind of corrosive influences come at you as a man. The antifeminism is a way that a lot of men have found to respond to their perceived decline over the last few decades. It fits very nicely into traditional masculinity. Someone screwed you—you don't get mad, you get even."

Look at the subtitle of a book that was published in 2011: *Manning Up: How the Rise of Women Has Turned Men into Boys.* A woman, Kay Hymowitz, wrote this book, and it is another account of young men who seem to be stalled in a prolonged adolescent phase. She describes young men who fill their spare time with video games and Adam Sandler movies, while the women their age outpace them in education and career. Hymowitz argues that the young men who are "wait-listed for adulthood" are responding to uncertainty about what it means to be men in today's culture. Their old role as providers and protectors seems to be disappearing. As women move ahead without them, it serves to "legitimize men's attachment to the sandbox," she wrote in a *Wall Street Journal* column based on her book. "Why should they grow up? No one needs them anyway. There's nothing they have to do. They might as well just have another beer." If this is so, and men are falling behind—and perhaps wanting to hibernate in man caves—because the old notions of masculinity are no longer working for them, then what is the solution? That women should regress, throw over feminism, and get back to the kitchen so these guys can feel better about themselves?

I agree with Hymowitz that this can be a confusing time to be a young man. Part of what I am arguing is that mothers can play an important role in helping their sons through this transition by giving them the skills they need to help them mature and succeed in school and in the workplace. Yet look at the message in Hymowitz's title—that it is somehow the success of women that is impeding men, implying that life is a zero-sum game in which only one gender can dominate. In truth, it serves both genders if men thrive, something that Hymowitz does acknowledge in the contents of her book. Questioning the way we raise boys to be men is not an attack on masculinity or on the importance of fathers. Why on earth would we want to do anything to harm men? *We are the mothers of sons.*

ꕔ Changing Course

We need a new road map for raising boys in the twenty-first century. When I make a wrong turn, my GPS navigator immediately pauses, lets me know it is recalculating, and then instructs me to "make the next legal U-turn." It is time to change course. We have been on the same unbending road for far too long. The old model for mothers and sons—to encourage him to separate young, to toughen up emotionally, to go it alone as a teenager, to not identify with any part of his mother—is not getting our boys to the place they need to be.

Many mothers have already changed direction and are heading down a new path. Now it is time for them to have some company on the journey. Our culture has been slow to recognize changes in how mothers are raising their boys, let alone supporting that change. Mothers and sons continue to be bombarded with messages to back off from each other, and it is coming from all sides—movies, commercials, literature, boy "experts," and even well-meaning family members who are hanging on to outdated theories about raising healthy boys.

Instead of having to defend their actions and combat the old "mama's boy" stereotypes, mothers should be encouraged to keep their sons close. Why do mothers deserve this support? Because we now know that a strong mother-son bond is good for boys' emotional health. Because we now know that it is good for boys' physical health. Because we now know that it better prepares boys for the world they live in. And because we've always known that one thing will never change—mothers want the very best for their sons.

Acknowledgments

ॐ

Many kind people held my hand and guided me through the process of writing this book. First, thank you to my agents, Susan Rabiner and Sydelle Kramer. The seeds of this book were planted in a conversation the three of us had on the day we met, during which time Susan and I waxed on about our sons, and Sydelle shared her insights on what we were really saying about the relationship. From that day on, they both shepherded me through every step of developing the project.

Special thanks to Carin Rubenstein, who encouraged me to move beyond daily journalism and get cracking on a book. She warned me about every pitfall along the way and was always on target. My fellow writer and good friend Joanne Dobson not only reviewed the manuscript with an English professor's sharp eye but also commiserated with me during my lows and celebrated my highs during multiple revisions. My writing group showed incredible patience as they read all those iterations—thanks to Ruth Earnest, Susan Hodara, Fran Alexander, Linda Atkinson, and Kristina Lindbergh for all of their ideas, edits, and support. My niece, Emily Stone Tucker, was getting her PhD, working, and expecting a baby and still found the time to help hunt down dozens of academic studies that I used in my research for the book. Thanks, Em.

This was my first book, and I wasn't sure what the professional editing process would be like. It turned out to be amazingly pleasant, thanks to Megan Newman, at Avery, and her able assistant, Miriam Rich. I couldn't have been luckier than to land in their capable hands.

To the hundreds of mothers and sons who answered my survey, allowed me to interview them, and shared their lives, many thanks. I have yet to meet the mother who does not want to talk about her son! Layne Gregory introduced me to the many great moms involved with Boys to Men, and I am grateful to her and to the organization's mothers' advisory committee for sharing so much of what they have learned about raising boys. Thanks also to the MOOBs (that's Mothers of Only Boys), a group in Rye, New York, for their hospitality and often hilarious comments.

Cate Dooley did very important academic work at the Jean Baker Miller Institute in the late 1990s on the topic of mothers and sons. I wondered when I approached her if she might be a bit proprietary about this topic. On the contrary, she was warm, generous with her time and research, and extremely helpful.

One son I interviewed described his mother as his "compass." I love the term because it can mean so many things. A compass keeps you oriented. It also means to encircle. It has another meaning as "comprehension" or "understanding." It has the same root as the word "compassion." My family is my compass. They help me navigate my way with unwavering love and support. To each of them, especially, I say thank you.

Notes

ꜱ

Chapter One. Defending the Bond

17 **"In the workshops with mothers of adult sons":** Interviews, Cate Dooley, April 2009 and May 2009.

20 **In my online survey of more than 1,100 mothers:** www.motherson bond.com—1,135 responses on online questionnaire, followed up by dozens of telephone and/or in-person interviews.

21 *Time* **magazine recently ran the following headline:** Eben Harrell, "Being a Mama's Boy: Good for Your Health?" *Time,* August 27, 2010.

21 **a research project presented in 2010 at the American Psychological Association:** C. E. Santos, "The Missing Story: Resistance to Norms of Masculinity in the Friendships of Adolescent Boys" (2010). Available from ProQuest Dissertations and Theses database (UMI No. 3426967).

22 **"The emotional language boys used when speaking of their mothers":** Interview, Carlos Santos, April 2011.

24 **his most recent research is making the connection between the extent to which boys embrace:** C. Santos, N. Way, and D. Hughes, "Racially and Ethnically Diverse Boys' Trajectories of Academic Engagement

and Resistance to Stereotypes of Masculinity During Middle School"
(2011). Paper presented at the biennial meeting of the Society for
Research in Child Development, Montreal, Quebec, Canada.

25 **Dooley and Fedele even suggest that the real label:** C. Dooley and
N. Fedele, "Mothers and Sons: Raising Relational Boys" (1999). Jean
Baker Miller Training Institute, Wellesley Centers for Women, Paper
No. 84, p. 4.

25 **teenagers who have warm, supportive relationships:** Michelle A.
Miller-Day, "Parent-Adolescent Communication about Alcohol, Tobacco,
and Other Drug Use," *Journal of Adolescent Research* (2002): Vol. 17,
No. 6, pp. 604–16.

25 **recent studies show that it is a teenage boy's mother who is the most
influential:** Evidence from multiple studies—R. W. Blum, "Mothers'
Influence on Teen Sex: Findings from the National Longitudinal Study
of Adolescent Health and Development" (2002), University of Minne-
sota: pp. 1–24; C. A. McNeely, M. L. Shew, T. Beuhring, R. Sieving, B.
C. Miller, and R. W. Blum, "Mother's Influence on Adolescents' Sexual
Debut," *Journal of Adolescent Health* (2002): Vol. 31, No. 3, pp. 256–65;
James Jaccard and Patricia Dittus, "Adolescent Perceptions of Maternal
Approval of Birth Control and Sexual Risk Behavior," *American Jour-
nal of Public Health* (2000): Vol. 90, No. 9, pp. 268–78; James Jaccard,
Patricia Dittus, and Vivian V. Gordon, "Maternal Correlates of Adoles-
cent Sexual and Contraceptive Behavior," *Family Planning Perspectives*
(1996): Vol. 28, No. 4, pp. 159–85; Patricia J. Dittus and James Jaccard,
"Adolescents' Perceptions of Maternal Disapproval of Sex: Relation-
ship to Sexual Outcomes," *Journal of Adolescent Health* (2000): Vol. 26,
No. 4, pp. 1426–30.

26 **Boys are at risk for becoming "emotionally illiterate":** Dan Kindlon
and Michael Thompson, *Raising Cain: Protecting the Emotional Life of
Boys* (New York: Ballantine Books, 1999).

26 **Dr. William Pollack, an assistant clinical professor of psychology at
Harvard Medical:** William Pollack, *Real Boys: Rescuing Our Sons from
the Myths of Boyhood* (New York: Holt Paperbacks, 1998).

27 **The author, Hanna Rosin, argues that:** Hanna Rosin, "The End of
Men," *The Atlantic*, July/August 2010.

28 **The social sector of the economy will gain 6.9 million jobs by 2018:**
Barry Bluestone and Mark A. Melnik, "After the Recovery: Help

Needed. The Coming Labor Shortage and How People in Encore Careers Can Help Solve It" (2010), Kitty and Michael Dukakis Center for Urban and Regional Policy, Northeastern University, Boston.

28 **Harvard just added a first-year curriculum course:** Adam Bryant, "Looking Ahead Behind the Log," *The New York Times*, July 22, 2011.

28 **"The postindustrial economy is indifferent to men's size and strength":** Rosin, "The End of Men."

29 **Actually, recent research on gender reveals that attributes like social intelligence, open communication:** Multiple sources: Janet Hyde, "The Gender Similarities Hypothesis," *American Psychologist* (2005): Vol. 60, No. 6, pp. 581–92; Leslie Brody, *Gender, Emotion and the Family* (Cambridge, MA: Harvard University Press, 1999); Leslie Brody, "Gender and Emotion: Beyond Stereotypes," *Journal of Social Issues* (1997): Vol. 53, No. 2, pp. 369–94; C. Z. Malatesta and J. M. Haviland, "Learning Display Rules: The Socialization of Emotion Expression in Infancy," *Child Development* (1982): Vol. 53, pp. 991–1003; Eleanor Maccoby, "Gender and Relationships," *American Psychologist* (1990): Vol. 45, No. 4, pp. 513–20; Pollack in *Real Boys* and Thompson and Kindlon in *Raising Cain* all cite evidence of boys' emotional suppression.

30 **In one national survey, nearly 40 percent of respondents:** Pew Social Trends Staff, "The Decline of Marriage and Rise of New Families," Pew Research Center, November 18, 2010.

30 **Four in ten mothers are the primary breadwinners in the family:** Richard Fry and D'Vera Cohn, "New Economics of Marriage: The Rise of Wives," the Pew Research Center, January 19, 2010.

30 **A Pew Research study published in 2010:** Ibid.

30 *Time* **concluded that "at the most basic level, the argument over where women belong is over":** Nancy Gibbs, "What Women Want Now," *Time*, October 14, 2009.

31 **"After all, what's more masculine: being a strong, silent, unemployed absentee father":** Andrew Romano and Tony Dokoupil, "Men's Lib," *Newsweek*, September 20, 2010.

31 **"The handy thing about being a father is that the historic standard is so pitifully low":** Michael Chabon, *Manhood for Amateurs: The Pleasures and Regrets of a Husband, Father and Son* (New York: HarperCollins, 2009), p. 11.

31   **"I expected to be chastised for doing so little":** Michael Lewis, *Home Game: An Accidental Guide to Fatherhood* (New York: W. W. Norton, 2009), p. 158.

34   **Studies have shown that parents observing newborns only a few hours old perceive the boys to be stronger and more active than the girls:** Katherine Hildebrandt Karraker, Dena Ann Vogel, and Margaret Ann Lake, "Parents' Gender-Stereotyped Perceptions of Newborns: The Eye of the Beholder Revisited," *Sex Roles* (1995): Vol. 22, Nos. 9/10, pp. 687–701.

Chapter Two. The Pink-and-Blue Divide

37   **Why do you think books like:** Landrum B. Shettles and David M. Rorvik, *How to Choose the Sex of Your Baby*, Fully Revised and Updated (New York: Broadway Books, 2006), also published under the titles *Your Baby's Sex* in 1970 and *Choose Your Baby's Sex* in 1977. Doubleday published further revised editions under the title *How to Choose the Sex of Your Baby* in 1984 and 1989, and by Broadway Books in 1997.

38   **"Our proven baby gender selection program":** www.choose-baby-sex.com.

42   **About half of all women say they would:** According to a study that looked at parents across a broad spectrum of race, class, and sexual orientation: Emily W. Kane, "'I Wanted a Soul Mate': Gendered Anticipation and Frameworks of Accountability in Parents' Preferences for Sons and Daughters," *Symbolic Interaction* (2009): Vol. 32, No. 4, pp. 372–89.

42   **Only 7 percent of couples enrolled in the trial are trying to prevent genetic disease; the other 93 percent are seeking "family balance":** Information provided by MicroSort, January 7, 2010.

43   **As one woman . . . put it, "I envisioned that a daughter":** Kane, "'I Wanted a Soul Mate,'" p. 383.

44   **"Some of these moms believe there's something magical about a relationship with daughters":** Interview, Joyce Venis, August 2008.

45   **research has revealed that boys who do have insecure attachments:** R. Pasco Fearon, Marian J. Bakermans-Kranenburg, Marinus H. VanIJzendoorn, Anne-Marie Laspley, and Glenn I. Roisman, "The Significance of Insecure Attachment and Disorganization in the Development of Children's Externalizing Behavior: A Meta-Analytic Study," *Child Development* (March/April 2010): Vol. 81, No. 2, pp. 435–56.

46   **research on the extent to which "girl behavior":** see note "Actually, recent research on gender reveals that attributes like social intelligence, open communication," for Chapter 1.

46   **New research on the brain disputes:** Cordelia Fine, *Delusions of Gender: How Our Minds, Society, and Neurosexism Create Difference* (New York: W. W. Norton & Company, 2010); Lise Eliot, *Pink Brain, Blue Brain: How Small Differences Grow into Troublesome Gaps–and What We Can Do About It* (New York: Houghton Mifflin Harcourt Publishing, 2009).

47   **boys might well begin life as more emotionally sensitive than girls:** Evidence from multiple studies: Leslie Brody, *Gender, Emotion, and the Family* (Cambridge, MA: Harvard University Press, 1999); E. Macoby and N. Jacklin, *The Psychology of Sex Differences* (Stanford, CA: Stanford University Press, 1974); E. Boatella-Costa, C. Costas-Moragas, F. Botet-Mussons, et al., "Behavioral Gender Differences in the Neonatal Period According to the Brazelton Scale," *Early Human Development* (2007): Vol. 83, pp. 91–97.

47   **In one study mothers were instructed to stop smiling, talking, and playing with their six-month-old babies:** M. Katherine Weinberg, Edward Z. Tronick, Jeffrey F. Cohn, and Karen l. Olsen, "Gender Differences in Emotional Expressivity and Self-Regulation During Early Infancy," *Developmental Psychology* (1999): Vol. 35, No. 1, pp. 175–88.

47   **Another study found that six-month-old boys exhibited:** Marta Katherine Weinberg, "Sex Differences in 6-Month-Old Infants' Affect and Behavior: Impact on Maternal Caregiving" (1992). Electronic doctoral dissertation, University of Massachusetts–Amherst.

48   **In a study published in the journal *Pediatrics*:** Wendy H. Oddy, Jianghong Li, Andrew J. O. Whitehouse, Stephen R. Zubrick, Eva Malacova, "Breastfeeding Duration and Academic Achievement at 10 Years," *Pediatrics* (February 1, 2011): Vol. 127, No. 2 (published online December 20, 2010).

48   **Why are boys more receptive:** Wendy Oddy quoted in www.medical newstoday.com, December 20, 2010.

48   **infant males are surprisingly more fragile than infant girls:** Eliot, *Pink Brain, Blue Brain*, pp. 47–48.

49   **parents tend to respond with far less comfort to their son's distress than they do to their daughter's:** Jeannette M. Haviland, "Sex-Related

Pragmatics in Infants," *Journal of Communication* (1977): Vol. 27, pp. 80–84; Daniel Stern, *The Interpersonal World of the Infant* (New York: Basic Books, 1985).

50 **Mothers of girls underestimated their daughter's abilities by a significant margin:** Emily Mondschein, Karen E. Adolph, and Catherine S. Tamis-LeMonda, "Gender Bias in Mothers' Expectations About Infant Crawling," *Journal of Experimental Child Psychology* (2000): Vol. 77, pp. 304–16.

58 **In 1918, toward the end of World War I:** Jeanne Maglaty, "When Did Girls Start Wearing Pink?" Smithsonian.com, April 8, 2011.

58 **"It's pink, it's girly, and it's all about them!":** Irena Silverman, "The Pinking of Preschool," *The New York Times*, The 6th Floor, posted March 24, 2011.

58 **"I'd sooner send my daughters to learn to field-dress a deer":** KJ Dell'Antonia, "Would You Send Your Daughter to an All-Girls Preschool? *Slate*, XX Factor, posted March 14, 2011.

59 **A Fox News commentator opined that it was:** Dr. Keith Ablow, Fox News Contributor, www.health.foxnews.mobi, posted April 11, 2011.

59 **Erin R. Brown of the conservative Culture and Media Institute:** Erin R. Brown, "J. Crew Pushes Transgendered Child Propaganda," Culture and Media Institute, www.mrc.org, posted April 8, 2011.

61 **In one study of preschool children:** Emily W. Kane, "'No Way My Boys Are Going to Be Like That!' Parents' Responses to Children's Gender Nonconformity," *Gender and Society* (2006): Vol. 20, No. 2, pp. 149–76.

61 **"Occasionally, if he's not doing something":** Ibid., p. 159.

61 **"Sometimes I get so annoyed":** Ibid., p. 161.

62 **"There are things that are meant for girls":** Ibid., pp. 162–63.

63 **from a 1957 copy of Dr. Benjamin Spock's *The Common Sense Book of Baby and Child Care*:** Benjamin Spock, *The Common Sense Book of Baby and Child Care* (New York: Pocket Books, 1957), pp. 577–78.

64 **According to sociologist C. J. Pascoe, who spent a year studying homophobia:** C. J. Pascoe, *Dude, You're a Fag: Masculinity and Sexuality in High School* (Berkeley and Los Angeles: University of California Press, 2007).

65 **In her book about the American women's movement:** Gail Collins, *When Everything Changed: The Amazing Journey of American Women, from 1960 to the Present* (New York: Little, Brown and Company, 2009).

65   **Men make up only 9 percent of the country's public elementary school teachers:** *Status of the American Public School Teacher 2005–2006* (released March 2010), National Education Association Research, Washington, D.C.

65   **only 6 percent of nurses are male:** www.nursingadvocacy.org.

Chapter Three. Oedipus Wrecks

69   **Oedipus at a greeting card rack:** Hillary Price, "Oedipus at the Card Rack," Rhymes with Orange, *Journal News,* May 2, 2008.

70   **Freud had a penchant for using mythical texts:** Sigmund Freud, *The Interpretation of Dreams* (1899), translation copy (New York: Avon, 1965), Chapter V, "The Material and Sources of Dreams," p. 296: "[I]t is the fate of all of us, perhaps, to direct our first sexual impulse towards our mother and our first hatred and our first murderous wish against our father. Our dreams convince us that this is so. King Oedipus, who slew his father Laius and married his mother Jocasta, merely shows us the fulfillment of our own childhood wishes."

71   **"Freud's use of Oedipus":** Interview, Michael Kimmel, March 2011.

72   **"the nuclear complex of neuroses" :** Alain de Mijolla, ed., "Complex," *International Dictionary of Psychoanalysis* (Gale Cengage, 2005), eNotes .com, 2006, http://www.enotes.com/psychoanalysis-encyclopedia/complex.

73   **She called him her "Golden Sigi":** Peter Gay, "Sigmund Freud: Psychoanalyst," *Time,* March 29, 1999.

73   **Later in life, Freud would say:** Ernest Jones, *Life and Works of Sigmund Freud,* Vol. 1 (London: Hogarth Press, 1953), p. 5.

75   **The feminist activist Betty Friedan:** Betty Friedan, *The Feminine Mystique* (New York: W. W. Norton & Co., 1963), chapter 5.

75   **In her 1970 book:** Kate Millett, *Sexual Politics* (New York: Doubleday, 1970, and Simon & Schuster, 1990).

76   **In 1976, Jean Baker Miller's:** Jean Baker Miller, *Toward a New Psychology of Women* (Boston: Beacon Press, 1976).

76   **Harvard psychologist Carol Gilligan:** Carol Gilligan, *In a Different Voice: Psychological Theory and Women's Development* (Cambridge, MA: Harvard University Press, 1982).

77   **In 1935, he wrote a letter responding:** Letter reprinted in Ernest Jones, *Life and Works of Sigmund Freud* (London: Hogarth Press, 1953), pp. 208–9.

79   **The most popular publication issued by the national nonprofit group:** *Our Daughters and Sons: Questions and Answers for Parents of Gay, Lesbian and Bisexual People*, Parents and Friends of Lesbians and Gays, 2006.

79   **contemporary researchers have looked at genetics:** For overview of research, see Neil Swidey, "What Makes People Gay?" *Boston Globe Magazine*, August 14, 2005; also "The Science of Sexual Orientation," *60 Minutes*, CBS News, aired March 12, 2006.

81   **"How can a mother expect":** Rev. John C. Abbott, *Mother at Home: Or the Principles of Maternal Duty* (New York: American Tract Society, 1833), p. 62.

81   **"The mother is the angel-spirit":** Rev. Samuel Phillips, *The Christian Home* (Springfield, MA: G. & F. Bill, 1859), p. 18.

82   **"Strip the Christian family":** Ibid., p. 31.

83   **Schizophrenia was believed:** Carol Eadie Hartwell, "The Schizophrenogenic Mother Concept in American Psychiatry," *Psychiatry: Interpersonal and Biological Processes* (August 1996): Vol. 59, No. 3, pp. 274–97.

83   **In 1960, psychiatrist Leo Kanner gave an interview:** "Medicine: The Child Is Father," *Time*, July 25, 1960.

83   **Influential child psychologist Bruno Bettelheim:** Bruno Bettelheim, *The Empty Fortress: Infantile Autism and the Birth of Self* (New York: Free Press, 1972; London: Collier-Macmillan Ltd, 1967), p. 125.

85   **"Nothing gets better for women over time":** Interview, Paula J. Caplan, June 2009.

85   **Caplan conducted a study:** Paula J. Caplan, *Don't Blame Mother: Mending the Mother-Daughter Relationship* (New York: Routledge, 2000).

87   **Probably the most well-known book:** D. H. Lawrence, *Sons and Lovers* (London: Gerald Duckworth Company Ltd, 1913; New York: Modern Library, 1999).

87   **"As her sons grow she selects them as lovers":** D. H. Lawrence, in a letter to Edward Garnett, in Aldous Huxley, ed., *The Letters of D. H. Lawrence* (New York: Viking, 1932).

88   **Feminists such as Simone de Beauvoir and Kate Millett:** Simone de Beauvoir, *The Second Sex* (New York: Alfred A. Knopf, 1952); Millett, *Sexual Politics*.

88   **In Maugham's observation, "Few misfortunes can befall a boy":** "W. Somerset Maugham," Great-Quotes.com, Gledhill Enterprises, 2011, http://www.great-quotes.com/quote/1367138.

88   **"He was all she had in the world":** Somerset Maugham, "The Mother," *The Complete Short Stories of Somerset Maugham*, Vol. 2 (New York: Doubleday, 1922, 1930), pp. 303.

89   **Far more vicious was the sociological attack:** Philip Wylie, *A Generation of Vipers* (Champaign–London: Dalkey Archive Press, 1942, 2007), pp. 194–217.

90   **Dr. Edward Strecker, a psychiatrist and contemporary of Wylie:** Edward Strecker, *Their Mothers' Sons* (Philadelphia: J. B. Lippincott Co., 1946).

90   **An editorial on "momism":** "Momism," *Washington Post*, February 11, 1951, p. B4.

90   **Maugham was said to have been devastated:** Ted Morgan, *Somerset Maugham: A Life* (New York: Alfred A. Knopf, 1980), pp. 8–9.

90   **in a television interview:** Mike Wallace interview with Philip Wylie, aired on May 12, 1957. Transcript: http://www.hrc.utexas.edu/multimedia/video/2008/wallace/wylie_philip_t.html.

91   **In a 1952 journal he wrote of:** John Cheever, *The Journals of John Cheever* (New York, Alfred A. Knopf, 1990), p. 10.

91   **Another famous rant about emasculating mothers:** Philip Roth, *Portnoy's Complaint* (New York: Vintage Books, 1967).

91   **Reviewer Eric Weiner put it this way:** Eric Weiner, "Portnoy's Complaint: Self-Love and Self Loathing," National Public Radio, April 7, 2008.

92   **The New York Times hailed Jonathan Franzen's 2010 novel:** Sam Tanenhaus, "Peace and War," *The New York Times*, August 19, 2010.

93   **"Patty was undeniably very into her son":** Jonathan Franzen, *Freedom* (New York: Farrar, Straus and Giroux, 2010), p. 8.

93   **"the move was a stunning act":** Ibid., p. 21.

94   **The casting call for eligible men:** http://www.realitywanted.com/call/2570-mommas-boy-nbcryan-seacrest-now-casting.

95   **Tomei's character:** Manohla Dargis, "Mommy Dearest, You're Mine Forever," *The New York Times*, June 18, 2010.

Chapter Four. Moms and the "Boy Crisis"

98   **Moreover, studies have shown that:** C. E. Santos "The Missing Story: Resistance to Norms of Masculinity in the Friendships of Adolescent Boys" (2010). Available from ProQuest Dissertations and Theses database (UMI No. 3426967); R. Pasco Fearon, Marian J.

Bakermans-Kranenburg, Marinus H. VanlJzendoorn, Anne-Marie Laspley, and Glenn I. Roisman, "The Significance of Insecure Attachment and Disorganization in the Development of Children's Externalizing Behavior: A Meta-Analytic Study," *Child Development* (March/April 2010): Vol. 81, No. 2, pp. 435–56.

99 **Nonetheless, some advocates:** Leonard Sax, *Why Gender Matters: What Parents and Teachers Need to Know about the Emerging Science of Sex Differences* (New York: Doubleday, 2005); Michael Gurian, Kathy Stevens, and Peggy Daniels, *Successful Single-Sex Classrooms: A Practical Guide to Teaching Boys and Girls Separately* (San Francisco: Jossey-Bass, 2009).

101 **"The Boy Crisis" on the cover of Newsweek:** *Newsweek*, January 30, 2006.

101 **In 1992, the American Association of University Women (AAUW):** *How Schools Shortchange Girls: A Study of Major Findings on Girls and Education*, commissioned by the American Association of University Women Educational Foundation, 1992.

101 **The following year, Mary Pipher published:** Mary Pipher, *Reviving Ophelia: Saving the Selves of Adolescent Girls* (New York: Ballantine Books, 1994).

102 **In 2000, *The Atlantic* published an article:** Christina Hoff Sommers, "The War Against Boys," *The Atlantic*, May 2000.

102 **The pendulum kept swinging, and the AAUW came out with another report in 2008:** "Where the Girls Are: The Facts About Gender Equity in Education," American Association of University Women Educational Foundation, 2008.

103 **Dr. Rosalind Barnett, a senior scientist:** Rosalind Barnett and Caryl Rivers, *Same Difference: How Gender Myths Are Hurting Our Relations, Our Children, and Our Jobs* (New York: Basic Books, 2004).

104 **A mother's education and aspirations:** Katherine A. Magnuson and Sharon M. McGroder, "The Effect of Increasing Welfare Mothers' Education on Their Children's Academic Problems and School Readiness," Joint Center for Poverty Research, Northwestern University (2002); Dale Walker, Charles Greenwood, Betty Hart, and Judith Carta, "Prediction of School Outcomes Based on Early Language Production and Socioeconomic Factors," *Child Development* (1994), Vol. 65, No. 2, pp. 606–12; David L. Stevenson and David P. Parker, "The Family-

School Relation and the Child's School Performance," *Child Development* (1987), Vol. 58, No. 5, pp. 1348–58.

104 **boys are more likely to be diagnosed:** In the United States, boys (13.2%) were more likely than girls (5.6%) to have ever been diagnosed with Attention Deficit/Hyperactivity Disorder. Source: Center for Disease Control and Prevention.

104 **girls are more likely to be given a diagnosis:** National Institute of Mental Health, www.nimh.nih.gov. The lifetime prevalence of girls thirteen to eighteen years old diagnosed with major depressive disorder is 15 percent; for boys it is 7.5 percent. The prevalence of general depression among thirteen- to seventeen-year-olds is nearly three times as high for girls as for boys; 12.4 percent of girls in that age group are diagnosed as depressed, compared to 4.3 percent for boys.

104 **Boys are more likely to kill themselves:** Ibid. Nearly five times as many males as females ages fifteen to nineteen died by suicide in 2007.

105 **His treatise on new manhood, *Iron John*:** Robert Bly, *Iron John: A Book About Men* (Cambridge, MA: De Capo Press, 1990).

105 **"Women can change the embryo to a boy":** Ibid., p. 16.

106 **The use of the word "sissy":** www.dictionary.reference.com/etymology.

106 **He exhorted young men to "avoid books":** Rosalind Barnett and Caryn Rivers, "The Myth of 'The Boy Crisis,'" *Washington Post*, April 9, 2006.

107 **In 2010 the Boy Scouts of America:** William Yardley, "$18.5 Million in Liability for Scouts in Abuse Case," *The New York Times*, April 23, 2010.

108 **Barack Obama has touched on the theme every Father's Day:** "President Obama to Discuss Importance of Fatherhood and Personal Responsibility," White House Advisory, June 19, 2009.

108 **"I think sometimes that had I known":** Barack Obama, *Dreams from My Father: A Story of Race and Inheritance* (New York: Three Rivers Press, 1995), p. xii.

109 **studies have shown that a mother's support:** C. P. Cowan, P. A. Cowan, N. Cohen, M. K. Pruett, and K. Pruett, "Supporting Fathers' Engagement with Kids." In Jill Duerr Berrick and Neil Gilbert, eds., *Raising Children: Emerging Needs, Modern Risks, and Social Responses* (New York: Oxford University Press, 2008), pp. 44–80; P. A. Cowan, C. P. Cowan, M. K. Pruett, and K. Pruett, "Six Barriers to Father Involvement and Suggestions for Overcoming Them," *National Council*

of Family Relations Report (Spring 2009): F1–F4; P. A. Cowan, C. P. Cowan, M. K. Pruett, K. D. Pruett, and J. Wong, "Promoting Fathers' Engagement with Children: Preventive Interventions for Low-Income Families," *Journal of Marriage and the Family* (2009): Vol. 71, pp. 663–79.

110 **For Bly, a boy must be ready:** Bly, *Iron John*, p. xiii.

111 **"Boys with a more positive mother-son relationship":** Kim A. Jones, Teresa L. Kramer, Tracey Armitage, and Keith Williams, "The Impact of Father Absence on Adolescent Separation-Individuation," *Genetic, Social & General Monographs* (February 2003): Vol. 129, No. 1, p. 89.

111 **Take therapist Dr. Kenneth M. Adams's:** Kenneth Adams and Alexander Morgan, *When He's Married to Mom: How to Help Mother-Enmeshed Men Open Their Hearts to True Love and Commitment* (New York: Fireside, 2007).

112 **Michael Gurian, who is yet another popular champion:** Michael Gurian, *Mothers, Sons & Lovers: How a Man's Relationship with His Mother Affects the Rest of His Life* (Boston: Shambhala Publications, 1994).

113 **Fathers are often "absent, distant, abusive or passive":** Ibid., p. 64.

113 **"Separating from our mothers is a primordial door":** Ibid., p. 23.

113 **Mothers of sons, he writes, consider it their job to "hold back the coming of manhood":** Ibid., p. 24.

114 **"It is as if we are naked over a gorge":** Ibid., p. 42.

114 **"Our mothers have devoured, or eaten away, parts of our masculine psyche":** Ibid., p. 87.

114 **When fathers are withdrawn or absent, and mothers are angry about it, the son perceives that "manhood has been devoured by the Goddess, found lacking, spit out":** Gurian, *Mothers, Sons & Lovers*, p. 73.

115 **Gurian now runs an institute:** The Gurian Institute, wwwgurianinstitute.com.

115 **In 2010 he reissued his guide for teachers and parents:** Michael Gurian, *Boys and Girls Learn Differently! A Guide for Teachers and Parents*, Revised 10th Anniversary Edition (San Francisco: Jossey-Bass, 2011).

115 **Girls, he has written, "are less able to separate emotion from reason":** Michael Gurian, Patricia Henley, and Terry Trueman, *Boys and Girls Learn Differently: A Guide for Teachers and Parents* (San Francisco: Jossey-Bass, 2001), p. 36.

115 **Boys' higher level of testosterone:** Ibid., p. 29.

115 **"His claims are bogus":** Interview, Rosalind Barnett, May 26, 2009.

116 **"The argument that boys and girls need different educational experiences because 'their brains are different' is patently absurd":** Lise Eliot, *Pink Brain, Blue Brain: How Small Differences Grow into Troublesome Gaps—and What We Can Do About* It (New York: Houghton Mifflin Harcourt Publishing, 2009), p. 305.

116 **the American Council for Coeducational Schooling:** http://lives .clas.asu.edu.

116 **As of January 2011, at least 524 public schools in the United States had some single-sex offerings:** National Association for Single Sex Public Education, www.singlesexschools.org.

118 **In his book *Manhood in America*:** Michael Kimmel, *Manhood in America: A Cultural History* (New York: Free Press, 1996).

120 **"The underpinning for a boy's achievement of 'healthy' masculinity, instead, is founded upon a secure and involved":** Michael Diamond, "The Shaping of Masculinity: Revisioning Boys Turning Away from Their Mothers to Construct Male Gender Identity," *International Journal of Psychoanalysis* (2004): Vol. 85, pp. 359–80, abstract.

120 **masculinity is reworked throughout a man's life:** Michael J. Diamond, "Masculinity Unraveled: The Roots of Male Gender Identity and the Shifting of Male Ego Ideals Throughout Life," *Journal of the American Psychoanalytic Association* (2006): Vol. 54, No. 4, pp. 1099–130.

120 **Ken Corbett, a psychology professor at New York University:** Ken Corbett, *Boyhoods: Rethinking Masculinities.* Published with assistance from the foundation established in memory of Philip Hamilton McMillan of Class of 1894, Yale College, 2009.

121 **Kimmel points to the psychological damage:** Interview, Michael Kimmel, March 23, 2011.

121 **One recent study examined "healthy" masculinity in a literal way:** Arik Marcell, Carol Ford, Joseph Pleck, and Freya Sonenstein, "Masculine Beliefs, Parental Communication and Male Adolescents' Health Care Use," *Pediatrics* (2007), Vol. 119, No. 4, pp. e966–75.

122 **Dr. Ronald F. Levant, a psychology professor at the University of Akron who:** Interview, Dr. Ronald Levant, April 8, 2011.

123 **Levant's academic research focuses on:** Ronald Levant, Rosalie Hall, Christine Williams, and Nadia Hasan, "Gender Differences in

Alexithymia," *Psychology of Men & Masculinity* (2009): Vol. 10, No. 3, pp. 190–203.

124 **Currently there are roughly 9.8 million single mothers:** United States Census Bureau.

124 **In 2008, a record four in ten births (41 percent) were to unmarried women:** Gretchen Livingston and D'Vera Cohn, "New Demography of Motherhood," Pew Research Center, August 19, 2010.

124 **Between 8 and 10 million children in the United States are being raised in gay and lesbian families:** U.S. Department of Health and Human Services, Child Welfare Information Gateway.

128 **Two economists who reviewed census data:** Gordon Dahl and Enrico Moretti, "The Demand for Sons," *Review of Economic Studies* (October 2008): Vol. 75, No. 4, pp. 1085–120.

128 **But their research raises the question of why "boys hold marriages together, and girls break them up":** Steven E. Landsburg, "Oh, No: It's a Girl!" *Slate*, posted on October 2, 2003.

129 **"I've had women in my practice express":** Interview, Dr. Christine Nicholson, March 2009.

131 **"Single moms get a lot of pressure":** Interview, Michael Kimmel, March 2011.

131 **The argument that children need both a mother and a father:** Timothy Biblarz and Judith Stacey, "How Does the Gender of Parents Matter?" *Journal of Marriage and Family* (February 2010): Vol. 72, No. 1, pp. 3–22.

132 **Nanette Gartrelle, a researcher at the University of California:** Nanette Gartelle, Amy Banks, Nancy Reed, Jean Hamilton, Carla Rodas, and Amalia Deck, "The National Lesbian Family Study: 3. Interviews with Mothers of Five-Year-Olds," *American Journal of Orthopsychiatry* (October 2000): Vol. 70, No. 4, pp. 542–48.

132 **But in a study published in the *American Journal of Sociology*:** Timothy Biblarz and Adrian Raftery, "Family Structure, Educational Attainment, and Socioeconomic Success: Rethinking the 'Pathology of Matriarchy,'" *American Journal of Sociology* (September 1999): Vol. 105, No. 2, pp. 321–65. Further argument: Timothy Biblarz, Adrian Raftery, and Alexander Bucur, "Family Structure and Social Mobility," *Social Forces* (June 1997): Vol. 75, No. 4, pp. 1319–41; Timothy Biblarz and Judith Stacy, "Ideal Families and Social Science Ideals," *Journal of Marriage and Family* (February 2010): Vol. 72, No. 1, pp. 41–44.

133   **More than one in four fathers with children eighteen and under now live apart from their children:** Gretchen Livingston and Kim Parker, "A Tale of Two Fathers," Pew Research Center, June 15, 2011, p. 1.

133   **In a nationwide survey conducted in 2010 by both Pew and *Time*:** "The Decline of Marriage and Rise of New Families," the Pew Research Center, November 18, 2010.

134   **In *Raising Cain: Protecting the Emotional Life of Boys*, the authors:** Dan Kindlon and Michael Thompson, *Raising Cain: Protecting the Emotional Life of Boys* (New York: Ballantine Books, 1999).

134   **"Most important, a boy needs male modeling of a rich emotional life":** Ibid., p. 7.

135   **"Fathers tend to fall back on what they have been taught":** Ibid., p. 96.

138   **"When I shared the subtitle . . . with a school administrator":** Ibid., p. 291.

138   **Thompson describes his mother as:** Ibid., p. xiv.

138   **"War and baseball—it's almost a cliché":** Ibid., p. xviii.

139   **Olga Silverstein calls the way mothers separate:** Olga Silverstein and Beth Rashbaum, *The Courage to Raise Good Men* (New York: Penguin Books, 1994).

141   **"the picture I keep seeing in my mind's eye":** Ibid., p. 113.

141   **Babette Smith, an Australian author and journalist:** Babette Smith, *Mothers and Sons* (St. Leonards, Australia: Allen & Unwin Pty Ltd, 1995).

141   **William Pollack also began speaking:** William Pollack, *Real Boys: Rescuing Our Sons from the Myths of Boyhood* (New York: Holt Paperbacks, 1998).

142   **"I do go out on a limb with that term":** Interview, William Pollack, April 2011.

143   **"The moms of older sons were in pain":** Interview, Cate Dooley, April 2009 and May 2009.

Chapter Five. Car Talk

150   **An academic study done at the University of Arizona:** Matthias Mehl, Simine Vazire, Shannon Holleran, and Shelby Clark, "Eavesdropping on Happiness: Well-Being Is Related to Having Less Small Talk and More Substantive Conversations," *Psychological Science* (February 18, 2010): Vol. 21, No. 4, pp. 539–41.

151 **"I don't think boys don't have words for feelings":** Interview, William Pollack, April 21, 2011.

151 **Research shows that by the time they are school age:** Deborah Tannen, "Gender Differences in Topical Coherence: Creating Involvement in Best Friend's Talk," *Discourse Processes* (1990): Vol. 13, No. 1, pp. 73–90; Carol Gilligan, *In a Different Voice: Psychological Theory and Women's Development* (Cambridge, MA: Harvard University Press, 1982); E. Maccoby, "Gender and Relationships: A Developmental Account," *American Psychologist* (April 1990): Vol. 45, No. 4, pp. 513–20.

151 **Scholars have established that girls generally learn:** J. Bretheron Dunn and P. Munn, "Conversation about Feeling States between Mothers and Their Children," *Developmental Psychology* (1987): Vol. 23, pp. 132–39.

152 **Studies have shown that mothers encourage baby girls' talking:** Multiple sources: Christi A. Cervantes and Maureen A. Callanan, "Labels and Explanations in Mother-Child Emotion Talk: Age and Gender Differentiation," *Developmental Psychology* (January 1998): Vol. 34, No. 1, pp. 88–98; Leslie Brody, *Gender, Emotion and the Family* (Cambridge, MA: Harvard University Press, 1999); Susan Adams, Janet Kuebli, Patricia Boyle, and Robyn Fivush, "Gender Differences in Parent-Child Conversations about Past Emotions: A Longitudinal Investigation," *Sex Roles* (1998): Vol. 33, Nos. 5–6, pp. 309–23.

152 **Men Are from Mars:** John Gray, *Men Are from Mars, Women Are from Venus: A Practical Guide for Improving Communication and Getting What You Want in Your Relationships* (New York: HarperCollins, 1992).

152 **Deborah Tannen's book:** Deborah Tannen, *You Just Don't Understand: Women and Men in Conversation* (New York: William Morrow and Company, 1990).

153 **With respect to communication skills, the new scientific literature:** Lise Eliot, *Pink Brain, Blue Brain: How Small Differences Grow into Troublesome Gaps—and What We Can Do About It* (New York: Houghton Mifflin Harcourt Publishing, 2009), pp. 67–72.

153 **One study of four-and-a-half-year-old twins:** Michael J. Galworthy, Ginette Dionne, Philip S. Dale, and Robert Plomin, "Sex Differences in Early Verbal and Nonverbal Cognitive Development," *Developmental Science* (May 2000): Vol. 3, No. 2, pp. 206–15.

153 **A study of 395 families conducted by Brigham Young University:**
L. M. Padilla-Walker, J. M. Harper, and A. C. Jensen, "Self-Regulation
as a Mediator between Sibling Relationship Quality and Early Adolescents' Positive and Negative Outcomes," *Journal of Family Psychology*
(2010): Vol. 24, pp. 419–28.

162 **In *Packaging Boyhood*:** *Saving Our Sons from Superheroes*: Sharon
Lamb, Lyn Mikel Brown, and Mark Tappan, *Packaging Boyhood: Saving
Our Sons from Superheroes, Slackers, and Other Media Stereotypes* (New
York: St. Martin's Press, 2009).

162 **Mark Tappan, a professor of education and human development:**
Interview, Mark Tappan, April 2011.

164 **Disney has come under repeated criticism:** Mia Adessa Towbin, Shel-
ley A. Haddock, Toni Schindler Zimmerman, Lori K. Lund, and Litsa
Renee Tanner, "Images of Gender, Race, Age, and Sexual Orientation
in Disney Feature-Length Animated Films," *Journal of Feminist Fam-
ily Therapy* (2004): Vol. 15, No. 4; Lauren Dundes, "Disney's Modern
Heroine Pocahontas: Revealing Age-Old Gender Stereotypes and Role
Discontinuity under a Façade of Liberation," *The Social Science Journal*
(Autumn 2001): Vol. 38, No. 3, pp. 353–65.

167 **"The fear of alienating a male child from 'his' culture seems to go
deep":** Adrienne Rich, *Of Woman Born: Motherhood as Experience and
Institution* (New York: W. W. Norton, 1976).

168 **"Feminism was obviously about challenging patriarchs":** Interview,
Andrea O'Reilly, May 2009.

170 **In a story reported in *The New York Times*:** Jan Hoffman, "As Bullies Go
Digital, Parents Play Catch-Up," *The New York Times*, December 4, 2010.

180 **"My mother had a passion for improving the male of the species,
which in my case took the form":** Russell Baker, *Growing Up* (New
York: Putnam, 1982), p. 8.

182 **"Cry and you are out of here":** Stephanie Rosenbloom, "Big Girls
Don't Cry," *The New York Times*, October 13, 2005.

184 **But a 2006 study found that despite the surge of women in the
workforce:** Suzanne Bianchi, John P. Robinson, and Melissa A. Milkie,
"Changing Rhythms of American Family Life," Russell Sage Foundation, 2006.

185 **In a survey conducted by the Families and Work Institute:** Ellen
Galinsky, Kerstin Aumann, and James T. Bond, "Times Are Changing:

Gender and Generation at Work and at Home," 2008 National Study of the Changing Workforce, Families and Work Institute.

187 **In one study, scholars set out to look at the differences:** Jose F. Domene, Rubab G. Arim, and Richard A. Young, "Gender and Career Development Projects in Early Adolescence: Similarities and Differences between Mother-Daughter and Mother-Son Dyads," *Qualitative Research in Psychology* (2007): Vol. 4, No. 1, pp. 107–26.

Chapter Six. Moms and Teenage Boys

194 **"Most adolescent boys are attracted to women":** Anthony E. Wolf, *Get Out of My Life: But First Could You Drive Me and Cheryl to the Mall?* (New York: HarperCollins, 1991), p. 29.

198 **"Do mothers and sons sometimes tread on something that feels sexual?"** Interview, William Pollack, April 21, 2011.

200 **Angry, risk-taking adolescents:** Tiffany Field, "Violence and Touch Deprivation in Adolescents," *Adolescence* (2002): Vol. 37, No. 148, pp. 735–50.

200 **The aggressive boys were also less liked by their peers:** Carol MacKinnon-Lewis and Amy Lofquist, "Antecedents and Consequences of Boys' Depression and Aggression: Family and School Linkages," *Journal of Family Psychology* (1996): Vol. 10, No. 4, pp. 490–500.

203 **But statistics show that sexual abuse is much more prevalent:** National Data Archive on Child Abuse and Neglect, "Fourth National Incident of Child Abuse and Neglect" (NIS 4). Report to Congress, U.S. Department of Health and Human Services, Administration for Children and Families, Office of Planning, Research, and Evaluation, Children's Bureau, 2010.

203 **Studies have shown that adult males abusing young females:** Ibid.

203 **Less than 5 percent of reported sexual abuse:** National Archive of Criminal Justice Data; Myriam S. Denov, "The Myth of Innocence: Sexual Scripts and the Recognition of Child Sexual Abuse by Female Perpetrators," *The Journal of Sex Research* (August 2003): Vol. 40, No. 3, pp. 303–4.

203 **The registration form:** www.trianglefatherdaughter.com.

207 **"Mothers are no less necessary in the lives":** Interview, Michael Kimmel, 2011.

208   **In interviews of more than four hundred boys and men:** Michael Kimmel, *Guyland: The Perilous World Where Boys Become Men* (New York: HarperCollins, 2008).

213   **studies have shown that teenagers who have good communication:** Michelle A. Miller-Day, "Parent-Adolescent Communication about Alcohol, Tobacco, and Other Drug Use," *Journal of Adolescent Research* (November 2002): Vol. 17, No. 6, pp. 604–16; R. W. Blum and P. M. Rinehart, "Protecting Teens: Beyond Race, Income and Family Structure," Minneapolis Division of General Pediatrics and Adolescent Health, University of Minnesota Adolescent Health Program, 2002.

213   **One study of inner-city teenagers reveals:** James Jaccard and Patricia Dittus, "Adolescent Perceptions of Maternal Approval of Birth Control and Sexual Risk Behavior," *American Journal of Public Health* (September 2000): Vol. 90, No. 9, pp. 1426–30.

214   **In fact, mothers are so influential and effective:** Miller-Day, "Parent-Adolescent Communication," p. 612 ["Given that adolescents may choose to talk with mothers rather than anyone else about risky issues and that they feel closer to their mothers, mothers may be logical targets for drug education and intervention programs."]

217   **Most mothers of adolescents tend to be more attuned:** National Longitudinal Survey of Youth–1997; Kristin Anderson Moore, Rosemary Chalk, Juliet Scarpa, and Sharon Vandivere, "Family Strengths: Often Overlooked, But Real," 2002 Child Trends Research Brief.

222   **Studies have shown that teenagers—both boys and girls:** Christopher Daddis and Danielle Randolph, "Dating and Disclosure: Adolescent Management of Information Regarding Romantic Involvement," *Journal of Adolescence* (April 2010): Vol. 33, No. 2, pp. 309–20; "Every Child, Every Promise, Turning Failure into Action," America's Promise Alliance, national sample of 2,000 teenagers and their parents, with Child's Trends.

222   **Moreover, teenagers who report high levels of closeness to their mothers:** R. W. Blum, "Mothers' Influence on Teen Sex: Connections That Promote Postponing Sexual Intercourse" (2002), monograph based on Add Health Survey from the National Longitudinal Study of Adolescent Health, Center for Adolescent Health and Development, University of Minnesota.

222 **A study that focused on inner-city black teenagers:** James Jaccard, Patricia J. Dittus, and Vivian V. Gordon, "Maternal Correlates of Adolescent Sexual and Contraceptive Behavior," *Family Planning Perspectives* (July/August 1996): Vol. 28, No. 4, pp. 159–65, 185.

223 **A study . . . revealed that mothers are nearly twice as likely to recommend:** Clea McNeely, Marcia L. Shew, Trisha Beuhring, Renee Sieving, Brent Miller, and Robert Blum, "Mothers' Influence on the Timing of First Sex among 14- and 15-year-olds," *Journal of Adolescent Health* (2002): Vol. 31, No. 3, pp. 256–65; R. W. Blum, "Mothers' Influence on Teen Sex: Findings from the National Longitudinal Study of Adolescent Health and Development" (2002), University of Minnesota.

225 **Studies have shown that mothers are more likely than fathers:** C. Lammers, M. Ireland, M. D. Resnick, and R. W. Blum, "Influences on Adolescents' Decision to Postpone Onset of Sexual Intercourse: A Survival Analysis of Virginity Among Youth Ages 13 to 18," *Journal of Adolescent Health* (2000): Vol. 26, No. 1, pp. 42–48; McNeely et al., "Mothers' Influence on the Timing of First Sex among 14- and 15-yearolds"; Add Health Survey from the National Longitudinal Study of Adolescent Health, 2002.

225 **This is particularly important because:** Arik Marcell, Carol Ford, Joseph Pleck, and Freya Sonenstein, "Masculine Beliefs, Parental Communication and Male Adolescents' Health Care Use," *Pediatrics* (April 2007): Vol. 119, No. 4, pp. e966–75; Ronald Levant, David Wimer, Christine Williams, K. Bryant Smalley, and Delilah Noronha, "The Relationships between Masculinity Variables, Health Risk Behaviors and Attitudes toward Seeking Psychological Help," *International Journal of Men's Health* (Spring 2009): Vol. 8, No. 1, pp. 3–21; Abigail K. Mansfield, Michael E. Addis, and Will Courtenay, "Measurement of Men's Help Seeking: Development and Evaluation of the Barriers to Help Seeking Scale," *Psychology of Men & Masculinity* (2005): Vol. 6, No. 2, pp. 95–108; Michael E. Addis and James R. Mahalik, "Men, Masculinity, and the Contexts of Help Seeking," *American Psychologist* (January 2003): Vol. 58, No. 1, pp. 5–14.

230 **"What moms can say to their sons":** Interview, Michael Kimmel, March 2011.

231 **Until her death, she insisted, "Al's a good boy":** Carole Klein, *Mothers and Sons* (Boston: Houghton Mifflin, 1984): pp. 218–19.

Chapter Seven. Let's Hear It from the Boys

237   **"Are You Still a Mama's Boy?" asks a headline from a recent article in *Details* magazine:** Kayleen Schaefer, "Are You Still a Mama's Boy?" *Details*, October 20, 2009.

240   **In her research on boys' friendships, Way found:** Niobe Way, *Deep Secrets: Boys' Friendships and the Crisis of Connection* (Cambridge, MA: Harvard University Press, 2011).

240   **"By the time they're eighteen, if you ask them":** Interview, Niobe Way, January 2010.

242   **a wealth of research shows that people who are more emotionally and socially connected:** Ursula Belt, "The Role of Autonomy-Connectedness in Depression and Anxiety," *Depression and Anxiety* (2006): Vol. 23, No. 5, pp. 274–80; Lyndal Bond, Helen Butler, Lyndal Thomas, John Carlin, Sara Glover, Glenn Bowes, and George Patton, "Social and School Connectedness in Early Secondary School as Predictors of Late Teenage Substance Use, Mental Health, and Academic Outcomes," *Journal of Adolescent Health* (2007): Vol. 40, No. 4, p. 357; Diann M. Ackard, Dianne Neumark-Sztainer, Mary Story, and Cheryl Perry, "Parent-Child Connectedness and Behavioral and Emotional Health Among Adolescents," *American Journal of Preventive Medicine* (2006): Vol. 30, No.1, pp. 59–66.

243   **Suicide rates:** WISQARS Injury Mortality Report, Center for Disease Control. In 2007, there were roughly 1.23 suicides per 100,000 boys in the United States between the ages of 10 and 14, 11.03 suicides per 100,000 boys between the ages of 15 and 19, and 20.64 suicides per 100,000 males between the ages of 20 and 24.

243   **"There's this very harsh and ultimately negative idea":** Interview, William Pollack, April 2011.

247   **Academics who study masculinity:** Ronald F. Levant and Katherine Richmond, "A Review of Research on Masculinity Ideologies Using the Male Role Norms Inventory," *The Journal of Men's Studies* (Spring 2007): Vol. 15, No. 2, pp. 130–46.

250   **"If a son sees that a loving and mature woman":** Interview, William Pollack, 2011.

254   **"What we know about the children":** Interview, Michael Kimmel, March 2011.

255   **As *Ebony* magazine put it:** Lynn Norment and Kevin Chappell, "The Truth About Mama's Boy and Daddy's Girl," *Ebony*, July 1998.

256   **In a 2008 study, David Perrett, a professor at the University of St. Andrews:** David Perrett, *In Your Face: The New Science of Human Attraction* (New York: Palgrave Macmillan, 2010).

257   **A recent in-depth study of romantic attraction:** Paul W. Eastwick and Eli J. Finke, "Sex Differences in Mate Preferences Revisited: Do People Know What They Initially Desire in a Romantic Partner," *Journal of Personality and Social Psychology* (2008): Vol. 94, No. 2, pp. 245–64.

257   **"The earning-power effect as well as":** Pat Vaughan Tremmel, "Rethinking What We Want in a Partner," Northwestern University New Center, February 13, 2008.

257   **Researchers at the University of Iowa found:** "Study Finds Education and Money Attract a Mate; Chastity Sinks in Importance," University of Iowa New Service, February 5, 2009; Christine Whalen, *Marry Smart: The Intelligent Woman's Guide to True Love* (New York: Simon & Schuster, 2006).

258   **"The baby boomer mothers and the generation after":** Interview, Christine Whalen, May 2011.

262   **"When Mr. Right Is a 'Mama's Boy'":** Lynn Harris, "When Mr. Right Is a 'Mama's Boy,'" *Ladies' Home Journal*, LHJ.com.

262   **"Ladies, the Best Catch Is a Man":** Sathnam Sanghera, "Ladies, the Best Catch Is a Man Who Loves His Mum," *London Times*, September 2, 2008. http://www.timesonline.co.uk/tol/comment/columnists/article4653744 .ece.

262   **"Mummy's Boy = Best Husband":** Tim Utton, *Daily Mail Online*. http://www.dailymail.co.uk/femail/article.-187165/Mummys-boy-best-husband.html.

262   **Their study of thirty-three couples reveals a correlation:** Sarah R. Roberts and Sharon E. Stein, "Mama's Boy or Lady's Man," paper presented at American Psychological Society, May 2003.

262   **Sarah Roberts, the study's lead researcher, suggested in an interview with Reuters:** Reported by Netscape, "No. 1 Reason Men Become Good Husbands," http://webcenters.netscape.compuserve.com/love/package.jsp?name=fte/goodhusbands/goodhusbands.

263   **"When you think about it, if the relationship has been good":** Interview, William Pollock, April 2011.

264 *Science* **magazine reported that:** Kristen Minogue, "Mama's Boys Get the Girls," *Science*, August 31, 2010. http://news. sciencemag.org/science now/2010/08/mamas-boys-get-the-girls.html.

265 **New York Giants quarterback Eli Manning:** Karen Crouse, "Eli Manning Took Cues from Mother," *The New York Times*, January 29, 2008.

266 **"I got to know more about her":** Ibid.

266 **According to father Archie Manning, "Eli and Olivia are":** Ibid.

267 **"This is a new, overwhelming time in their lives":** Interview, Wilma McNabb, May 2011.

269 **"I hear her at the games":** Ray Rice, quoted by Linda Lobroso, "Giving Thanks for Mothers' Love, Wisdom," *Journal News*, May 8, 2011.

269 **"I guess I just want to see my mom":** Michael Phelps, quoted by Karen Crouse, *The New York Times*, April 18, 2008.

270 **"My mama is my best friend":** "Kanye West Pays Tribute to His Mom, Donda," *MTV*, November 13, 2007.

270 **"Now I think of the phrase in very positive ways":** Donda West, *Raising Kanye* (New York: Pocket Books, 2007), p. 60.

271 **"The moral of the story is, Listen to your mother":** Tom Hooper, quoted by Melena Ryzik, "It's Back to the Studio, as Oscar Season Ends," *The New York Times*, March 3, 2011.

Chapter Eight. Looking Forward

273 **"Our conference the year before on mothers and daughters"** Interview, Andrea O'Reilly, May 2009.

274 **"It's funny that you are asking me":** Interview, Layne Gregory, April 2009.

277 **It was the early modern feminists:** Andrea O'Reilly, *Mothers & Sons: Feminism, Masculinity, and the Struggle to Raise Our Sons* (New York: Routledge, 2001); Judith Arcana, *Every Mother's Son: The Role of Mothers in the Making of Men* (New York: Doubleday, 1983); Linda Rennie Forcey, *Mothers of Sons: Toward an Understanding of Responsibility* (New York: Praeger, 1987).

277 **"We are creating and nurturing the agents of our own oppression":** Arcana, *Every Mother's Son*, p. 3.

278 **"I told mothers, 'You know the depth of your own pain'":** Interview, Cate Dooley, April and May 2009.

280 **nearly every study on happiness points:** Overview of research: Joshua Wolf Shenk, "What Makes Us Happy?" *The Atlantic*, June 2009; James

Fowler and Nicholas A. Christakis, "Dynamic Spread of Happiness in a Large Social Network: Longitudinal Analysis over 20 Years in the Framingham Heart Study," *BMJ*, December 4, 2008; Claudia Wallis, "The New Science of Happiness," *Time*, January 9, 2005.

282 **"a sanctuary dedicated to masculine awesomeness"**: "The 15 Best Man Caves on the Internet," www.brobible.com.

282 **"Men are reacting to the increased demands"**: Interview, Dr. Ronald Levant, April 2011.

283 **Look at the subtitle of a book:** Kay Hymowitz, *Manning Up: How the Rise of Women Has Turned Men into Boys* (New York: Basic Books, 2011).

283 **"Why should they grow up? No one needs them anyway"**: Kay S. Hymowitz, "Where have the Good Men Gone?," *Wall Street Journal*, February 19, 2011.

Index

∽

Levant, Ronald F., 122, 282–83
Lewis, Michael, 31

male role models
  absence of, 98, 106–11, 123–28,
    130–33, 134, 137
  emotional modeling, 10–11,
    134–35, 137, 248–49
  negative models, 248–49
"Mama's Boy or Lady's Man?"
  (Roberts), 262
manhood. *See* masculinity
Manhood for Amateurs (Chabon), 31
Manhood in America (Kimmel), 118
Manning, Eli, 265–66
Manning Up (Hymowitz), 283–84
masculinity
  acceptable emotions and behaviors,
    23, 26–27, 43, 134
  ambivalence of mothers
    concerning, 165–71, 182
  antifeminism, 282–84
  blame of mothers for undermining,
    95–96
  boys' alienation from, 98, 100, 105
  commercial messages about,
    162–63
  complexity of concept, 118–21
  concealment of vulnerability,
    208–9
  emasculating and feminizing
    mother, 5, 9, 62–64, 98, 100,
    107, 110–15, 205
  men's perceptions and
    interpretations of, 247–48, 250
  mixed messages about, 34, 169
  mothers' help in defining, 100
  premature separation from mother
    and, 121, 139–42
  sexist media messages, 226–30

toughness, 10, 17, 21–23, 25–26,
  49–50, 100
unavailability of male role models,
  98, 106–11, 123–28, 130–33,
  134
unhealthy consequences of
  traditional view, 121–23
Maugham, W. Somerset, 13,
  88–89, 90
McNabb, Wilma "Char," 265,
  266–67, 269
media. *See* popular culture
*Men Are from Mars, Women Are from
  Venus* (Gray), 152–53
MicroSort, 42
Miller, Jean Baker, 76, 144
Millet, Kate, 76, 88
Moretti, Enrico, 128
"Mother, The" (Maugham), 89
Mother at Home (Abbott), 81
Mothers and Sons (Smith), 141
"Mothers and Sons" conference,
  273–74
mother-son closeness
  cultural disapproval of, 9, 11,
    14–15, 33, 53–56
  maternal instinct for, 9, 11–12,
    16–17, 29, 144–46
  versus mother-daughter
    relationships, 2–3, 13, 19
  new attitudes concerning, 20–21,
    26–27, 29, 143–44
  prevalence of close relationships,
    2, 6, 11, 20
  scientific research supporting,
    21–23, 213, 280
  secretiveness concerning, 3–5,
    6, 16
  See also sons' experience of mother-
    son closeness; *specific issues*

emotional expression, 46–47,
49–50, 97, 123, 152
gender-associated attributes, 29,
32, 57
verbal skills, 152, 153–54
Sommers, Christina Hoff, 102
sons' experience of mother-son
closeness
among celebrities, 269–70
among football players, 265–69
attraction to women resembling
mothers, 255–60
versus closeness to fathers, 248–50
comfort and confidence in
discussing, 245–46
housekeeping skills and self-
reliance, 252–53
longing for closeness, 51–53, 73,
142, 144
mama's boy stereotype, 237–39
modeling of emotional strength,
248–51
perception as unable to mature,
243–44
preparation for nontraditional
home life, 254
prevalence of close relationships,
246–47
public embarrassment over, 235–37,
239–40
romantic relationships and, 260–64
Sons and Lovers (Lawrence), 87–88
Spock, Benjamin, 63
Stacey, Judith, 131–32
stereotypes
depiction of parents, 162
gender preconceptions, 34, 37,
40, 50
mama's boy, 4, 15, 237–39, 262–63
masculinity, 21, 24, 26, 134

noncommunicative male,
149–50, 151
promotion of, by single-sex
education, 116
as self-fulfilling prophecies, 50
sexual stereotypes, 164
See also gender norms; popular
culture
Stewart, Jon, 59
Strecker, Edward, 90
Surbeck, Martin, 264

Take Our Daughters to Work
Day, 101
talk. *See* conversation
Tannen, Deborah, 147, 152–53
Tappan, Mark, 162–63
teenage years
age-appropriate physical contact,
197–200
anger and hostility, 199–200, 208,
209–10
attunement of mothers to details,
217–18
breakups with girlfriends, 218–20
conflation of maternal love with
sexuality, 194–97, 201–5
discussions about sex, 220–25
distancing from male friendships,
240–42
father-son versus mother-son
communication, 214–18
feminization, 205–6
Freud's Oedipus theory, 195–96
idolization of son, 230–33
isolation and confusion, 208–10,
242–43
mothers' sense of loss, 200–201
quiet companionship and
comforting presence, 211–12